The Adventure of
Working Abroad

Joyce Sautters Osland

The Adventure of Working Abroad

Hero Tales from the Global Frontier

Jossey-Bass Publishers
San Francisco

Substantial discounts on bulk quantities of Jossey-Bass books are available to corporations, professional associations, and other organizations. For details and discount information, contact the special sales department at Jossey-Bass Inc., Publishers. (415) 433–1740; Fax (800) 605–2665.

For sales outside the United States, please contact your local Paramount Publishing International office.

 Manufactured in the United States of America on Lyons Falls Pathfinder Tradebook. This paper is acid-free and 100 percent totally chlorine-free.

Credits are on p. 245.

Library of Congress Cataloging-in-Publication Data

Osland, Joyce
    The adventure of working abroad : hero tales from the global frontier / Joyce Sautters Osland.
      p.   cm. — (The Jossey-Bass management series)
    Includes bibliographical references and index.
    ISBN 0-7879-0108-3
    1. Americans—Employment—Foreign countries.   2. International business enterprises—Personnel management.   3. Cross-cultural orientation—United States.   I. Title.   II. Series.
    HF5549.5.E4508   1995
    650.14—dc20   95-8629

FIRST EDITION
HB Printing   10 9 8 7 6 5 4 3 2 1

Furthermore, we have not even to risk the adventure alone, for the heroes of all time have gone before us. The labyrinth is thoroughly known. We have only to follow the thread of the hero path, and where we had thought to find an abomination, we shall find a god. And where we had thought to slay another, we shall slay ourselves. Where we had thought to travel outward, we will come to the center of our own existence. And where we had thought to be alone, we will be one with all the world.

—Joseph Campbell
Hero with a Thousand Faces

Contents

I dedicate this book to my parents,
Charles and Eleanor Sautters,
and my parents-in-law,
Ketil and Bergit Osland,
who, in addition to
other sterling qualities
and good works
too numerous to mention,
never begrudged us our adventures.

Preface

⋅ ⋅

The expatriate experience has shaped my life—and it is shaping the lives and careers of an increasing number of people as more organizations become international. Traditionally, expatriates share their experiences among themselves, but apart from this interaction, there are few resources—formal or informal—to help expatriates and potential expatriates make sense of the often radical changes that working abroad can make in their lives. I realized that such resources were needed when I repeatedly heard these questions from the expatriates I interviewed: "Is my experience normal? Have you heard similar stories from other expatriates?" The realization that others have taken the same journey and pondered the same questions is comforting and makes the transition, first to overseas and then back home, more manageable, freeing the expatriate to focus more fully on his or her work. Some aspects of each individual's experience naturally are unique, but there is much that expatriates share and can teach one another. In this book, I have tried to gather together the commonalties of their subjective experience within a framework that reveals the shared threads in their stories.

Origins of the Book

I returned to the United States in 1984 after living and working abroad for eleven years. Although my beady quasi-sociologist's eye had been trained primarily upon the local people in the various countries in which my family and I lived, I could not help observing numerous expatriates over the years. Some of these were Americans I was training for overseas jobs; others were old-time expatriates who served as cultural mentors for me, or newcomers for whom I returned the favor. But the great majority were friends or acquaintances from other countries who kept me entertained at innumerable dinner parties (the common diversion of expatriates living in out-of-the-way places) with their tales of expatriate life.

When I returned to academic life in the United States and began reading what scholars had to say about expatriates, I was disappointed to find nothing written on the key issues I had repeatedly heard discussed abroad. What I read in no way captured the essence of the experience, nor its significance. After conversations with human resource managers, I was even more surprised to find that many multinationals were doing little to prepare expatriates for overseas assignments and subsequent repatriation. Therefore, as part of a research study, I began interviewing returned expatriate businesspeople, both to test whether the hunches about expatriates I had developed over the years were valid and to discover what else I could learn. Their fascinating stories leave little doubt that, for many of them, their time abroad was one of the most significant experiences of their lives. Once again, I heard the same threads running through their stories—the mastery that resulted from successfully grappling with a foreign language and foreign customs; the heroic flavor of their tales about rising to difficult occasions and accomplishing what had previously seemed impossible; the paradoxes they pondered; and the personal transformation they experienced as a result of opening themselves up to another culture. For many expatriates, the overseas experience is a time of accelerated challenge and learning that leaves its unique mark. The threads of their stories reflect the same journey that mythical heroes traverse, as described by Joseph Campbell in his book *Hero with a Thousand Faces* (1968). Campbell's insightful portrayal of the common stages in hero adventure myths provided a metaphorical framework that helped me interpret the expatriate experience in a new way.

Purpose of the Book

It is my hope that this book will prove useful to prospective, current, and returning expatriates, as well as to the managers and human resource specialists who work with them. My purpose is to capture the "oral tradition" of expatriate stories, to show how the experience of living and working abroad changes the expatriates' lives, stimulating both personal and professional growth and learning. The basis for the book is my research on returned expatriate managers, the body of previously published work on expatriates and sojourners, and my own overseas years of participant-observation with expatriates, including a recent three-year stint at the Central American Institute of Business Administration (INCAE), a Harvard-affiliated business school located in Costa Rica.

The Adventure of Working Abroad responds to three specific concerns regarding expatriates:

1. *Nowhere in my research did I find a description of the expatriate experience that rang true, or one that I felt could help expatriates and managers understand the significance of working overseas.* Although there are a number of books that convey practical advice to expatriates about the mechanics of adapting to another culture and setting up house, very few authors really focus on the subjective experience of expatriates. Only in fiction, such as E. M. Forster's *Passage to India* and George Orwell's "On Shooting an Elephant," and in autobiographical books like Leonard Woolf's *Growing* and Aldous Huxley's *Jesting Pilate* do we find rich descriptions of expatriate experience (Storti, 1990; Lewis and Jungman, 1986). However, that genre naturally stays at the level of narrative and lacks the conceptual frameworks that help expatriates make sense of their experiences.

When I looked to academic writing for information and ideas that might be useful for expatriates, I found numerous studies done with Peace Corps volunteers, educational advisors, and international students. Expatriate businesspeople differ significantly, however, from these groups, both in their goals abroad and in the higher status they often possess in relation to people from the local culture due to their managerial positions. Academic studies relevant to expatriate businesspeople are limited primarily to selection, training, adjustment, effectiveness, and repatriation, but there is more to the expatriate experience than commonly meets the eye. It is the less tangible and, in a sense, more subjective aspect of the experience that quite naturally eludes those who have never lived abroad. By gathering and sharing expatriate stories, I hoped to create a resource to help prospective expatriates obtain more realistic ideas of what to expect and to allow them to benefit from the experience of those who have gone before them.

2. *Not only is lack of information a problem for expatriates, but it is also a problem for companies.* Studies have shown that U.S. companies do a worse job than both European and Japanese firms of preparing people to work abroad and, as a result, have a higher early-return rate (Tung, 1987). The failure rate for U.S. expatriates is estimated at 20 to 50 percent (Mendenhall, Dunbar, and Oddou, 1987). Given that expatriates who return home early cost their companies between $55,000 to $150,000 in direct costs alone (Mendenhall, Dunbar, and Oddou, 1987), this failure rate is a serious problem. Another sobering but little-publicized statistic is the high resignation rate, approximately 20 percent, of expatriates when they return from abroad (Adler, 1981; Black and Gregersen, 1991). In principle, these employees have survived the overseas experience and are returning with valuable international skills. Why then do they quit and seek other employment?

The statistics seem to indicate that U.S. companies are missing the boat when it comes to understanding what really happens with expatriates. Although a few companies have been increasing their efforts in recent years, the majority of U.S. companies do not prepare expatriates adequately for overseas assignments or help them deal with all the changes and challenges facing them. To shed more light on this topic, I have included suggestions, both my own and those of the expatriates I interviewed, about how companies should handle overseas assignments and what expatriates themselves can do to ensure a more successful sojourn.

3. *Human resource (HR) people also need expertise on the expatriate experience if they are to prepare, support, and debrief expatriates as effectively as possible.* Occasionally, expatriate assignments are made more difficult by U.S.–based employees who have not had sufficient exposure to expatriate issues. For example, when HR managers are asked why repatriation is so difficult, they are likely to state that expatriates simply miss the autonomy, prestige, perks, and lifestyle they had abroad. I hope to provide a broader and more complex explanation for repatriation blues. Most HR managers have never lived abroad, and some mistakenly treat expatriates as if they were no different from domestic employees. In an international transfer, expatriates deal with more complicated circumstances and emotions than people making a domestic move. When they complain about the difficulty of moving their family to another country, mastering a new language and culture, weathering adjustment problems, and handling socially isolated spouses, some HR staffers begin to regard them as well-paid whiners rather than people in desperate need of an understanding listener.

Furthermore, managers without international experience sometimes place expatriates in unnecessarily difficult positions because they do not understand the local cultural constraints upon the expatriates' behavior. This occurred, for example, when one corporation insisted than an expatriate manager negotiate a land purchase in a country where ownership by a foreign corporation symbolizes an infringement of national sovereignty. The attempt failed, as the hapless expatriate knew it would, because this strategy did not take the local political conditions and cultural beliefs into account. Although there is no substitute for international experience, my goal with this book is to bridge the gap by providing HR managers and those who supervise expatriates with the expatriate perspective and graphic vignettes of life abroad.

With these unfulfilled needs in mind, I wrote *The Adventure of Working Abroad* to accomplish the following objectives:

1. To provide a better understanding of the complex, transformational nature of the expatriate experience

2. To help prepare people for international assignments and repatriation by letting them hear through the words of others what it is really like and by providing practical advice for dealing with the experience

3. To provide current and returned expatriates with a framework for making sense of their experience

4. To help those who have never lived abroad better understand the subjective meaning of the expatriate experience, and to provide ideas for improving the way companies handle overseas assignments

Audiences for the Book

I have written this book primarily for prospective, current, and returning expatriates. Although the expatriates I interviewed were businesspeople, their stories are remarkably similar to those of international volunteers and developers, foreign service personnel, and missionaries, who will also find the book useful. In addition, I hope to educate and increase the effectiveness of those who work with expatriates—their supervisors both abroad and back at headquarters, international human resource managers, and cross-cultural trainers. As one of the few qualitative descriptions of expatriates, this book will, I hope, also be of interest to academic researchers, professors, and students of international management, human resources, organizational behavior, and cross-cultural psychology.

Overview of the Contents

Chapter One discusses the importance of understanding the expatriate experience and briefly describes the study that is the basis of the book. It introduces the major themes of mastery, transformation, and heroism. It draws an analogy between mythical heroes and expatriates, outlines the plot of the myth of the hero's adventure, and presents the various categories of "hero talk" in expatriate stories.

Chapters Two through Seven, which are named after Campbell's stages in the myth of the hero's adventure (1968), portray the relationship between mythical heroes and expatriates at each stage of their journey. Chapter Two describes the first stage of the hero's adventure for both mythical heroes and expatriates. It explains the differences between the offer of a domestic assignment and the offer of an international assignment. The chapter depicts expatriates' varied reactions to the international "call to adventure." It presents the relationship between the expatriate's feelings about going abroad and his or her subsequent success overseas. The chapter also describes what happens when both mythical heroes and expatriates refuse the call.

Chapter Three examines the first months abroad, when expatriates are crossing both geographic and cultural boundaries and struggling to learn about and adapt to the host culture. It identifies the threshold guardians that keep expatriates from becoming integrated into the other culture. The chapter also explains acculturation strategies and the expatriate pecking order that results.

Chapter Four highlights the importance of cultural mentors and others who guide the expatriate through the shoals of the host culture and help him or her survive and succeed abroad. It explains where expatriates find this type of help and identifies the advantages of having a cultural mentor. It also relates the crucial role of learning in an expatriate experience. The chapter ends with a compilation of expatriate advice on beginning the journey.

Chapter Five portrays the obstacles and paradoxes that typically confront expatriates. It presents a new concept, expatriate paradoxes, that has never before been studied or articulated in an organized manner. Paradoxes are situations involving the presence of contradictory, mutually exclusive elements that operate equally at the same time (Quinn and Cameron, 1988). The chapter includes expatriates' descriptions of their experience with paradoxes and how they learned to resolve them.

Chapter Six describes the transformational process that expatriates undergo in terms of "letting go" of and "taking on" various factors. It reveals how expatriates believe they have changed abroad. It details the boons or skills they bring home with them. The chapter also contains practical advice about the paradoxes and transformation that expatriates undergo in this stage of their adventure.

Chapter Seven discusses the repatriation process and identifies why it can be difficult. The expatriates' description of repatriation blues goes beyond commonly held wisdom. The concept of differentiation and integration provides another way to understand what occurs when expatriates return home.

Chapter Eight focuses on the need for companies to learn from their experiences with expatriates. It also provides a description of recommended practices regarding expatriate assignments, along with extensive guidance for HR personnel and managers who work with expatriates prior to, during, and after their assignments. Finally, details about the research on which the book is based are located at the end of the book.

My primary argument, constructed and presented throughout these chapters, is that expatriates undergo a transformational experience that is not yet fully understood or appreciated. The common threads of this experience are heroism and mastery, paradox, and accelerated learning, but seldom is everything necessary done to prepare expatriates for the experience ahead of time or to help them learn from it afterwards. Also, organizations are not always prepared to welcome back their own expatriates, who have changed and grown abroad, or to utilize their international skills. As a result, both expatriates and their organizations at times falter, suffer, and fail to take full advantage of the expatriate experience. I hope to show that the myth of the hero's adventure is a useful metaphor for understanding this transformation and mastering its demands.

Acknowledgments

A key figure in the myth of the hero's adventure is the magical friend who provides protection and aid to the hero. "For those who have not refused the call, the first encounter of the hero's journey is with a protective figure who provides the adventurer with amulets against the dragon forces he is about to pass" (Campbell, 1968, p. 69). Throughout the hero's adventure of writing a dissertation and a book, I have been surrounded by magical friends whom I would like to acknowledge. Gail Ambuske, Darlyne Bailey, Richard Boyatzis, David Kolb, Michael Manning, Anne McKee, Cecilia McMillen, Sybil Perlmutter, George Robinson, Michael Sokoloff, and, in particular, Eric Neilsen all made intellectual contributions to this project in addition to sharing their wisdom, skills, and friendship. I would like to extend my thanks to the business schools that supported me throughout this endeavor and let me raid their libraries. I am grateful to the entire learning community in the Organizational Behavior Department at Case Western Reserve University, where I began this research; to INCAE for providing me with yet another expatriate experience during the book's gestation; and to the University of Portland, and Bruce Drake and James Robertson in particular, for allowing me the time to complete the writing. I'd also like to thank Suzanne Adams and Tom Howe for their computer expertise, Neal Chandler, John Orr, Joan Saalfeld, and Karen Vaught-Alexander for their writing advice, and the wonderful reference librarians at the University of Portland for service above and beyond the call of duty.

I am indebted to the research participants who contributed time from their busy schedules and shared their experiences and wisdom to help other expatriates. In order to protect their privacy, the names used in the book are not their real ones.

The editors at Jossey-Bass, Bill Hicks, Barbara Hill, and Sarah Polster, have been extremely helpful and have made major contributions to the book, as did Marta Maretich and the anonymous reviewers.

In retrospect, one of the aspects of my own expatriate experience seems to be living in other people's houses prior to or after returning from abroad. My special thanks to Bruce and Eileen Drake, Gwen Eubank, Diane and Terry Pancoast, Juliann Spoth, and Sue and Rick Taft, who gave me shelter during various stages of researching and writing this book.

I would like to acknowledge the intellectual contribution that Joseph Campbell made to this book. His work on myths in *Hero with a Thousand Faces* (1968) provided both the inspiration and the framework for *The Adventure of Working Abroad*.

I owe my largest debt of gratitude to my favorite expatriate, my husband, Asbjorn Osland. As a very successful expatriate manager, he contributed large doses of his own formidable understanding of the expatriate experience and was generous with ideas, constructive criticism, and elegant phrases. Last but not least, I want to thank our children, Jessica, Michael, and Katrina, for being troopers both overseas and while I was chained to a computer. This book is written for them and for my nephews, Adam and Joshua Henson, as they, too, succumb to wanderlust and the lure of Peace Corps and Africa.

Portland, Oregon   Joyce Sautters Osland
May 1995

The Author

∙ ∙

JOYCE SAUTTERS OSLAND is assistant professor of organizational behavior at the School of Business Administration, University of Portland, Oregon. She received her B.A. degree (1970) from the University of Minnesota in social welfare with honors, her M.S.W. degree (1972) from the University of Washington, and her Ph.D. degree (1990) in organizational behavior from The Weatherhead School of Management, Case Western Reserve University.

Osland, a former Peace Corps volunteer, was an expatriate for fourteen years and has been repatriated three times. During her first eleven years abroad, she worked primarily in the field of nonprofit international development in Burkina Faso, Senegal, Colombia, Guatemala, and Scotland, with briefer stints in Ecuador and Peru. She worked as a community organizer, manager, researcher, training specialist, and consultant. When she returned to the United States, she began consulting with businesses in the areas of organization development and management education. Upon completion of her doctorate, Osland taught for three years in the MBA programs at INCAE, the Central American Institute of Business Administration, located in Costa Rica. She has traveled extensively throughout Latin America consulting and giving management seminars. In addition to expatriate research and training, her current interests focus on comparative management in Latin America. She is particularly interested in the characteristics and cultural differences of outstanding managers and female executives in South American countries. Osland has written several articles on organizational behavior, in addition to two textbooks, *The Organizational Behavior Reader* (1995) and *Organizational Behavior: An Experiential Approach* (1995, with D. Kolb and I. Rubin).

The Adventure of
Working Abroad

· ·

• •

From Innocence to Mastery

Expatriate Tales and the Myth of the Hero's Journey

Mankind's common instinct for reality . . . has always held the world to be essentially a theatre for heroism.
—William James, *The Varieties of Religious Experience*

Many people who work overseas fall into the role of racon-teur—teller of tales. While living abroad, we swap and pass on stories about the interesting, amusing, and outrageous incidents we have experienced or heard of secondhand. Sometimes we gossip about the seemingly inexplicable behavior of people from the local culture, in an effort to make sense of it or simply to entertain ourselves. Upon returning home, most expatriates are prone to repeating these exotic tales with little or no provocation and often at great social risk. If we took the time, however, to listen carefully to these stories, we would hear certain themes repeated again and again, themes that convey the meaning the overseas experience holds for expatriates.

During fourteen years in seven different countries, I have listened to hundreds of fellow expatriates of various nationalities talk about what they loved and hated about living overseas. I have sat by while a good number of them have agonized over the decision about whether to return home, and I have listened to the nostalgic reminiscences of former expatriates about life abroad. But when I began rummaging around in what has been written about business expatriates, I saw virtually no mention of the common themes I myself had heard in their stories and musings. For example, I found no mention of the changes expatriates undergo as a result of their time abroad, or of how these changes affect their efforts to fit back into a former life when they are repatriated. There were no descriptions of the mastery they feel when they crack the code of another culture, conquer the intricacies of a foreign language well enough to be mistaken for a native, or pull off "mission impossibles" at work. And few writers mentioned the ubiquitous paradoxes that characterize life overseas, or captured the heroic flavor of their exploits. This book aims to fill the void. It draws on the stories expatriates tell about their adventures, in an effort to provide prospective expatriates, seasoned expatriates, and the organizations that send them on their journeys with a better understanding of the expatriate experience.

The Expatriate Experience

Listening to expatriates' stories about how they had changed abroad reminded me of the accounts of people who have been deeply touched by mid-life crises, personal growth workshops, personal tragedy, or other unsettling, unique, and psychologically demanding experiences. The difference between these challenges and living in another culture is primarily a matter of degree. For better or worse, expatriates are upended by concurrent changes in culture, job context, and socioeconomic supports. There are some similarities between this experience and moving to a new job in a very different region of one's own country. However, the cross-cultural context is a unique milieu in which many individuals are led to question their basic assumptions about themselves, their culture, their interpersonal relationships, and their management style. According to one well-accepted theory (Holmes and Rahe, 1967), one's level of stress is related to the number of changes that are occurring concurrently in the different areas of one's life. A move abroad can produce simultaneous changes on virtually all fronts. The cross-cultural context provides numerous stressors, both positive (novelty and adventure) and negative (being forced to question one's values, feeling inadequate, and encountering family problems), in an accelerated and accentuated fashion. The cross-cultural setting can be so stressful that it demands that ordinary people rise to extraordinary and even heroic heights, and if they do, they usually find they have been transformed in the process and have unearthed strengths in themselves that were never required within their own culture. Many expatriates have to plumb the depths of their inner resources, first to survive the differences and changes, then to be effective, and finally, to develop explanations for the ambiguity of their new experiences. To enable their own personal transformation, they need to resolve, both intellectually and emotionally, the meaning of those experiences.

Obviously, we do not have to leave our native country to undergo this type of personal growth, but there is no question that the cross-cultural context is particularly fertile ground for personal development. Still, not all expatriates take advantage of this opportunity. People go abroad for a variety of reasons, some of which have nothing to do with a hero's adventure. Some people are motivated solely by hardship pay and a reputedly glamorous lifestyle; others are merely polishing their resume for future job hopping, while a handful grab at an international assignment as a last-chance option before termination or as an escape from personal, family, or even legal problems. Most of the people I interviewed or spent time with did not fit these profiles, and this book does not describe such experiences. Instead, this book is about and for the majority of expatriates, whose experiences are a variation of the hero's adventure.

The Myth of the Hero's Journey

When I stumbled upon the myth of the hero's adventure (Campbell, 1968), it occurred to me that this story could be a vehicle or a framework for helping expatriates make sense of their experience.

Joseph Campbell, renowned expert on mythology, studied myths from all over the world and identified their common plots and stages. All hero's adventure myths—one of the most common mythical themes—share the same basic plot: *separation* from the world, *initiation* involving penetration to some source of power, and a life-enhancing *return*. For example, "Jason sailed through the Clashing Rocks into a sea of marvels, circumvented the dragon that guarded the Golden Fleece, and returned with the fleece and the power to wrest his rightful throne from a usurper" (Campbell, 1968, p. 30). Mythical heroes either seek to find their destiny outside their known world or inadvertently stumble into another world. In either case, there is an "awakening of the self," as mystics have termed it (Underhill, 1911). Heroes are helped by magical friends who guide them past the dangerous guardians of a different world. Next, they undergo a series of trials that ends with a decisive victory and brings them to the realization of a higher consciousness or a power hidden within themselves. After this transformation, heroes return home from their journey with the power to share with their compatriots (fellow citizens) the boons (benefits or blessings) they acquired on their adventure, such as the gift of fire or spiritual illumination. Campbell notes that the attempt to reintegrate themselves back into their original society is often the most difficult part of the heroes' journey. Like prophets, people are not always accepted as heroes in their own land. I was struck by the similarity between this mythical plot and the expatriate stories I had heard abroad.

Although I did not put a name to it at the time, I remember when I first began to conceptualize the idea of mastery and heroism among expatriates. A friend and returned expatriate was recounting how he had gained admission to a prestigious graduate school after the admission deadline had already passed. He stormed his way into the dean's office, slammed his fist down on the desk, muttered something about having just come back from driving a jeep through the wilds of South Asia delivering CARE food, which was certainly a lot more difficult than graduate school would ever be, and demanded admission. It worked! He described this incident as having put on his "shitkicker boots." I recognized immediately what he was talking about, because I had heard similar stories from other expatriates and had lived through similar experiences myself. All these anecdotes were about accomplishing seemingly impossible tasks abroad, made possible by the expatriate's tenacity, ingenuity, and, at times, audacity. The result was a feeling of mastery and self-efficacy that would not be daunted by small obstacles like graduate school deadlines. Some overseas assignments are so difficult that the obstacles in one's own culture pale in comparison.

For example, when I was first learning to speak Spanish as a Peace Corps volunteer twenty years back, I was asked to give a speech to a community group. I wanted to make a good impression because I was scheduled to work in the neighborhood for the next two years. At that point, my verbal communication in Spanish was on a par with a precocious Latino preschooler, so to speak before a group was clearly a challenge. I had to look up every other word in the dictionary; only my audience knows how many archaic words and false cognates I slipped into the text. Next, I memorized the entire speech because most of the words were totally new and meant nothing to me. No one snickered during the speech, which tells you a great deal about the innate courtesy of Colombians. Occasionally I think back on what was then a fairly terrifying experience, and chuckle, wondering what I actually told those people. Yet the lesson I learned from that experience has always stayed with me: if I could survive giving a speech in a language I barely spoke, public speaking in my own language should lose its terror and, for the most part, it has. Expatriates who have overcome innumerable obstacles abroad are like athletes or Outward Bound participants who have tested their endurance and live with the confidence that comes from successfully pushing back one's limits.

This was the case with Mark, an articulate, charming young man who looked like he was on the fast track at the well-known multinational where he worked. He had been referred to me by another expatriate in his company as someone who might meet my research criteria and be willing to talk about his experiences. Indeed, he talked at great length about his transfer to London, which turned out to be a highly significant experience. As a member of a culturally diverse team, he traveled extensively throughout Europe and Asia giving training programs. When he returned to the States, he heard a rumor via the grapevine that, rather than receiving the job he had been promised, he was going to be assigned to a major client who would consume all his time and take him in a career direction in which he did not want to go. He strode into the boss's office, demanded an immediate audience, and asked, "What the hell is going on here?" Mark said that it could have been the president of the United States in that office; the truth is he didn't care if he had to quit that day, even though he had the highest respect for the company. Since he seemed to be a person who cared a great deal about his career and wouldn't want to jeopardize it, I asked what had happened to him abroad that caused him to react this way.

• • • • • • •

I guess just the confidence in knowing that you went over there and you had this challenge. From the minute you touched the elevator button, you didn't know what was up there, who was up there, how you were going to be treated, how you were going to live. You didn't have a flat, you didn't have anything. You managed all of this on your own. . . . I have always been fairly confident in my abilities, but that was a real test in my mind. And it was like, "Well, I handled that. And I was in London and it was a big city and this is not. I don't have to take this!" I guess there is a lot of, maybe, over-importance, or being charged up.

• • • • • • •

On one level, maybe Mark and my graduate school friend are guilty of self-importance, but there are too many similarities in stories like these to dismiss that there is something about the experience that fosters this type of behavior in returned expatriates. Another explanation is that they are acting like heroes who have just returned from an adventure and a real test that involved mastery, transformation, and even heroism.

Though it may seem an unlikely comparison at first glance, expatriate businesspeople (and most other types of expatriates) have much in common with mythical heroes, and their experience overseas has much in common with the stages of the hero's adventure. Expatriates consider and eventually accept the request to go abroad, leaving behind the domestic office of the organization and the social support of an established life. They embark on the fascinating, adventurous but initially lonely overseas assignment. The location is shrouded in the ambiguity of unknown languages and customs. The expatriates' tasks are challenging, often well beyond what they would have been asked to accomplish in the United States in terms of autonomy and in the degree and breadth of responsibility. Unfamiliar obstacles of all stripes and colors appear. They force the adventuring heroes to question their own identity, their values, and their assumptions about numerous aspects of everyday life previously taken for granted. Some of these obstacles appear in the form of paradoxes the expatriates must learn to resolve, such as how much of their identity they must give up to be accepted by the other culture. When they perform their tasks successfully and learn to adapt to another culture, expatriates experience a solid sense of satisfaction, mastery, and self-efficacy. Their return to the United States is often marked by a sense of loss at leaving behind the magical charm and fulfillment of the sojourn. But among other changes, they return with greater understanding of foreign lands, increased self-confidence and interpersonal skills, and tolerance for differences in people. Some companies treat them as heroes and make use of the skills they developed or honed abroad; others do not.

The Stages in the Myth of the Hero's Adventure

Roger Harrison and Richard Hopkins (1967) wrote years ago that many Peace Corps volunteers return to the United States with a suitcase, or more likely a duffel bag, full of anecdotes that are seldom converted to abstract ideas and generalizations. There are, in fact, few models or theories to help expatriates put their experiences into a broader perspective. In addition to providing a structure for expatriate anecdotes, the metaphor of the hero's adventure also promotes a deeper understanding of the expatriate experience. Before I discovered this metaphor, I thought I knew a good deal about expatriates, yet it allowed me to see and comprehend much more because it organized disparate anecdotes into a logical framework. In subsequent chapters, each stage of the myth is described in detail. But first, to give you a sense of how the structure works, the stages and subphases are briefly defined here, followed by a short explanation of how they relate to expatriates.

Separation or Departure

The call to adventure, or refusal of the call, is the first phase of the hero's journey. Mythical heroes are visited by an unknown figure who asks them to accept a quest, or they accidentally fall into an unknown land and an adventure, triggering a mystical "awakening of the self." Not everyone, however, wants an adventure, and some heroes refuse the call. For expatriates, the call to adventure occurs when they are offered an overseas assignment. Some accept immediately, while others struggle with the decision or initially turn down the opportunity for career- or family-related reasons.

The crossing of the first threshold and the entering of the belly of the whale occurs when mythical heroes step over the portal into the unknown. This threshold is protected by guardians, such as gorgons or ogres, so that only the worthy can begin the adventure. The belly of the whale, as in the biblical story of Jonah, represents the womb where spiritual rebirth takes place and heroes begin the process of transformation. For expatriates, crossing the threshold means leaving behind their own culture to cross both physical and cultural boundaries. This stage encompasses the difficult settling-in and adjustment period expatriates often undergo. The threshold guardians, such as the inability to speak the foreign language and a restrictive expatriate community, attempt to prevent expatriates from entering and immersing themselves in the host culture.

The supernatural aid of a protective figure—a magical friend—provides a magic weapon or the assurance of success to the hero. Mythical examples of magical friends are the animals that warn heroes of danger or the old crones who dispense the wisdom that allows the heroes to succeed on their quest. For expatriates, this type of assistance is found primarily in the form of cultural mentors who interpret the local culture and guide them through its shoals. Magical friends can also be experienced resident expatriates, the nodes of social networks (international schools, churches, and social-athletic clubs), and career mentors back at headquarters.

Initiation

The road of trials, the first part of the initiation stage, refers to the tests and ordeals that strew the path of the mythical heroes, such as slaying dragons or ignoring the call of the sirens. The expatriate road of trials consists of the numerous obstacles encountered in learning to live and work effectively in another culture. The less well-known trials are the paradoxes of expatriate life—such as being both powerful and powerless, feeling at ease anywhere but belonging nowhere, being both free and not free of cultural norms—that must be resolved.

The ultimate boon, the transformation of heroes, occurs as a result of exposure to trials and illuminating revelations. Mythical heroes penetrate to a source of power, such as a higher consciousness or a sense of the universal power within each person (Campbell, 1968). The process of mythical transformation is symbolized as death and rebirth. Expatriates describe their own transformation in terms of "letting go" and "taking on." Their consciousness is transformed by exposure to cultural differences, trials, and paradoxes, sometimes with the aid of a cultural mentor. The source of power or the higher consciousness for expatriates is a bicultural perspective, increased self-awareness, and the knowledge that they possess the inner resources to master a difficult situation. Their boons are the skills and greater cultural understanding they gain abroad.

Return

The refusal to return and the rescue from without occur when mythical heroes do not want to end their journey and are reluctant to return home. In some instances, they are forced back into the world by deities. When applied to expatriates, this phase is experienced by the small number who are sent home against their wishes before their tour of duty is complete.

The crossing of the return threshold takes place when the mythical heroes end their journey and return home. This phase corresponds to repatriation for expatriates, and involves their readjustment to their homeland.

Master of two worlds and freedom to live represent the ability of mythical heroes to move back and forth between two different planes—the everyday world, and a higher, spiritual consciousness. For expatriates, the mastery of two worlds obviously is biculturalism, along with the ability to use the skills they learned abroad, and a heightened consciousness of themselves and the world.

Why use myth and metaphor to help understand human behavior? Myths are like universal poetry; they are metaphors that help us understand basic human truths and provide us with guidance. Like metaphors, myths allow us to step back from the messy and at times overwhelming stimuli and minutiae of our lives in order to reinterpret our experiences from a higher level of abstraction and generalization. Both metaphors and myths capture the essence of life. My purpose in using the metaphorical perspective of the myth of the hero's adventure is to help capture the often heroic essence of the expatriate experience.

Expatriate Stories

I interviewed thirty-five returned U.S. expatriates and analyzed the transcripts of the interviews to see whether the concepts of heroism and mastery, paradox, and transformation were in fact important to expatriate businesspeople, and to determine whether their stories reflect the hero's adventure (Osland, 1990). Demographic data on the subjects are presented along with the interview protocol in the appendix at the end of the book.

Before describing the interviews, I would like to state a few caveats concerning passages from the transcripts that are included in later chapters. At times you will read comments about other nationalities that may or may not be valid; they reflect the perception of the expatriates, and I do not necessarily share these views. There are numerous references to "Americans" throughout the book. I realize this term rightfully applies to people of the entire hemisphere, but U.S. citizens refer to themselves as Americans in these interviews and there is no graceful substitute for the word. Therefore, I beg the pardon of other American nationalities for using the term in this book to apply only to U.S. citizens.

The overall feeling I received from the interviews is that the opportunity to talk about their experiences was, with few exceptions, very welcome. There was minimal or no organizational pressure upon them to participate in the study, and all the participants could have pleaded a heavy workload or international travel had they felt in need of a good excuse. I was surprised but gratified by their willingness to talk to a stranger; many commented that no one else was willing to listen to their stories and thoughts about living abroad. One person referred to the interview as a "rare luxury." Several participants laughingly mentioned that family or friends would ask what it was like to live in the country where they'd been assigned, but after one or two sentences, or a couple of minutes, whichever came first, they would break in, saying, "How 'bout them (insert name of local professional sports team)?" and change the subject.

Although it was possible to complete the interview in an hour, some people talked for three hours; one animated subject followed me to my car, still talking, wanting to know if we could extend the interview over lunch or have another session. It would be flattering to chalk this warm reception up to my personal charms, but a more accurate interpretation is that many of these people had a previously unmet need to talk about their experiences. For most of them, the excitement and affect with which they related their feelings, thoughts, and adventures made it evident that their overseas experience was one of the most profound challenges and events of their lives.

The words that most commonly appeared in the interviews were "learn," "adventure," and "challenge." Both adventure and challenge seem directly related to the hero's adventure myth, and although the expatriates I spoke with did not openly refer to themselves as heroes, their conversation was full of "hero talk." We must bear in mind Campbell's caveat that the hero gets the adventure he or she is ready for (1988, p. 129). The interviews and transcripts revealed to me that there are different forms of expatriate experiences and different forms of "heroism." The expatriates' stories included one or more of seven different types of "hero talk":

1.   *Succeeding at difficult work assignments.* Expatriate assignments vary according to their purpose, and some are more challenging than others. For example, jobs that provide international exposure but involve the same type of tasks performed at home are much less demanding than unstructured jobs, like assessing the local management to see whether the person in charge should be replaced, building a new market in Asia, or turning around a failing subsidiary. Expatriates talk about the unstructured jobs as if they were difficult mythical quests.

2.   *Accomplishing work goals under less than favorable conditions.* Many expatriates tell stories about their job successes in the face of difficult odds such as high rates of inflation, political instability, or extreme logistical difficulties. The nature of numerous overseas assignments is that people are granted more responsibility than they would have at home; either because they possess greater power or

because the overseas organization is smaller, they often feel they have a greater impact at work. Certainly, many expatriates experience greater autonomy abroad, and some assume the role of "intrapreneurs"—people who function like entrepreneurs inside larger organizations (Pinchot, 1985). Many speak with great pride about what they achieved at work after overcoming the numerous obstacles one finds in overseas settings. Thus, expatriates are like mythical heroes who have proved their mettle and succeeded, in spite of the road of trials.

3. *Making it "on their own" or "going it alone."* Simply leaving their culture and family constitutes both an adventure and an act of courage for some people. For expatriates sent abroad by large corporations, it is often the first time they have ever worked alone. This responsibility provides yet another opportunity to prove oneself, much like Native American rites of passage that require adolescent boys to spend time alone in the wilderness. In some ways, going abroad is the final frontier. Like mythical heroes, some expatriates are consciously looking for adventure and seeking to prove themselves.

4. *Feeling "special."* Many expatriates talk about feeling special overseas for a variety of reasons. Simply being a foreigner draws attention, which is positive for the most part. The local people are curious about the foreigner's opinions and culture, and many expatriates assume the role of unofficial ambassadors for their countries. Like mythical heroes, many expatriates see themselves as being set apart from other people, undergoing a special experience.

Although I had never consciously thought about feeling special until it cropped up repeatedly in the interviews, I realize that I have experienced it many times abroad. When I was a Peace Corps volunteer in Cartagena, Colombia, I worked in a relocation neighborhood with former residents of what had been one of Latin America's most famous slums. I did community development work and nonformal education programs based at a convent that had a day care and food distribution program. When I descended from the bus to enter the neighborhood, I could hear the cries of the children ricocheting off their tightly packed, new cement homes, "The gringa is coming, the gringa is coming." Since they didn't have TV or Nintendo, I (the gringa with the strange version of Spanish) was a major source of entertainment for them. They would race out and put their often grubby little hands in mine as I passed, one of the highlights of my day. Their parents also came out to pat my arm or shake my hand and wish me a good day, or to ask my advice on some family matter. This was heady stuff for a twenty-two-year-old; such a daily welcome always made me feel special. When I look back on my life abroad, I see that the particular form of "feeling special" varied from country to country, but it was always present.

5.   *Taking pride in the ability to acculturate and adapt to changes.* A more specific way of feeling special relates to the expatriates' pride in their ability to survive and master the overseas experience. Each expatriate decides how "heroic" an experience he or she desires. For some, sheer survival qualifies as heroic, because mastering ordinary tasks overseas feels like an extraordinary achievement. Going beyond simple survival to work effectively within another culture, speak fluently in a foreign language, and become integrated into an unfamiliar society requires much more effort. Expatriates take pride in these accomplishments and perceive them as heroic because they, like mythical heroes, attempt to master the challenges in an unknown land.

6.   *Succeeding in comparison with other expatriates.* Taking pride in one's acculturation often comes from comparison with other expatriates who are in some way less successful. Expatriates are constantly exposed, through physical proximity, anecdotes, or comparisons made by host-country nationals, to compatriots who are miserably maladapted and who may even need to return home before their tour of duty is completed. It is virtually impossible for an expatriate to have no knowledge about those who have failed to succeed or cope with the expatriate experience. In comparison, the survivors often see themselves as heroes, who have what it takes to adapt.

7. *Experiencing a sense of mastery and self-confidence.* Most of the preceding categories of hero talk describe heroic efforts at work or in adapting to a foreign culture. This final category refers to expatriates' feelings of mastery and self-confidence that evolve from the heroic acts they accomplished overseas. Most of the expatriates I listened to were quite explicit in their belief that they had indeed done something difficult and worthy of pride. Like mythical heroes, they had returned from an adventure having "passed the test."

How, then, do expatriates adjust to crossing the return threshold? Mark, whom I introduced earlier, is a typical example. For two years, he had a steady diet of novelty and international travel. He finds it difficult to return to the life he once enjoyed in the United States.

• • • • • • • •

You have such an egocentric view of the world, and you go over— and my eyes were just opened. I can't remember another two-year period where I learned as much—appreciating different cultures and nationalities. I miss that very much. . . . There is something about coming back here. The drive down to [my suburb], although that is probably one of the prettiest drives you could have, but there's just something about it after driving down Piccadilly and Hyde Park. There is no challenge to it after two years of challenge and just everything new, from catching the subway to finding out what time British railroads go to Dover and the flights to de Gaulle . . . and all of a sudden, back to (the suburb). And there is no challenge to this city. . . . I don't have to get out a map or anything. . . . For two years, I carried a map in my briefcase. I must admit I am not thrilled at all with the thought of "this is it." I get up in the morning, I back up in my driveway, and I say, "It is a beautiful home and it is a nice, comfortable life, but . . ."

• • • • • • •

It seems to me that the following passage explains in part why repatriation is so difficult for Mark and other expatriates.

• • • • • • •

People say that what we're all seeking is a meaning for life. I don't think that's what we're really seeking. I think that what we're seeking is an experience of being alive, so that our life experiences on the purely physical plane will have resonances within our own innermost being and reality, so that we actually feel the rapture of being alive [Campbell, 1988, p. 3].

• • • • • • •

Expatriates feel more alive overseas because of the adventure, the challenge, and the learning inherent in the experience. This is why so many of them describe it as the most significant experience of their lives. They are challenged to learn and master new skills and settings in a way that has never been necessary in their own culture. When they return home they are no longer the same people they were when they left, because, like mythical heroes, they have been transformed during the journey.

The Call to Adventure

Accepting the Challenge

> *A legendary hero is usually the founder of some-*
> *thing—the founder of a new age, the founder of a*
> *new religion, the founder of a new city, the founder of*
> *a new way of life. In order to found something new,*
> *one has to leave the old and go in quest of the seed*
> *idea, a germinal idea that will have the potentiality of*
> *bringing forth that new thing. . . . You might also say*
> *that the founder of a life—your life or mine, if we live*
> *our own lives, instead of imitating everybody else's*
> *life—comes from a quest as well.*
>
> —Joseph Campbell, *The Power of Myth*

What can we learn by using the metaphor of the hero's adventure myth to understand the stories of expatriates who have "gone before us on the hero path" (Campbell, 1988, p. 123)? The first phase of the hero's adventure signifies the separation from the world and is called the departure stage. It is composed of three substages: (1) the call to adventure or refusal of the call; (2) the crossing of the first threshold and the entering of the belly of the whale; and (3) supernatural aid of a protective figure—the magical friend. This chapter focuses on the beginning phase of the myth—the call to adventure or refusal of the call.

The call to adventure is the point at which the mythical hero either decides to pursue a quest or stumbles innocently into an adventure while chasing something else. For example, Theseus wanted to become a great hero like his cousin Hercules; his call occurred when he learned that seven maidens and seven youths of Athens were to be eaten by the Minotaur. He vowed to kill the beast, and thus his deliberate adventure began. An example of stumbling into an adventure appears in the legend of an Arapaho Indian girl who spies a porcupine. She wants its quills and follows the porcupine higher and higher into a cottonwood tree. Even though her friends call her to return, she continues climbing until she reaches the sky. In both cases, destiny has summoned the hero, and the call of the unknown is more powerful than that of the known. Joseph Campbell describes the call:

* * * * * * *

[The usual hero adventure begins with someone from whom something has been taken, or with someone who feels there is something lacking in the normal experiences available or permitted to the members of this society.] This person then takes off on a series of adventures beyond the ordinary, either to recover what has been lost or to discover some life-giving elixir [1988, p. 123].

* * * * * * *

Expatriates can be heard to remark that something is lacking in the normal experiences available in their own culture. Both Sam and his wife were actively looking for an overseas adventure. Sam is a pleasant, down-to-earth midwesterner who talked passionately about his experiences in South Africa. He was twenty-seven years old when he finally received the call to work abroad for his accounting firm as an audit manager. However, he and his wife were offered more of an adventure than they had in mind. They had hoped to go to Europe or the United Kingdom; they were offered, instead, a choice between Capetown and Johannesburg. It was 1985, and South Africa's deteriorating political situation made daily headlines.

• • • • • • •

We'd been planning to go overseas on this two-year exchange program since we were married. We never bought a house; we waited
on having children, things like that. . . . We had a choice,
Capetown or Johannesburg. And, you know, when I told my wife,
it was a hard time. I didn't know if I wanted to go. She didn't
know if she wanted to go. And we decided we didn't want to go,
because I was scared. . . . I probably would have had to make a
career change [if I had turned down the assignment] but I felt
other things are more important, like my wife's happiness and
safety. Because the unknown is always something you are not sure
of. . . . And we had kind of made up our minds that we weren't
going to go [but] my wife had second thoughts and she decided,
"Let's go!" We had no children, no responsibilities. "If we don't
like it, we can always leave. Let's take advantage of the situation."
And then things got really bad in South Africa. It was kind of a
difficult period before we left, because here we are, excited and
anxious to go, and people around us are saying, "How can you go
there? Jesus, aren't you scared?"

• • • • • • •

And so they went, and learned firsthand about the complexities
of South Africa's racial situation. Sam described their time abroad
as magical and special.

For the majority of the expatriates in my study, the offer of an
overseas assignment was seen as a call to adventure, a chance for
career advancement, or both. For others, it was a source of conster-
nation and ambivalence as they carefully weighed the pros and cons
of such a move. For a small minority, the call was not welcome, but
they felt compelled to accept it anyway.

I remember when the phone rang one hot, humid day in
Tumaco, Colombia. Did we want to accept a transfer to Upper
Volta? My husband, Asbjorn, turned to me and asked if I was willing
to go. After reassuring me that we were talking Africa and not

Russia (some of us are doomed to experience geography before the world map takes its proper shape in our minds), I enthusiastically nodded my agreement. Asbjorn hung up and we both raced for the atlas to figure out where in the world Upper Volta was located. (I don't advise that you do the same because the country has since changed its name to Burkina Faso. It is located in the interior of West Africa, bordered by the Ivory Coast, Ghana, and Benin to the south, Niger to the east, and Mali, home of Timbuktu, to the north and east. If these clues don't help, perhaps you should dig out the atlas.) We were thrilled to think of setting off on another adventure, especially one that would allow us to experience a different part of the world. It's obvious, in retrospect, that adventure and advanced wanderlust were our major criteria; we certainly did not make a rational decision based on information about the country.

I have heard many similar stories about split-second decisions from other expatriates. Like Sam, Hugh works for a major accounting firm. He too had requested an international assignment. Finally, the long-awaited call came from headquarters one day at 5:00 P.M.: "Do you want to go to Venezuela or Mexico?" Hugh replied, "Give me a hint where Venezuela is and I'll find out something about it." He had to let them know his decision by 8:30 the next morning. He opted for Venezuela and spent his free time traveling all over South America.

One possible explanation for how it was possible to quickly make these decisions is that some people are subject to impulsive behavior; another explanation is that something else is operating here—namely, a visceral, gut-level response to a call to adventure. When people are looking for excitement, the particular destination is less important than taking off for the unknown.

A transfer within one's own country can provoke a somewhat similar rush of joy, but the offer of an overseas assignment differs from domestic assignments in four aspects. First, an overseas assignment entails a more pronounced journey into the unknown than most domestic assignments. In many corporations, there is no guarantee that the expatriate will be rewarded with a promotion upon repatriation. There are even instances of expatriates being stranded abroad because no job awaits them back home. And while there are clear-cut regional differences within one's own country, there are enough commonalties and media information to support accurate expectations. However, there is no way to know what life in another culture is like until it is actually experienced (Schutz, 1944). Therefore, moving abroad involves leaving behind the known for the unknown to a degree that is seldom replicated within one's own culture.

A second difference is the greater physical separation from one's organization, extended family, and friends that going abroad creates. This substantial geographical separation leaves expatriates to face the unknown without the benefit of their accustomed anchors. On the positive side, an international experience often unites the nuclear family, partly because they lack these other anchors and "circle the wagons" to survive the challenge. But for those who accept the call, there is a sense of uneasy responsibility and uncertainty in uprooting a family with no guarantee that every member will adjust to the new culture or that the accompanying spouse will also find employment, gainful or otherwise.

Thus, a third difference is greater uncertainty about the potential adjustment of other family members to life in another country. Occasionally, children or spouses who adjusted beautifully to previous countries are surprisingly miserable in a particular culture and never do adapt.

Finally, the fourth difference between the domestic and international assignment concerns the nature of the cross-cultural experience. Usually, one's normal defense mechanisms and mental maps must be reorganized to cope with a different culture. Before that process is complete, the expatriate, like the mythical hero, will endure a high degree of uncertainty, anxiety, and unavoidable adventure. Not everyone is willing to withstand the discomfort. Many expatriates, however, are like the heroes who accept the call to adventure because they feel there is something lacking in their lives. Those who are ready for an adventure and willing to make the necessary sacrifices are likely to have a gut-level reaction to the call. It is therefore more important for potential expatriates to pay attention to their emotional response to the call of an international assignment than it is for those reassigned domestically.

Of the many expatriates I spoke with, the vast majority reported that they were extremely excited when they first heard about the possibility of going abroad. They described it as a rare opportunity and a flight into the romantic unknown. According to one person, "Our first reason for actually accepting the assignment probably would have been just the adventure of going out and trying something different." Many used the phrase "I'd always wanted to go" when they spoke about accepting an assignment. Several decided instantaneously, or hesitated only long enough to obtain the agreement of their spouses. And even though it had occurred years earlier, many recounted the actual moment of "the call" with the same total recall and enthusiasm usually given to marriage proposals.

Jack, an urbane, intelligent man, is an expatriate's expatriate. He is the hub of the loose expatriate network in his city because he counsels many expatriates-to-be on visa requirements and international legal matters. Jack spent several years abroad and still travels so extensively on business that he feels he has not really left Europe. His fascination with Europe began when he did his secondary studies abroad. Jack received the call to go to Belgium approximately eleven years prior to recounting the following story:

* * * * * * *

I remember sitting in my office downstairs on the eighteenth floor and the managing partner of the corporate practice group came to my office. I was still a fairly young attorney here and I thought immediately, "Holy Toledo, what did I do wrong that he's coming to see me?" He told me that . . . the firm had an office in Brussels . . . and the workload was increasing and they needed to send somebody there and would I be prepared to take an assignment of a year or two in Brussels? I said yes immediately! And he said, "Well, don't you want to think about it?" and I said, "I'll think about it overnight, but I don't think my answer's going to change."

* * * * * * * *

In an interesting study of Swedish expatriates, Ingemar Torbiorn (1982) writes that expatriates should have a spontaneous desire to work abroad and even an element of idealism or a sense of mission. Otherwise, they are not likely to make the necessary sacrifices or be committed to achieving a real understanding or acceptance of the conditions in the other country. This sounds very much like a call to adventure that will require heroic sacrifices. There is some disagreement, however, in what has been written about expatriates concerning the validity of a motivation such as the lust for adventure or a pioneering spirit. While Chorafas (1967) and Voris (1975) consider these acceptable motivations for going abroad, Fayerweather (1959) suggests that exaggerated or romantic expectations result in greater disappointment with the reality of the new setting. Failed expectations about an overseas assignment can definitely cause problems, but they can be partially avoided if companies provide prospective expatriates with realistic job previews and accurate information on the country. The results of my own investigation indicate that a sense of adventure is in fact an acceptable motivation and one that many of the expatriates I interviewed said they would use as a criterion for selecting prospective expatriates.

Just as there are different types of mythical heroes—those who choose to undertake the journey and those who blunder into it—there are similar differences among expatriates. Some immediately see going abroad as a call to adventure and require very little information about either the country or the job before they accept. Other expatriates are more cautious and need to reflect and gather more information before they agree to go. Still others go not because they want to but for career reasons or because the company will not allow them to refuse. Once abroad, cautious or reluctant expatriates may or may not allow themselves to be swept away by the adventure of life abroad.

Even when people have sought out an overseas assignment, they may have second thoughts. Mark, the returned expatriate introduced in the first chapter who kicked up a fuss when his boss tried to switch job assignments on him, actively campaigned for an international post as part of his company's management development program. His following words capture both the exhilaration and the reluctance to pull up roots:

* * * * * * *

And I remember the phone call came and [my manager said], "You are going to London!" And I remember the exact moment. I was sitting in a car on West Sixty-Fifth Street and I remember the thought was just excitement and, on the other hand, I felt a tear because I said [to myself], Geez, what am I doing? Because the family life is great, the work life is great, I enjoy the city. And all of a sudden it was like, I am leaving it all. I remember just being so torn for probably about a week or so and then [I] talked to people who had been on tours [of overseas duty] and that sort of thing. Once I got over that first week, I bought into it and it was just pure excitement. . . . [On the way to London], in New York, I remember I had a two-hour layover. And I remember then I was just choked up. Because I was extremely emotional, and I am not a terribly emotional person. And I remember calling my father saying, "I don't know if I am doing the right thing here." And he said, "You are, you are, just go. We will miss you, but you can always take a flight home." So there it was, you know, off on this big mission. And it was just terrific!

* * * * * * *

For other expatriates, as for the mythical heroes who fall into an adventure, the ambivalence occurred before the call was accepted. Of the people I interviewed, the few who reported difficulty deciding whether or not to go abroad were ambivalent due to fears about the adjustment of their family and/or concerns about the job. Allen, a bespectacled engineer working for a chemical company, was thirty-four when he was offered a challenging job in Argentina. At this point, he had already spent about eight years working in his company's international department. He was chosen for the assignment in Argentina because the company wanted him to get overseas experience and because his particular technical expertise was not available there.

* * * * * * *

The first crisis of course is just to make the decision to go. I mean that was a very tough decision, having a wife who had a job . . . a career; two children; a mother who was a widow; and so on. Just making the decision to go . . . took a long time. There were many sleepless nights, many long conversations weighing pros and cons. . . . Finally, my wife said, "Why don't we go for it?" I think deep down inside I really wanted to go for it, because that is the reason I came to International. I knew when I came to International that eventually I would be asked to take an overseas assignment. So the decision part was long and drawn out.

* * * * * * *

After a rocky start, Allen and his wife adjusted very well. When Allen was unexpectedly transferred back to the States several years ahead of schedule, his wife cried.

Bruce, a tall, athletic forty-year-old banker, was offered a high-level staff position in a Hong Kong bank because there were no local employees who could handle the particular job. Unlike most international assignments, this one had less autonomy than his stateside job in a regional office.

* * * * * * *

[Two bosses] both approached me to take a job in Hong Kong. It happened to be on a day when we were having a golf outing . . . and I thought they were just trying to unnerve me before the golf game. But it turned out to be a serious request and I can remember calling my wife shortly before our guests came to the golf outing and telling her. She asked what my reaction was and I said, "Well, I was going to think about the offer." And she said, "If you wait more than thirty seconds before you say yes, you are crazy!" . . . My concerns about going at that time were more related to the position I would be in. I have always been in a line position and prefer customer contact work. The job that was offered to me was a staff position, more administrative, albeit in a much more exotic spot. . . . So, while I initially would have jumped at the chance to go to Hong Kong, my reservations were about whether the job was right.

· · · · · · ·

The reaction of ambivalent expatriates was a cognitive, rational approach that centered on what the assignment would mean for their career and family. Some were concerned about moving high-school aged children. In one case, the expatriate initially decided against moving his teenage children, even though the assignment would be good for his career development. However, after visiting the foreign country and gaining a clearer picture of what they could expect, the family as a whole decided to go. With very few exceptions, the spouses in my study were very willing to go abroad and adjusted well. Several subjects mentioned that their wives were more adventurous than they and had really encouraged them to accept the assignment. The spouse's failure to adjust is often cited as a reason why expatriates return early, but my interviews indicate that, in many cases, it is also the spouse who encourages the expatriate to accept the call. Authorities on expatriates acknowledge the importance of the spouse's reaction and commitment to making the experience successful. In my own experience, it is usually the positive attitude of the spouse who takes care of the children that determines whether the children will adjust well. The chances that the spouse and children will not adjust are greater when they themselves do not perceive the chance to live abroad as their own hero's adventure.

As expatriates become older and more experienced, many are more picky about the calls they are willing to answer. A common statement by high-level executives with a good track record and people with previous expatriate experience is "I'll go under certain conditions and if I'm my own boss."

Ron is a candid, take-charge kind of guy whom I interviewed a few weeks after he returned from a highly successful assignment in Europe. He had worked abroad before for the large chemical company that employs him, so when they asked him to turn around a poorly functioning plant in Holland, he carefully checked out the situation before accepting the job.

. . . .

We got the word back here that the whole problem was in the plant. When I went over and talked with the different people, it wasn't all in the plant. There were a lot of management problems. So I said, "If you want me to go back there on a two or three year assignment, then I want to know definitely that I've got two years minimum." And I had estimated that we were going to need about three quarters of a million dollars to turn the business around. I said, "I need the commitment on that. . . ." After some *keen* discussions with the president of the division, he agreed. So I went over, and after eighteen months we started making money, and it went up from there.

. . . .

Ron was trying to ensure that he would have both the time and resources to get the job done. Some overseas jobs have built-in obstacles that one learns to avoid. For example, many of the staff and advisory jobs with foreign governments are frustrating because one has little or no influence with host-country counterparts. Occasionally, the person who requested the expatriate either leaves the agency or assigns the expatriate to other managers who did not request outside help. Furthermore, some subsidiaries resent having to pay a higher U.S. salary and benefits for an American expatriate from headquarters when they think a local employee could do the job better and cheaper. Although the experienced expatriates I interviewed enjoyed living abroad, they were also concerned that future calls include jobs that would allow them to be effective and avoid the pitfalls they had observed in foreign assignments.

In some companies, expatriates are forced to accept an international assignment because there is an unwritten norm that you can only turn down such an assignment once without jeopardizing your career. "Acceptable" reasons for turning down the offer are usually personal or family reasons. The second call, however, must be accepted to show one's loyalty to the company and one's support for an international focus. In reality, this norm may be counterproductive. Both the expatriates I interviewed and those I observed abroad who had been ambivalent or downright unhappy about going abroad tended to be less adjusted, in their own opinion, than those who had wanted to go. This makes sense if we recall Torbiorn's (1982) warning that succeeding abroad requires considerable energy and commitment. People who do not want to live abroad seldom make the necessary effort; thus, they remain either marginalized in solitude or "enclaved" with other unhappy compatriots. As a result, they receive little gratification or reinforcement from the overseas setting; this makes them try even less to adjust, setting in motion a vicious cycle. It is logical that companies intent on developing global capacity encourage and reward people for getting international experience. However, an unanticipated consequence of corporate policies that insist on international experience for top management positions is that some people are forced to choose between two equally distasteful options—accepting an international assignment they do not want, or risking career stagnation. Although I believe in the positive value of an international experience, forcing reluctant managers to go abroad may result in an early return or failure on the job. Most experienced expatriates come to have strong feelings about selection criteria, because they have seen so many failures and because they know how much damage disgruntled expatriates can do to the company's reputation and profitability. So much of being an effective expatriate has to do with one's attitude toward the experience that it is risky to send people who have been forced to accept a call they do not want to answer.

If people find themselves in this position of being forced to go abroad, it is time for serious soul-searching about why they do not want to go and about the strength of their dislike compared to the importance of their career. How flexible or rigid are they in their attitudes? Vowing to work on their attitude and make the best of a time-limited assignment is the answer for some reluctant expatriates. Most people can salvage something from an overseas experience, even if they do not enjoy it as much as others do. I would not recommend, however, that people with rigid personalities and ethnocentric views toward the other culture be pressured to go abroad.

It is easier at certain points in life to answer a call to adventure. Going abroad as a single person, a childless couple, or a couple with very young children is relatively uncomplicated. A spouse's career and children's schooling, however, become extremely important considerations and constraints. In many countries, it is illegal for spouses to work, so their career options are severely limited. The entire family has to answer the call or at least make a commitment to work at adjusting. If the expatriate makes such an important decision alone without consulting the family, answering the call can be the prelude to personal tragedy. At the same time, a refusal to answer the call can lead to stagnation. Thus, for some expatriates, opting for the hero's adventure is clearly a high risk–high gain proposition.

Refusal of the Call

In mythology, a refusal of the call is dealt with harshly. Minos had prayed to the god Poseidon to raise up a bull out of the sea as a sign that he was the rightful owner of the throne in Crete. In return, he promised to sacrifice the animal immediately to demonstrate his allegiance and service to the god. Poseidon gave King Minos a divine bull, but when Minos saw it, he decided it would be to his advantage to sacrifice a substitute and add the majestic bull to his own herd. The sacrifice of the bull during Minos's investiture was to symbolize his selfless submission to his role as king. His kingdom prospered economically but, as punishment for reneging on his promise, Poseidon made Minos's wife fall madly in love with the bull and she bore him a son, the Minotaur, half bull, half human.

Another example of the refusal of the call is Daphne, daughter of the river-god Peneus, and an independent young woman who did not wish to marry. When Apollo saw her beauty, he chased her, but she refused to stop. Just before Apollo caught her, she asked her father to change her and destroy her beauty. Immediately she was transformed into a laurel tree.

Campbell describes what the refusal of the call has meant in mythology:

• • • • • • •

Refusal of the summons converts the adventure into its negative. Walled in boredom, hard work, or "culture," the subject loses the power of significant affirmative action and becomes a victim to be saved. His flowering world becomes a wasteland of dry stones and his life feels meaningless. . . . All he can do is create new problems for himself and await the gradual approach of his disintegration. . . . The myths and folk tales of the whole world make clear that the refusal is essentially a refusal to give up what one takes to be one's own interest. The future is regarded not in terms of an unremitting series of death and births, but as though one's present system of ideals, virtues, goals, and advantages were to be fixed and made secure [1968, pp. 59–60].

• • • • • • •

Some of the expatriates reported that had they refused the assignment, they would have spent the rest of their life wondering what they had missed.

A perilous journey across dark seas to the unknown makes the adventure more explicit, but we do not have to leave our borders to respond to a call to adventure. This was the theme of the popular film _Dead Poets Society,_ in which "Seize the day!" is the exhortation of the prep school teacher encouraging his students to follow their dreams and live up to their potential. "Follow your bliss" was the advice Campbell gave to his own students. Yet, if one can answer the call and have a hero's adventure at home, one can also go abroad and still refuse the call.

This was the case with Sandra, one of the few female expatriates I was able to locate. After passing through a security check that rivaled some border crossings, I was elevated to the upper regions of the multinational where Sandra works. I found a businesslike woman who exuded competence in a senior management position. Sandra sought out an international experience solely for career reasons. She spent almost all her time abroad working. She insisted that there were no cultural differences between the United States and England. She did, however, feel that her expertise was more respected by the British. Sandra was very successful in her overseas job and developed good relationships with colleagues and subordinates. Yet in her own eyes, she had a very limited adventure. She explains, "London worked out exactly as I wanted it to, but it wasn't a life. It wasn't very satisfying working all the time. . . . You succeed but it's not what you wanted—'Is that all there is?'. . . I did what I wanted to do and it wasn't enough."

Campbell states that the price of the refusal of the call is meaninglessness, which is clearly a theme in Sandra's story. Furthermore, in mythology a refusal of the call represents a reluctance to set aside one's personal interests, which may also be evident in Sandra's phrase, "I did what I wanted to do and it wasn't enough." She went abroad, but apparently refused the call to adventure.

One finds a wide variety of expatriates overseas. Some are off on their own unique hero's adventure. Others began their settlement in a foreign country years ago as an adventure, but as the years passed, the unknown became the known and evolved into a routine that no longer requires heroic effort. For some of these long-term, one-country expatriates, returning to their native country would be the more heroic adventure. Other expatriates, those who accepted the overseas assignment but refused the call to adventure or did not perceive that one was being proffered, are not enacting heroism but simply living their lives abroad for personal, career, financial, or other reasons. The message is not that these people are leading meaningless or selfish lives, but that some metaphor other than the hero's adventure would be more appropriate for understanding their experience. My purpose here is not to develop metaphors for all types of expatriates, but to focus on the one that seems most prevalent.

As we see in the following chapter, the next step in the journey for both heroes and expatriates who accept the call entails leaving behind the known world for the unknown.

The Belly of the Whale

Stepping into an Unknown World

The Stranger within my gate,
He may be true or kind,
But he does not talk my talk—
I cannot feel his mind.
I see the face and the eyes and the mouth,
But not the soul behind.

> —Rudyard Kipling, *"Stranger"*

In hero myths, the call to adventure is succeeded by the appearance of a magical friend who protects and guides the heroes as they cross the first threshold and begin their journey. The first threshold occurs at the moment when heroes step outside their normal world and enter the unknown. For most expatriates, the presence of a magical friend is more likely to come after the crossing of this threshold, once they are living in the unknown world of another culture. Joseph Campbell describes crossing the first threshold as follows: "The adventure is always and everywhere a passage beyond the veil of the known into the unknown; the powers that watch at the boundary are dangerous; to deal with them is risky; yet for anyone with competence and courage the danger fades" (1968, p. 82).

There are two key points in the preceding passage. One is the idea of *crossing a threshold,* the boundary of the hero's present sphere. For expatriates, this step involves leaving the known quantity of their life in the United States and venturing forth into a strange culture. The uncertainty and difficulty of their first months in a new country are the result of their having crossed this boundary. The second key point refers to the presence in hero myths of *threshold guardians*, whose job is to watch the established boundaries and prevent the unworthy from entering.

The earliest example of the universal tar-baby myths, Prince Five-Weapons, illustrates this stage of the hero's adventure. The prince had just finished studying military skills with a renowned teacher. Because of his achievements, his teacher rewarded him with the gift of five weapons. On his way home, the prince came to a forest. People warned him not to enter the forest because therein lived an ogre named Sticky Hair who killed every man he saw. Nevertheless, the prince left the safety of the road and entered the forest, leaving the known for the unknown and crossing the first threshold. When he reached the heart of the forest, the ogre demanded to know where he was going and threatened him. The prince showed no fear, but all five of his weapons stuck to the ogre and when he tried hand-to-ogre combat, he himself stuck to the ogre. He warned the ogre that the ogre too would die if he ate the prince, who claimed to have a thunderbolt for a weapon in his stomach. Since the prince was the first man to show no fear of either death or the ogre, the monster became afraid and freed the prince, who was an early incarnation of the future Buddha. The thunderbolt represented the weapon of knowledge. The Prince preached his doctrine to the ogre, who was then transformed into a spirit and ceased to prey upon men. The ogre in this myth is a threshold guardian. The prince was warned to avoid the unknown forest and the ogre, but only by leaving the safety of the known path and courageously confronting the ogre did he find within himself the most effective weapon of all, knowledge.

The next sections explain in detail how these two aspects of the departure stage of the hero's adventure—crossing the threshold and threshold guardians—relate to the expatriate experience.

Crossing the Threshold

In myths like the tale of Prince Five-Weapons, most people avoid the forest because fear of the unknown keeps them within the established boundaries of their world.

* * * * * * *

> Beyond . . . is darkness, the unknown, and danger. . . . The usual person is more than content, he is even proud, to remain within the indicated bounds, and popular belief gives him every reason to fear so much as the first step into the unexplored. . . . The regions of the unknown (desert, jungle, deep sea, alien land, etc.) are free fields for the projection of unconscious content. Incestuous *libido* and patricidal *destrudo* are thence reflected back against the individual and his society, suggesting threats of violence and fancied dangerous delight—not only as ogres but also as sirens of mysteriously seductive, nostalgic beauty [Campbell, 1968, pp. 77–79].

* * * * * * *

Two analogies in this passage shed light on the way we talk about going to live in a foreign land. First, many individuals, "the usual people" in Campbell's words, are indeed proud of staying in their own country. They make comments like, "I don't see why you have to traipse off to other countries. The United States (or Senegal, Costa Rica, and so on) is good enough for me." The unspoken portion of the last sentence is sometimes, "Why isn't it good enough for you?" These same people are also likely to assume many negatives about other countries and to feel sorry for expatriates. Bruce, the banker introduced in Chapter Two whose wife insisted that he accept a Hong Kong assignment, described it best:

* * * * * * *

> I found it interesting, when I came back, that a lot of people said, "Oh, gosh, you must be really glad to be back!" How do you respond to a question like that? . . . To some degree, I am glad to be back; to some degree, I am not glad to be back. But the fact

that people asked the question in that way, indicating that, "Gosh, it must have been a horrible experience!" and you just sit there and say [to yourself], "Gosh, that's kind of narrow-minded!". . . I am so glad I had the experience, I can't tell you. And I think it is unfortunate that more people aren't open-minded enough to say that everybody would like to do it. And I do feel sorry for some people who live in the same spot their entire lives and think the whole world revolves around that spot.

• • • • • • •

In his words we can glimpse the essential lack of understanding that sometimes exists between the adventurers, who go beyond the indicated bounds, and the "usual" people, who are content and proud to stay within those bounds. Both feel somewhat sorry for the other and have difficulty understanding the other's perspective. How is it that some people perceive living in another country as an exotic adventure while others see only danger and discomfort? Just like the regions of the unknown in myths, "alien lands" can be blank screens upon which people project their own unconscious thoughts. Had Sam and his wife been swayed by the newspaper reports about South Africa, they would have missed what he called "the experience of a lifetime." They found their fears about the country were unjustified. In fact, with the exception of war zones, life in other countries is seldom as negative as people imagine or project. Americans often grimace when I mention that we lived in Central America. "Weren't you scared?" they ask. "After Cleveland?" we respond. Cleveland is actually a very pleasant city, but all countries have hazards, and the ones from unknown countries apparently loom larger. Most expatriates quickly learn to accept and avoid whatever brand of danger a particular country offers. The important point is that people often project their fears (danger, health threats) and desires (the siren call of Tahiti, Hawaii) onto foreign countries because they represent the unknown. If we allow it, projected dangers can become threshold guardians that prevent us from ever crossing the first threshold, or from really experiencing the other culture.

What is the actual crossing like for expatriates? It is usually very stressful. Apparently I am not unique among expatriates when I admit that the only (non-family-related) temper tantrums I have ever thrown occur during the first few months in a new country when my tether is noticeably shorter than usual. Moving, starting a new job, and making new friends all at once is always difficult. However, the inherent difficulty of moving and creating a new life structure is exacerbated by crossing the threshold of another culture.

A prominent source of concern are the ordinary details of living. How do I get a telephone installed and the lights turned on? How do I locate the nine different stores or markets that are the equivalent of my favorite discount store? How do I figure out that baking soda is sold in pharmacies rather than grocery stores? And how do I go about ransoming my household effects from customs? Ordinary tasks can become extraordinarily difficult abroad, and it is not until expatriates have developed a routine that they feel settled in. The following stories portray some of the uncertainty and difficulty of the expatriates' first days abroad.

I first met Carl, a tall, rangy man with a wry sense of humor, in a focus group for returned expatriates. Compared with other expatriates, Carl and his family were very much "on their own" overseas. Most business expatriates are assigned to established overseas offices with staff who meet them at the airport and provide at least some guidance or help in settling in. Carl, a scientist with a chemical firm, went to a German university to study a technology that was essential to his company's research and development (R&D) effort. He was on his own with no organizational support, except his paycheck. Before the actual move, Carl and his wife flew to Germany to make the final arrangements with the university and find housing and a school for their two children. In spite of this advance preparation, their first few days were full of unexpected difficulties with tasks that would have presented no problem at all in their own country.

• • • • • • •

> We arrived on a Saturday morning around 10:00 or 11:00 in the morning. Figured we could go out and stock up on some things on Saturday afternoon, except all the shops closed at noon on Saturday and we were just out of luck until Monday morning. . . . The second thing we had to do once we got there, we had to start buying furniture. Now this sounds like an easy task, filling a house full of furniture [but] . . . dealing with everybody in German! But we managed to get through it and we soon had enough furniture to move into the house. And there were a lot of ups and downs at first, I would say six months to a year. And then things settled down and we were more or less into a routine.

• • • • • • •

I encountered George, a mild-mannered auditor, when he was referred by another expatriate in his company. He had spent almost two years based in London, in charge of his Fortune 500 company's European auditing function. It was obvious from the joking around that accompanied my tour of George's department that his co-workers were used to being entertained by his stories about life abroad. Indeed, he had a host of hilarious stories to tell about the series of obstacles he encountered in his assignment. When I asked him what the first few days were like, he gave the following response:

• • • • • • •

> Sheer panic. Other than that, hey, no problem. There wasn't a lot of time to indoctrinate me. . . . My very first day in England I went into work just to get the car. . . . It was a stick shift. I drove a stick shift about fifteen years ago for about a month. . . . Now let's see, a stick shift. How does that work? . . . The manager who was leaving drove me to a petrol station, filled it up for me and said, "Okay, here is your driving lesson." So I jerked back [to the office about a

mile or two away] and he proceeded to show me where all of the little gizmos were on the car. He said, "Okay, you are on your own!" And there I was with the car and no map and two hundred miles to drive that day with a stick shift, sitting on the wrong side of the front seat. It was a little terrifying, a white-knuckle drive. The first few days were typical in that respect.

• • • • • • • •

People often expect fewer difficulties when they move to a country where the same language is spoken, but this is usually a mistake. Even without a language barrier, the culture can present enough differences to make adjustment a challenge. Mack, a reserved engineer in his thirties, was very surprised by his reaction to England. He was assigned to London as a project manager and technical specialist by his oil company. He and his wife, along with their two children, rented a house in a neighborhood that was not especially welcoming to either expatriates or children. Mack's major worry was his family's adjustment, and he summed up his first six months with a classic description of culture shock:

• • • • • • •

Uncomfortable and unhappy. It's hard to believe that it would be, because the first six months we did a lot of traveling too, and interspersed among those general unhappy feelings were a lot of good times and things that we never would have seen. And maybe that's another way to sum it up. It was like a yo-yo. One moment you'd be way up, you'd be really enjoying yourself, seeing something [new] and maybe you'd found somebody friendly and it'd be really a good feeling. And the next minute you'd have that feeling of a mixture of everything bad—homesick, lost, can't understand everything that's said to you even though it's English. All of it together so you were just up and down . . . on the whole, pretty uncomfortable.

• • • • • • •

Moving to Burkina Faso was one of the most difficult physical thresholds my husband and I crossed. We arrived with a one-month-old baby at what turned out to be not deepest, darkest Africa but brightest, flattest Africa. There was only one available house to rent in the small town of Kaya. It was a small cement-block house with no ventilation, on top of a laterite hill that supported very little vegetation. Since we were worried that the baby might get malaria from the numerous mosquitoes, we quickly put up screens on the windows and doors, prompting our French neighbors to ask, with flawless logic, "How will the flies get out of the house?" With some difficulty, we even screened the vent pipes that theoretically let hot air escape from the false ceiling. Even so, the inside walls of the house were too hot to touch during the dry season. The town had electricity only from 6:00 to 10:00 P.M., and shortly afterwards we discovered why no one else had ever screened the vent pipes. When the house went dark, the bats who lived in the false ceiling and used the vent pipes as their nightly exit came down into the house, looking for a way to get outside. They swooshed through our humble home, occasionally careening into our mosquito net. Nothing in Doctor Spock had prepared me for flying rodents, and I was terrified a bat would bite the baby if she rolled against her mosquito net. In retrospect, perhaps we should have simply removed the screens from the vents but, as a brand new mother, I didn't like the idea of sharing a tiny house with forty bats. We decided to evict them and experimented with several methods. In one of our first attempts, we both held an end of the volley ball net and tried to snag bats by moving the net up and down. This was complicated by the fact that we had no illumination at this time of night other than the flashlight wedged in my armpit. After a bat was diverted into my hair by this technique, we decided to try something else. (This was about the time of my Burkina Faso temper tantrum, triggered by finding a dead bat in the baby's toy basket.) I beamed the flashlight around the living room like a searchlight while my husband swatted the bats with a tennis racket that somehow eluded their radar system. By the time our belongings arrived a mere six months later, we had a batless house. We managed to liberate our crate of household effects from customs just before the customs building burned down. As I stood on our porch gazing fondly at the long awaited crate, I noticed a black tide moving toward the door. On closer inspection, the crate was full of thousands of black ants, apparently intent on taking over the house. I emitted a ladylike shriek and ran to put the baby in a safe place while I drowned the ants. A passing African grabbed the hose and together we repulsed the invaders. Life settled down somewhat after those first six months and assumed a more predictable pattern.

When crossing the threshold, there is always the chance that one's belongings may go astray or arrive in an altered state. One expatriate family opened their crate to discover that their rocking chair had apparently not fit the box, so the Afghan movers had simply cut off the offending part of the rockers and inserted them alongside the chair. Another embassy official steamed along with his belongings after his crate was left moldering in the tropical rain on a Nigerian dock for several weeks; but he went ballistic when they bulldozed his crate to smithereens to make more room for incoming cargo. There are enough awful customs stories from many countries to drive a materialist to minimalism. Not only can you not emancipate your belongings because of red tape, but you are charged for each additional day they are held in the customs warehouse where, adding insult to injury, customs workers may help themselves to whatever strikes their fancy. Sometimes your belongings arrive without a hitch, but it's an uncertain proposition. I usually plan on not seeing them for six months, if ever.

Governmental red tape is a major logistical headache, particularly in less developed countries. Acquiring a visa can take months, years, or literally forever in many countries, and the visa may be a prerequisite for other transactions like renting a house, buying a car, or opening up a bank account. In Guatemala, an entire industry has sprung up to provide relief for foreigners and locals alike who have an aversion to dealing with governmental bureaucracy or who cannot afford the time it involves. *Transpapeladores* ("paper passers") expedite government paperwork on behalf of clients. Twenty years back, a group of expatriates in Colombia agreed that the most infamous-red-tape case in that country was a customs process at the Santa Fe de Bogotá airport that involved thirteen signatures on a form. However, the need for thirteen signatures in itself was not enough to capture the infamous title—it was the fact that one person's signature was required on this form in four different spaces *but* he could only sign after the person whose name preceded his on the list had signed the form. This meant tracking the same man down and waiting to see him on four separate occasions!

In some countries, obtaining the required signatures and stamps for the simplest government form feels like a diabolical scavenger hunt or the proverbial catch-22. Once Asbjorn had to send his passport to the Peruvian ministry of foreign relations for a new visa. In the 1970s, governmental red tape was raised to an art form in Peru (eleven signatures for a lost driver's license). Although it was a routine procedure, the ministry failed to process the application in six months, and we were due to leave the country for another post. When repeated requests and lawyerly, bureaucratic machinations failed to free his passport, Asbjorn took to calling himself a political prisoner. He was rescued by our maid, another magical friend, who had a relative working for the government; the relative sneaked into the government building after hours and liberated the passport in time for us to catch our flight.

The degree of difficulty experienced in crossing the first threshold may vary for spouses. For the working spouse, the majority of whom are men, crossing the threshold may be somewhat smoother because having a job provides some degree of consistency with their previous life and structure in their new environment, lessening the unknown. Some expatriates use their office as a safety zone until they feel comfortable enough to cross the threshold of the foreign culture. This was Dan's strategy. He is a self-described loner who worked in Brazil as an operations manager for a large multinational. While he enjoyed what he called the adventure of learning how to buy and cook the right cut of meat, he left all the settling-in problems to his wife, who was more outgoing. The downside to this strategy was that it took him longer to cross the cultural threshold because he barricaded himself at work.

* * * * * * *

And I had the fort of the office. And very often I would work seven days a week. Just because it was comfortable. I had my desk and my stapler; and the people there, all the guards and everything, knew who I was and would take care of me. Brought me my water and tea and made sandwiches and things like that. So it was more comfortable for me inside the fence and it took a while to get out on the street. It just took a while. It was a strain on the family because I left it all to them, you know. I left the problems to them while I went to work. There was a lot to do, too.

* * * * * * *

Researchers have written about the greater difficulty of nonworking expatriate wives (Adler, 1986; Gaylord, 1979) as they struggle with the initial logistical arrangements and the lack of structure in their lives. Whether the accompanying spouse is male or female, nonworking spouses are faced with the task of composing a life "from scratch," a challenge for which few people are prepared.

Many of the male expatriates I interviewed acknowledged that the initial challenges were greater for their wives. For example, Eric believes that their two international moves were more difficult for his wife than for him because he "arrives one day and goes to work the next," leaving her to get the family settled at home and school. Eric is an exuberant marketing executive whom I interviewed in his home, which was full of Asian art. He and his family had recently returned from Korea and were still getting settled. He was quite proud of his wife's capacity to manage everything overseas. She had established her own export company, showing the same initiative she had exhibited on the first day of an earlier assignment in Japan.

* * * * * * *

> The first day we got to Japan, well, first of all they lost our bags, which was typical. But I told my wife, who was staying at a hotel in Tokyo, "Take the train out to the bus and get on the bus and our stop is like the ninth stop and the house is right there," because I had bought the house and she had never seen it. So she got to the train station, had enough money to get onto the train. She got off the train at the right place and went down to get the bus. She got to the bus, went to get onto the bus and then she ran out of money, change. So she went into a Pachinko parlor [where a game is played with steel balls] and asked for change and they pointed to a machine and she put a thousand yen into a machine, and got a big plastic bucket of Pachinko balls. And she thought that they were tokens for the bus. . . . And that box of Pachinko balls is here somewhere. We kept it with the thought in mind that anytime you felt stupid about something you did—just drag those babies out.

* * * * * * *

People often feel stupid in their first months in a strange country. In addition to making assumptions that things are similar to life at home when they are not, one experiences an enormous amount of uncertainty. How do we interpret the verbal and nonverbal messages we receive from people in the other culture? What do we have to say and do to get the same kind of responses, or social reinforcement, that we are accustomed to at home? How do we express complex thoughts in the vocabulary of a two-year-old?

Expatriates who make the effort to learn another language experience tremendous mental fatigue in the beginning as they struggle to understand a torrent of meaningless sounds. One expatriate described the emotional low point of his entire sojourn as "dealing with some person on the phone who is speaking a mile a minute, and you don't understand a word that they are saying." It is these moments of total frustration that make expatriates wonder if they will ever survive and be productive. Even after attaining a certain level of fluency, there are periodic vocabulary challenges as one's exposure to another culture expands. For example, one might easily master work-related technical terms, but dealing with having a baby in that language might send one rummaging quickly for the dictionary to look up technical childbirth terms.

In the same way that the nature of the first threshold varies for spouses, it also varies for different expatriates. For example, it is fairly easy to move to a country where there is an established office and to take over the household (even to the point of inheriting the servants) of one's predecessor. It is harder to be the advance person for one's organization and arrive in a country where both the office and the household must be organized from the bottom up. Some unlucky souls arrive to find that the job they thought was theirs no longer exists. Others find themselves with a job so loosely defined that they must struggle to carve out a role for themselves. Still others discover that the locals resent their presence before they even set foot in the office. Expatriates assigned to a number of regional offices often face a greater challenge than expatriates working in only one country. They have to undergo a crash course in regional cultures, languages, management styles, products, and travel arrangements.

Expatriate managers invariably run into different ways of doing business or getting things done at work. Paul, an enthusiastic engineer in his late thirties, was sent to be technical director for a Mexican manufacturing plant. He quickly ran into a common cultural obstacle: "getting your work request into the queue."

. . . .

Procedures for filling out a maintenance request were very slow. There are forms to do that here [in the United States], and you get results. If you fill out forms down there, you get no results at all.

But on the other hand, if you go to the maintenance supervisor and say, "Come on buddy, I need some help," in a minute he'll cut off the other guy that came to him yesterday and go fix my equipment. There's no point in going on a Wednesday morning and saying, "Can you be here Friday morning?" because, of course, he'll say yes. But that precludes the possibility that someone is going to meet him at the gate on Friday morning and take priority.

* * * * * * *

Another threshold problem is the testing period that sometimes occurs in the beginning of an assignment. Especially in cultures that are organized in terms of in-groups and out-groups, it takes foreigners quite a while to earn their acceptance. Foreigners are, by definition, part of the out-group and are usually treated with distrust and suspicion by the in-group (Triandis and others, 1988). It is not uncommon for expatriates in some situations to be treated discourteously in the beginning and made to cool their heels until they have gained the respect of the local people. This was often the case when expatriates dealt with government bureaucrats in West Africa. Because of the colonial history, Africans sometimes put white expatriates through a testing period to see whether they will prove to be arrogant or respectful.

Lack of knowledge about how to implement changes in a foreign culture is another problem that appears especially during this stage. Most expatriate managers have cross-cultural failures to confess. Paul was concerned that his Mexican engineering supervisors were working too much overtime. They were not paid by the hour but they spent too much time at work during the weekends. Paul tried to institute cross-training so that they could cover for each other on weekends. However, he ran smack dab into their reluctance to trust each other to not make mistakes in each other's turf. This was more important to them than having time off. He also discovered that they preferred hanging out at the plant on weekends to having time off.

For some people, crossing the threshold brings unpleasant "surprises"—the discrepancy between one's expectations and the reality one finds (Louis, 1980). It is easy to have mistaken perceptions about foreign lands because of the distance involved and the siren song they represent to us. The more unrealistic the expectations, the harder the crossing, and at some point expatriates may begin to question the wisdom of their decision to go abroad.

Both cultural and physical thresholds involve learning. The expatriates I interviewed mentioned repeatedly that their first six months abroad were a time of accelerated learning. Among the numerous demands at work, expatriates also struggle to bone up on meaningful history and to decipher strange policies and operating procedures. They learn to decipher who the key figures are and how they should relate to them. They perceive and adapt to a new set of constraints, developing ways to work around them. In order to cross the cultural threshold, they learn to crack the code of the other culture and figure out what behaviors are acceptable and what are unacceptable.

Expatriates describe the threshold period as a time of strangeness, exhilaration, difficulties, uncertainty, and intense learning. For most people, this period ends around the sixth month, when they have established a routine and begin to feel comfortable.

The Threshold Guardian

The second aspect of the departure stage in the hero's adventure are the threshold guardians. In myths, the guardians of the threshold are often ogres, dragons, or monsters whose purpose is to keep the unworthy from passing into another region. Only courageous and clever heroes survive their encounters with these guardians.

A few expatriates complained to me about specific individuals in the overseas office who had assumed ogre-like proportions in their eyes and kept them from accomplishing their mission—for example, "Initially I had difficulty working with my boss but I worked that out; it was like being in a Vegematic—you knew eventually you would escape, but you'd have a lot of scar tissue." For the most part, the threshold guardians for expatriates come in less obvious forms, such as (1) lack of language ability, (2) the impermeability of certain cultures, (3) the tight leash of a company headquarters, and (4) the restrictive nature of expatriate communities.

Lack of Language Ability

Learning a new language is one type of threshold for expatriates to cross, and one that is directly related to expatriates' effectiveness in their jobs (Osland, 1990). When expatriates speak the local language, the local people are more likely to accept them and to open up and share more information about both work and cultural matters. People are often grateful when expatriates make the effort to learn their language, and they manifest that gratitude in better treatment. Many expatriates consider learning the language to be common courtesy. There are fewer opportunities for misunderstandings and awkward relationships when expatriates are fluent in the local language. Many people tend to assume that foreigners who cannot speak the local language are either stupid or gullible. In turn, expatriates feel more a part of the local culture and experience it more fully when they are fluent. When I rode the bus to work on the extroverted northern coast of Colombia, I would eavesdrop shamelessly on the boisterous conversations that took place around me. People would often scream ribald comments to friends on the street, and the whole bus would chortle in appreciation. It would have been a shame to miss out on that slice of life by not understanding the language.

Cultural Impermeability

Many authors have written about cultural characteristics, similarities, and values (Hofstede, 1984; Kluckhohn and Strodtbeck, 1961; Torbiorn, 1982), but there are apparently no studies that compare the permeability of various cultures—their willingness to accept and integrate foreigners. Yet this factor may have much more impact upon the expatriate's ability to enter another culture than the similarity of the new culture's values to the values of his or her native culture. For example, the British are perhaps most similar to Americans in their cultural value patterns; however, many of the expatriates I interviewed report that it is difficult for Americans to be accepted in Britain. Numerous expatriates mentioned the anti-American feeling that exists in many parts of Europe; this sentiment also inhibits relationships, in spite of what many Americans perceive as a common cultural heritage. Expatriates mention such countries as England, Luxembourg, the Netherlands, Japan, Hong Kong, and Korea as cultures in which it is most difficult for Americans to find acceptance. I would like, however, to state a caveat, that there is always the danger that expatriates may assume that their individual difficulties in another culture are experienced by all expatriates. In other words, if I have offended the local people somehow and they avoid me, I may mistakenly attribute their rejection to their attitudes about foreigners rather than to my own inappropriate behavior. Before concluding, therefore, that these particular cultures are more impermeable than others, I would want to do an exhaustive study on cultural impermeability with a large sample of expatriates. In any case, the concept of cultural impermeability is highly significant. A few examples will serve to illustrate.

Several expatriates described the Luxembourgers as "cliquish," especially if one does not speak their language (French, German, and Luxembourgian are all spoken by the locals). Expatriates say that Luxembourgers keep to themselves for historical reasons—they grew weary of being overrun by a succession of foreign armies. Whatever the reason, the expatriates' efforts to fit in met with limited success.

Neil, a perceptive, confident man, has a high-level position in international banking. He and his wife worked very hard to take full advantage of an expatriate experience in Japan. Their goals were to become fluent in Japanese and to learn as much as possible about the country. Neil's wife succeeded so well that she coauthored a best-selling book on Japanese art.

* * * * * * *

> We started out socializing with transient expatriates. And we ended up avoiding [them] and spending all of our time with Japanese friends or American friends among the permanent expatriate community. . . . I think it is very difficult to become friends with the Japanese. I should say that the Japanese also become very distrustful of Americans who appear too acclimated, assimilated to the country. It was interesting that we found that our proficiency in Japanese opened a number of doors to us when we first arrived, when we were first still learning. But after we learned Japanese well enough that we started to lose our American accents and where we could speak on the telephone and have other Japanese think that we were Japanese. . . . that's when the Japanese would become distrustful. Distrustful is the wrong word. They lose their standard ways to deal with Americans. They know you can see through the facade. . . . They wonder if you have compromised your own national identity in order to learn their language so well. And that type of compromise, generically speaking, would not be well regarded among Japanese. . . . It's a very important concept to them.

* * * * * * *

Neil never regretted learning the language, but despite his best efforts, he knew he would never be fully accepted in Japan. Although many expatriates manage to cross the threshold and enter the cultures they described as "tougher," it seems that frequently their efforts are met with resistance because of the culture's attitude toward foreigners. They accustom themselves to what feels like rejection, keep making initiatives, sharpen their language skills, and work harder to understand the cultural norms and get beyond this particular threshold guardian.

Headquarters Constraints

Sometimes it is the organization that places constraints on expatriates that make it difficult for them to enter other cultures. For example, the travel time required by certain jobs makes it virtually impossible for some expatriates to learn a local language or develop local friends. Other companies ignore the advice of the expatriates and force them to do things that are so culturally inappropriate that the expatriates' credibility with the local culture suffers. The allegiance of the expatriate is a concern at some headquarters. Rather than encouraging their expatriates to become acculturated, they emphasize adherence to the parent company's attitudes and ways of doing business. Nancy Adler (1986) found that the less acculturated expatriates were perceived by headquarters as being most effective, because their allegiance was never in question. Becoming too acculturated and adopting the management style of your host country may not be appreciated at some headquarters, and may work against you in the long run. This was Dan's experience in his job as operations manager. His assignment in Brazil lasted five years, which was long enough for him to develop a style that worked with his employees but was different from the style favored at headquarters.

· · · · · · · ·

> We met many people [Americans abroad] that were loud and didn't even know they were in a different place and really didn't have any respect. . . . We saw a lot of people push, the American kind of bullying and the due dates and all that which is expected here. I've been criticized for the way I handled those things [in Brazil]. I am looser than a normal American. I got rated very, very high in my performance with the South Americans. The review went on and on and I said [to the headquarters person], "Is this going to hold me back with a domestic position?" About knocked the guy right off his chair. He said, "Well, I am afraid to say it probably will." Because of the things I got rated [highly] for, compassion, working with the people and doing it their way, and

getting them to cooperate and all that stuff. . . . I didn't beat anyone up and swear at them.

· · · · · · ·

Many U.S. companies would congratulate a manager who had
moved beyond beating up on employees and swearing at them, but
the question remains: What happens when expatriates develop a
management style overseas that differs from the norm in the home
office? Expatriates do not have much choice about adapting their
management style to local conditions if they really want to be effective and produce results for the company. Perhaps they can protect
themselves by educating people at headquarters on local conditions
and requirements and demonstrating in their contact with headquarters staff that they are also proficient with the headquarters'
style. Even within one's own culture, competent managers diagnose
the setting and the people involved and employ the style that is
most effective; thus, the ability to adapt one's style should be perceived as an advantage rather than as a disadvantage.

Multinationals have different approaches for dealing with their
foreign operations, and some approaches constitute a threshold
guardian for expatriates. Unlike companies that make a sincere
effort to understand cultural differences and adapt to local conditions, the attitudes and behaviors found in some organizations are
ethnocentric and even xenophobic (fearful of the foreign). Expatriates are more likely to find themselves caught in double binds and
uncomfortable boundary-spanning situations when they work for
ethnocentric organizations.

I met Stewart and his wife through my own expatriate network
before they went overseas. As so often happens when people decide
to go abroad, they sought out returned expatriates for information
about life abroad and reassurance that they were making the right
decision. I interviewed Stewart, a thoughtful, conscientious attorney, shortly after he returned home from an assignment in Japan.
He had held a high-level position in an overseas administrative

office for a large multinational. His particular threshold guardian was a demand from headquarters regarding a brand new plant, that placed him in a difficult position and affected his credibility with the host culture.

. . . .

> When somebody you have respect for at headquarters gives an order to study closing down a plant in Japan with its emphasis upon the long term, and you know that's something you really can't do, [you are put into a very difficult situation]. I mean, you just opened the plant! You just moved machinery and equipment there. You just had all these people commit hours and hours of time to moving their families there. And now you are telling them with a straight face, "Well, let's study closing the plant." I think you try to represent the company as best you can . . . to make [the Japanese employees] feel that [the people back at headquarters] are not a bunch of idiots. . . . But sometimes you can't do that.

The Expatriate Community

The role of an overseas expatriate community is a fascinating one. For some people, the expatriate community serves as a cultural mentor. For others, it functions as an organizing principle around which they structure their lives. For still others, it allows them to "move away from [foreign] people" (Horney, 1950) and stay with "their own kind."

In the beginning of an assignment, expatriates often seek out their compatriots to get the information they need—advice about schools, neighborhoods, where to shop, how to deal with customs, what to avoid, and so forth—what one expatriate referred to as the "rules and regulations" of life in that country. This support speeds up the transition process. When so much of one's environment is new, it is a relief to speak one's own language with people who are more or less on a familiar wavelength. The common bond among most compatriots allows them to let down their hair and talk about their frustrations or events that are happening at home.

The comfort and ease people feel with their compatriots serves as a "safety zone," a time-out from the rigors of trying to learn about and fit into another culture (Ratiu, 1983). The expatriate community is also the one place where expatriates are not, by definition, marginal and relegated to the fringes. Among their own kind, they can be full members and even leaders if they wish, which is seldom possible in the local culture until many years have gone by.

Although it is difficult to generalize about them, the expatriate communities of different nationalities have some common characteristics. The Chinese, for example, tend to live in self-sufficient compounds, complete with their own imported-from-home cooks. French expatriate communities often have an extremely active social life—one shift of people for cocktails followed by another shift for dinner. Most of the American communities I have encountered overseas provide both a warm welcome and a fund of essential information to newcomers. This seems to be especially true in hardship posts and countries that are not overrun with Americans.

The transient nature of the community seems to affect people differently. Some make friends more rapidly overseas, wasting little time in the preliminary stages of friendship because they never know when people will be transferred. Other expatriates think temporary assignments encourage superficial relationships at the expense of deep friendships: "Let's not get to be too close, because we know that in a couple of years we're not going to see each other again anyway."

Expatriate communities sometimes function as threshold guardians. In such communities, members make little or no effort to move beyond the narrow confines of the expatriate community, and they discourage new members from doing so. By segregating themselves and taking a condescending manner toward the locals, such communities prevent expatriates from crossing the threshold and experiencing another world.

For their own peace of mind and to help them get past this sort of threshold guardian, expatriates must often distance themselves from the expatriate community's attitude about the local culture, even though this stance may be perceived as a defection. Paul, introduced earlier, underwent many struggles while adjusting to his job in a Mexican manufacturing plant. He eventually blossomed, however, in that culture and really enjoyed and respected the Mexicans. Perhaps because there are so many Americans living in Mexico, the expatriate community there did not put out the welcome mat for Paul and his family.

* * * * * * *

> My wife did get invited one time . . . to a gringa party. That was the day after she had met someone in the local Kmart place who told her they have a group of twenty-four American women who get together in one another's houses once a month to, quote, bitch about these Mexicans, unquote. No, "bitch about these *damn* Mexicans," and it was these damn Mexicans who helped us move in, who helped us find our way around town. And now that we were more or less settled, these aristocratic holier-than-thou's show up and decide they want to be our friends. No, thank you!

* * * * * * *

Expatriates may also limit their time with the expatriate community because they want to be more effective and integrated. Stewart and his family worked very hard to understand and appreciate Japanese culture and learn the language. This paid off, because he gained the confidence of his Japanese colleagues, who shared with him their concerns about the company's operations. "I think that if people had behaved the way we had in general, the company would have been better off. Some of the guys simply made no effort to learn the language. They were part of the American community and chose not to do anything but remain a part of it."

In summary, overseas expatriate communities have the capacity to be both a positive and a negative force in the lives of expatriates. In the beginning of an assignment, they are especially helpful in transmitting useful information and in providing a safety zone when the burden of acculturation and total immersion becomes onerous. They also provide a context in which the expatriate does not have to be marginal. However, when they prevent expatriates from developing positive attitudes toward the host culture and from integrating themselves into the other culture, they function like the threshold guardians in the hero myths.

The Belly of the Whale

Once mythical heroes leave the world they know, they no longer have the same measure of control over what occurs to them, because beyond the first threshold lies the "belly of the whale." In this stage of the adventure, heroes are swallowed alive, falling into an abyss of some sort over which they have no control; later on, they are resurrected. This death-and-resurrection theme is found in the myths of cultures throughout history. The mythological significance of this stage of the hero's adventure, according to Campbell, is as follows:

◆ ◆ ◆ ◆ ◆ ◆ ◆

The belly is the dark place where digestion takes place and new energy is created. The story of Jonah in the whale is an example of a mythic theme that is practically universal, of the hero going into a fish's belly and ultimately coming out again, transformed. . . . Metaphorically, water is the unconscious, and the creature in the water is the life or energy of the unconscious, which has overwhelmed the conscious personality and must be disempowered, overcome and controlled. . . . The conscious personality here has come in touch with a charge of unconscious energy which it is unable to handle and must now suffer all the trials and revelations of a terrifying night-sea journey, while learning how to come to terms with this power of the dark and emerge, at last, to a new way of life [1988, p. 146].

◆ ◆ ◆ ◆ ◆ ◆ ◆

This stage is the beginning of the journey inward that results in transformation. An important part of that journey is subjugating one's selfish needs or egoistic interests to the service of a larger cause. For expatriates, the belly of the whale represents throwing themselves into the other culture and opening themselves up to its influence. Up to this point, they have physically left behind their own country and crossed the first threshold of the other culture. The belly-of-the-whale phase depicts the psychological leave-taking of one's own culture. Perhaps for the first time, expatriates are forced to examine their lives, their basic assumptions and values, and the often-taken-for-granted superiority of their own culture (Schutz, 1944). This is the expatriate version of giving up control. When you are introduced in this manner to your own culture, when you open yourself up to learning about another culture, and when you relinquish some of your own freedom in order to respect its norms, it is impossible to foretell how the experience might change you and your view of the world. Once again, learning is a major theme in expatriate stories about this stage. Listen to Sam, the audit manager introduced in Chapter Two, reflect on his time in South Africa:

. . . .

We lived more in those two years than [in any others]. I am thirty years old now and I think in those two years I probably grew the most. You open yourself up more [abroad]. You find that you have to make friends because you are there by yourself. . . . You are just thrown into an environment completely new to you so you have to make friends. . . . [One of the partners] said I came over as a little boy and left as a man. That's kind of true. I went over as kind of a brash American, cocky, thinking that what you know is the best and no other way. And you leave humble and a little less brash . . . more understanding and sensitive to other cultures and other people. And I think I grew a lot in that area. . . . I just think Americans have this ego problem at times that needs to be bashed overseas. . . . I think I learned that there is a heck of a lot more than just putting your head down and working. There is a lot out there to see and do and experience, and you shouldn't just grind through your day.

· · · · · · · ·

Not all expatriates throw themselves into the belly of the whale to the same extent. Some merely take a cursory look inside the whale's mouth before buffering themselves from as much cross-cultural contact as possible. The degree of contact determines, however, how much of an adventure expatriates will have and the extent to which they may be transformed by their experience abroad. Campbell's quotation describing the belly of the whale points out the importance of allowing the unconscious to release "the power of life." In myths, heroes can only be transformed when they relinquish control and allow themselves to experience a higher level of consciousness. The meaning of the metaphor for expatriates is that immersion into another culture allows greater access to their unconscious and to the possibility of experiencing a higher level of consciousness, which also results in transformation. For the expatriates in my study, the higher level of consciousness is either biculturalism or the realization that they, like Prince Five-Weapons, carried within themselves the hidden strengths needed to overcome the difficulties of their overseas adventure.

Acculturation Strategy

The question of how far expatriates enter the belly of the whale is determined by their acculturation strategy. Expatriates generally believe that one's level of commitment to acculturation is positively related to a successful expatriate experience. The greater the degree of effort to integrate oneself into the other culture, the more likely one is to be successful. This seems obvious and is usually true, but it was noteworthy that this particular topic aroused the most "heat" in the interviews. Why were the expatriates so emphatic about the advantages and "rightness" of their own acculturation strategy and so critical of other expatriates who did not adopt the same strategy?

My conclusion is that acculturation strategies serve a dual function. On the surface, they represent the expatriate's conscious decision about how to "do oneself" in the other culture. What is less obvious and what explains the strong emotions aroused by this topic is that acculturation strategies appear to be one of the most important determinants of expatriate social status.

Within the United States, people use a variety of status markers (for example, titles, houses, belongings) to differentiate themselves into a societal pecking order. For many expatriates, these external indicators of status lose some of their significance abroad because the host country's social order assumes greater significance and/or the host country's nationals may or may not be impressed by the U.S. brand of social trappings.

One of the most hilarious evenings my husband and I spent in Burkina Faso occurred when some African friends stopped by our house after attending the moving sale of the Peace Corps director. The Africans had never before seen many of the items on sale and did not know their names. They described each item they did not recognize and we tried to guess what they were talking about. When we were successful and could explain what these items were used for, they would break into gales of laughter over the stupidity of the white man's paraphernalia. They would listen incredulously and ask, "Surely you don't really need that, do you?" Hearing it put like that, you begin to think twice about the absolute necessity of owning a woodlike slab that you plug in (the meat warmer). In this context, U.S. status symbols lose their importance, especially for expatriates living in less materialistic cultures.

This is not the case for groups of American expatriates who all work for the same organization, such as the foreign service or large multinationals; they bring with them their own social system with its unique status symbols. The general services officer at U.S. embassies often has the arduous task of ensuring that no one at a certain level has "more" (square feet of housing, fancier lawn furniture, and so forth) than others at the same grade and salary level.

Yet, many other expatriates feel somewhat removed from the status hierarchy and norms they left behind in the United States. Nevertheless, they do not completely liberate themselves from all comparisons, even if they are not in face-to-face contact with other Americans. Expatriates develop at least one unique pecking order abroad, and it has its basis in expatriate acculturation strategies. There are definitely variations on the status rankings I am about to present, but these are the principal groups that one hears expatriates talk about and compare. Many expatriates cannot be so neatly categorized; they fall somewhere along a continuum that includes these groups.

At the top of the hierarchy are those who have made a strong commitment to acculturation, sometimes by marrying into the local culture. These are the expatriates who speak the local language fluently; move freely in the other culture and perhaps in the international expatriate circle that includes various nationalities; possess extensive knowledge about the other culture; and are successful at work. They synthesize both cultures (Bochner, 1982) and come closest to being truly bicultural.

Further down the hierarchy we find two groups of Americans who seldom receive much respect outside their own social circles. The first group are the Americans who have "gone native" and have no contact with other Americans; they have rejected their own culture and embraced the host culture. In my personal experience, the few expatriates who totally reject their own culture are seldom well-balanced personalities. There is a difference between people who avoid all their compatriots because they dislike them and everything they stand for, and people who limit their contact with the expatriate community so it does not function as a threshold guardian. People who "go native" seem to be running from themselves when they idealize the local culture, and they incur the risk of identity problems (Bochner, 1982).

The second group that is criticized are those Americans who live in the "Golden Ghetto," a well-to-do area populated primarily by other Americans or expatriates. They limit their socializing to Americans or English-speaking internationals and do not learn the local language. By keeping to itself, this group rejects the host culture and idealizes its own culture (Bochner, 1982). Ethnocentric to a fault, members spend their time complaining about the locals and comparing unfavorably what they find abroad with what they left behind at home.

Pride is often an element in expatriates' stories when they talk about limiting contacts with other Americans or choosing *not* to live within the Golden Ghetto. As one expatriate put it, "When I was traveling, I didn't think I could learn anything about Peru hanging around with a bunch of Americans at the Hilton. . . . I'd rather stay in one of their nice hotels down the street and meet some people and you learn more about the country." This is a variation of a very common sentiment: "I didn't go overseas to be with Americans; I went to learn about the ———s." Many Americans seem to place a high value on learning about the other culture.

Given this hierarchy, in the eyes of many American expatriates acculturation seems to be a bell-shaped curve. Both ends of the spectrum—the Golden Ghetto approach that signals a total absence of integration, and the "going native" syndrome of complete integration with the other culture and no contact with other Americans—are perceived as negative. The expatriates I interviewed who lived in Golden Ghettos or who did not speak the local language seemed somewhat defensive on this point, going to great lengths to justify why they had made that choice even though no one was questioning it. This appears to indicate that whether it is explicit or implicit, expatriates see a degree of integration and acculturation as more desirable than isolation.

Many expatriates speak with surprising vehemence about how other Americans live abroad, whether or not they had personal contact with them. Why is it so important to expatriates how other Americans comport themselves abroad? Perhaps because outside the boundaries of our own culture, we still define ourselves in large part through comparisons with other Americans. Another reason may be that our ego boundaries often extend to include other Americans when we live abroad. Instead of limiting ourselves to worrying about our own behavior and its consequences, we correctly assume that the actions of other Americans also reflect upon us and may give us all a good or bad name. A Canadian expatriate in Senegal became inebriated and ran down a goat on his motorcycle in the wee hours of the morning. This was a serious faux pas in a devout Muslim neighborhood that highly valued both sobriety and their livestock. The reaction throughout the American expatriate community was identical: "Thank God, he's not an American!" Other times, we have not been so lucky.

Even though expatriates describe differing acculturation strategies, their stories have two aspects in common. First, they are quick to verbalize their strategy, which probably means that it is an important issue to them and one that may require a conscious decision. The second aspect is the instinctive comparisons people make about these strategies. Stan is a career expatriate in his fifties who is now director of a chemical company's international operations. He is a highly respected graybeard in the company. Abroad for nineteen years, he and his family both enjoyed and mastered the art of living overseas.

         · · · · · · ·

> We did try to get to know our neighbors. We did participate in activities in the communities in which we lived. We did make the effort to learn the languages. We were able to get by in the local languages in the three countries that we lived in. I have seen lots of people get turned off by Americans who never made any effort to get to know their next-door neighbor. Never made any effort to learn the language. Lived in a little cocoon. But I think if you make the effort, they [the local people] certainly appreciate it. And I think it makes your whole opportunity much richer for the effort that you put into it.

         · · · · · · ·

This is obviously good advice from an experienced expatriate. Yet along with the advice is the unspoken message that those expatriates who cocoon themselves by living in an enclave with their compatriots and who make little effort to acculturate are less admirable than those who try to integrate themselves.

At the very bottom of the expatriate pecking order are tourists. Many expatriates go to some length to avoid looking like tourists. Since most of us are tourists at one point or another, why do some expatriates look down on tourists and dislike being perceived as such? It is true that some American tourists can be loud and obnoxious; however, Americans do not have a monopoly on these traits and are not the worst tourists in the world. (While facilitating the strategic planning sessions for the tourism industry of a Latin American country, I watched in amazement when they unanimously voted to cross one country off their marketing list because its citizens were such disagreeable tourists.) It is also true that tourists are generally "prey" in places overrun by tourism, but I suspect that there are additional reasons why expatriates dislike being mistaken for tourists. Karen, a young scientist, had been working in a European research and development lab for four or five months when she described her visits to neighboring countries that attracted many American tourists. When she and her friends traveled to those countries on vacation, they spoke French so no one would know they were Americans. I asked why she did this and what she was thinking and feeling at the time.

* * * * * * *

We didn't want to feel like we belonged with all the other American tourists, I guess . . . because they talked too loud. . . . We went to the Heineken Brewery and everyone on that tour was American. . . . At first we kind of didn't want to be associated with them, but when we got to know just a small group, it was okay. They were just a bunch of normal people. [At the time we were] probably thinking that we were, and I hate to say this, a little superior because we knew at least some of the customs and we

> knew some of the things about them, that, say, someone who did live there would know. Kind of feeling that we knew more than the average person. But that didn't really make us better, it just kind of, in your own little way, you look down on other people. . . . it is like you . . . feel you are a member of a special little club, almost, and none of these other people know about it somehow.

◆ ◆ ◆ ◆ ◆ ◆ ◆

Wondering if this was more likely to occur in the beginning of an assignment, I asked whether she still felt this way at the end of her sojourn. She replied, "I still didn't want to be seen like a tourist. You wanted to feel you fit in a bit more. Knew enough of the culture that you wouldn't ask that question, or you would have already known the answer or stuff like that."

It seems to me that many expatriates enjoy being "in the know" about the history, geography, culture, and customs of the host country. Some of them use this knowledge to bolster a wobbly self-esteem (the snooty anglophiles, the self-proclaimed experts), but others take a simple pride in "knowing the ropes." They also take pride in "not standing out" which means, at a minimum, not looking like a tourist just off the boat. Like Karen, when they learn to fit in, they feel somewhat special and set apart from American tourists.

While chewing on this question, I was reminded of the times I have been mistaken for a tourist. On occasion when we approached individuals in other countries to request directions, they assumed that, because our appearance was foreign, we did not speak their language. This occurred even though we were speaking fluently (I've made great strides in Spanish since my Peace Corps days). It is interesting that their assumptions seemed to be based more on our appearance than on our ability to make ourselves understood in the local language. They would respond with words of pidgin English or with sign language while we tried to keep a straight face and/or restrain from grabbing what passed for lapels in that particular country and pointing out that we work, write, and teach in their language. It usually took a few minutes for them to realize that we were in fact speaking their language, and then the communication proceeded normally. But there was always a feeling of chagrin at being taken for a tourist when, unlike tourists, we had worked so hard to acculturate and learn the language. Americans who do speak the local language fluently receive so many compliments for doing so that it becomes a source of pride and something that sets them apart from and, consciously or unconsciously, above tourists.

Another reason expatriates dislike being taken for tourists has to do with stereotyping. Luke is a pleasant man in his thirties with an all-American look. He worked out of London for two years, setting up a European commercial banking network. Luke mentioned that every time he opened his mouth, the British would say, "Oh, you're a tourist." I asked him why he grew tired of being considered a tourist.

• • • • • • •

I guess it was just the fact that it limited things. There's an example that I used of when my son and I were walking around in a park. A British lady came up and asked directions. I started giving her directions and I'd gotten four or five words out of my mouth and her response was, "Oh, you're an American, you don't know." and she walked away. And it was kind of like, Why bother to try? Some merchants would assume people didn't understand exchange rates and the value-added tax and would try to add it on. And they'd try to cheat you. I got tired of that. . . . I guess I was tired of people assuming things, and assuming that you didn't know, assuming ignorance. I guess that's the thing that really bothered me the most about it.

• • • • • • •

The barrier in this instance came not from an assumption that foreigners cannot speak the language, but from the attitude that foreigners are by definition tourists who are not knowledgeable and

may even be "prey." Such attributions make it difficult for expatriates to feel either competent or integrated into the local culture.
Being a tourist does not require the hard work and sacrifice that is
demanded of successful expatriates; nor is it easy for tourists to be
"special" (except in their own eyes, of course) when there are so
many of them. Perhaps tourists are at the bottom of the expatriate
pecking order because other expatriates assume they are not
engaged in a hero's adventure, and because, due to their transient
status, they cannot immerse themselves in the other culture and
enter the belly of the whale.

The expatriate pecking order conveys the message that the
"ideal" expatriate makes a serious effort to acculturate and become
effective in the local culture. As the next chapter will show, the expatriate is helped in this endeavor by magical friends, who aid expatriates with the transformation that occurs in the belly of the whale
and with the obstacles they encounter in their journey.

4

The Magical Friend
Discovering a Cultural Mentor

*For those who have not refused the call, the first
encounter of the hero-journey is with a protective figure (often a little old crone or old man) who provides
the adventurer with amulets against the dragon forces
he is about to pass.*
— Joseph Campbell, Hero with a Thousand Faces

In mythology, the magical friend helps the hero on his or her journey either by explaining how to get beyond difficult obstacles or
by providing assurance that the hero will not be harmed. Ben
Kenobi, the elderly knight in the movie *Star Wars* who taught Luke
Skywalker how to use both a weapon and "the force," is an example of a magical friend. In myths, the guide, teacher, or ferryman are
other examples. Ariadne gave Theseus the thread that allowed him
to find his way out of the Minotaur's labyrinth. In Christianity, this
spiritual aid may be provided by the Holy Ghost or the Virgin Mary.
According to Joseph Campbell, the magical friend figure represents
the benign, protecting power of destiny. "One has only to know and
trust, and the ageless guardians will appear. Having responded to his
own call, and continuing to follow courageously as the consequences unfold, the hero finds all the forces of the unconscious at
his side" (Campbell, 1968, p. 72).

Expatriates, like mythical heroes, require help, protection, and encouragement. The following passage is an eloquent description of the challenges of mastering another culture:

. . . .

Learning to live in an alien society is much more than learning to speak a strange language, to eat unfamiliar food, and to observe different social customs. It involves a subtle but important change in one's expectations of oneself and of others and in the controls one feels over his [or her] emotions. One has to learn to do many new things and to stop a number of actions that are of long standing. But, more important, one has to cope with a loss of identity and familiarity and to get along without some of the social events that provide encouragement, direction, and meaning in our lives [Guthrie, 1966, p. 95].

. . . .

Learning to function in an unknown culture sometimes feels like one has been catapulted into a starring role in a foreign film without the benefit of either a script or subtitles. Culture shock results from not knowing how to gain social reinforcement in the foreign culture (Oberg, 1960; Furnham and Bochner, 1986). Behavior that is effective and perfectly acceptable at home may fail to produce the desired responses in others, or may even offend them. Even if expatriates have read extensively about the other culture and been forewarned about the major faux pas, they still have numerous questions that need to be answered before they can feel at home. Fortunate expatriates have cultural mentors, like the magical friends in hero myths, who explain the ropes to them and provide them with necessary encouragement when it feels like they will never "break the code" of the other culture and fit in comfortably. Cultural mentors contribute a great deal to reducing the uncertainty that expatriates feel.

Jack, the international lawyer introduced in Chapter Two who quickly responded to a call to Brussels, attributed his high degree of acculturation to a cultural mentor:

* * * * * * *

The person who became, in many respects, my mother . . . who I guess was a colleague of mine, not a contemporary in any sense of the word. She was in her early sixties when I went to Brussels. . . . She adopted me, gave me untold, unsolicited advice about how I should part my hair and what clothes I should wear and what language I should speak and how deferential I should be, all sorts of things. . . . She basically looked at me in the Ugly American role and viewed it as her job to educate me into the ways in which refined people in Europe conduct themselves. And so she would take me along to luncheons and dinner parties and introduce me to all the right people and make sure that I said the right things at the right time. . . . She's quite a character, but yes, she was my cultural mentor.

* * * * * * *

The extreme novelty and stress of entering another culture, coupled with expatriates' lack of knowledge about how to obtain social reinforcement in a new culture, compels them to seek help. For some, this signifies a forced return to childhood and dependency. Jack's reference to his cultural mentor as his "mother" may indicate the degree of dependency he felt in the beginning of his sojourn.

Jack was not the only expatriate to speak to me of his experience in terms of dependence and independence. Paul and his family had never been abroad before his transfer to Mexico. He struggled to learn the language and initially was both fascinated and baffled by Mexican behavior. His attitude toward Mexicans and toward his overseas experience was very positive. However, he was forced to request a transfer back to the United States because his children were not doing well in the local schools and his wife did not want them to fall behind. (Incidentally, of the thirty-five expatriates I interviewed, Paul was the only one who had to return because of his spouse and children.) I asked Paul to divide his overseas experience into a set of stages or chapters and to identify the major challenge of each stage.

* * * * * * *

[The first phase of my time abroad] was "social infancy" and the biggest problem was being so dependent. And the second one was making so many mistakes. . . . [I responded to that by] just observing what happened. I listened. I asked a lot of questions of people who could translate and explain not only what had been said but why they had said it. [In the next phase,] "adolescence," I was able to identify more and more of these things but I couldn't respond to everything. And there would be other cases where I'd either be cheated or laughed at or made fun of or used, . . . and I wouldn't even realize it! Getting into the [phase] I call "maturity"—all the other learning-curve episodes had passed. I was more in command of my situation at the plant and I was more independent out in the world and it was pretty enjoyable. The final phase I would call "autumn" although it's a little sad. By the end I was quite able to get along and at that point it was all cut off and [I came] back here.

* * * * * * *

The developmental life cycle is a good metaphor for describing the acculturation process. Paul did not have one major cultural mentor; instead, he asked questions of many people. Like most expatriates, he sought out people who could provide him with cultural explanations rather than simple translations.

When my husband, Asbjorn, was on his first African assignment, he realized that understanding the words in Burkina Faso was not enough. To be effective in that country, expatriates need a good command of French and a respectable smattering of Moré, the principal African dialect. One day he was sitting on a large mat on the ground, meeting with a group of Mossi villagers. An older man spoke a short phrase in Moré and everyone nodded in agreement. Seeing Asbjorn's puzzled look, someone translated the phrase into French, thinking that might help. It turned out to be a parable, the gist of which was something like, "the bird flew over." Since the

Mossi often employ parables and use them to capture the essence of what is occurring, Asbjorn's understanding of individual words was not enough; he needed an understanding of the cultural context as well.

Although cross-cultural communication difficulties were sometimes frustrating, part of our joy in living in West Africa was knowing that we were *not* on the same wavelength as the Africans; almost every day brought new revelations and cultural surprises that made life a constant source of novelty. We would not, however, have enjoyed the culture as much nor functioned very well in it had we not had a cultural mentor—Awa, a wise and witty African woman who taught us French and survival Moré. She answered innumerable questions about the culture, cooked us local food and taught us how to eat it with our hands without dripping oil all over our clothes, and explained what would be expected of us at various functions. Awa also provided invaluable work-related advice that helped both of us be more effective in our jobs.

Neil, the young banker introduced in Chapter Three who became quite fluent in Japanese and very knowledgeable about Japanese culture, was unique in that he was provided with an extensive overseas training program that evolved to include cultural mentoring.

* * * * * * *

I'd say there were two of my Japanese co-workers who I regarded as mentors, and they regarded me as their protégé to a certain extent. . . . Those were probably the closest relationships I had among my co-workers. And both those individuals were quite a bit senior to me in terms of age and certainly in life. . . . Now the fact that they have a consensus decision process working within a rigid hierarchy is not necessarily contradictory. The hierarchy is maintained by a very strict code of conduct and communication between yourself and various people elsewhere in the hierarchy. And . . . to assure that . . . those standards of communication are maintained, there is a detachment, a personal detachment between yourself and everybody else in the firm, that guarantees that there will never be a situation that would threaten that code of conduct. And so for that reason, I never really developed a close personal relationship with any of my colleagues. I had to have that aspect of doing business explained to me in very explicit terms by one of my mentors. Because I . . . became perplexed at my inability to become close with any of my workers. . . . The theme of that lecture was "being a manager is the loneliest job in the world."

* * * * * * *

When expatriates are trying to "break the code" of another culture, they function like scientists, forming hypotheses about the other culture, testing and discarding them, and trying to develop generalized rules that make behavior predictable. The trick is not to lock into attributions about the other culture before one really understands. Cultural mentors help expatriates test their hypotheses, provide missing explanations, and tell them when their conclusions about the other culture are incorrect.

Like Neil, many expatriate managers maintain a certain distance from their employees. It is quite common, however, for managers to develop a close relationship with one trusted subordinate. In South America, this person is called an *empleado de confianza*, someone who counsels the *jefe* (boss) and serves as a sounding board. If the *empleado de confianza* really has the expatriate's best interests at heart, the relationship can prevent the expatriate from making cultural errors.

Although we usually think of mentors as being older and more experienced than ourselves, this is not necessarily the case with cultural mentors. Good executive secretaries are often cultural mentors. When an expatriate boss was creating havoc in a Latin American organization, I went to his extremely competent secretary and politely asked if she had thought to warn him before he made his most recent cultural faux pas. She grimaced and said she knew that was part of her job; she'd done it for his predecessors. However, this particular expatriate would not accept any advice. He was eventually fired and left Latin America both puzzled and resentful.

Cultural mentoring is seldom a one-way flow of information. Expatriates also explain their own culture to their mentors and local friends, so the relationship is usually one of mutual sharing and co-inquiry about cultural differences. One day, a puzzled Brit came with a question for George (the auditor introduced in Chapter Three who experienced the white-knuckle drive on his first day in England). Their exchange sounds like a joke from *Reader's Digest*, but it's a good example of the kind of humorous give-and-take that occurs in overseas offices that manage diversity well.

· · · · · · · ·

"You know, George, I can understand why you [Americans] have so many different sayings and your accents are different when you consider the number of miles between us and the number of years that have passed. But one thing really bugs me, and that is the word 'schedule.' Don't you know the correct way to pronounce it is 'shedule'? Where did you ever learn how to say the word 'schedule' [with a hard c]?" George responded, "Well, in shool, of course!"

· · · · · · · ·

Cultural mentors are often members of the local culture who have lived abroad themselves and know what it feels like to be an expatriate, or who have had previous experience with Americans and other foreigners. They usually have a clear idea of what expatriates find most difficult to accept or learn about the local culture. Occasionally, these mentors are marginal people within their own culture who find it easier to be accepted by expatriates than by their own compatriots.

Research has shown that employees in U.S. companies who

have mentors within their organizations are more likely to succeed (Dreher and Ash, 1990). Similarly, the expatriates I studied who had cultural mentors in whom they could confide and who could explain the local culture to them (slightly more than half the group) generally fared better in four areas than those who did not have such mentors: (1) they were more fluent in the foreign language; (2) they perceived themselves as being better adapted to their work and general living conditions abroad; (3) they were more aware of the paradoxes of expatriate life, which indicates a higher degree of entry into and understanding of the other culture; and (4) they received higher performance appraisal ratings from both their superiors and themselves. In addition to these quantitative measures, expatriates with cultural mentors generally described their overseas experience in more glowing terms. This may be due to the fact that many cultural mentors provide social support, which not only moderates stress (Cobb, 1976) but also gives the expatriate a sense of belonging. Yet in spite of these advantages, only one company in my study has a program that might facilitate this type of relationship: Price Waterhouse assigns "host managers" to help new expatriates settle in.

Fortunately, the role of the magical friend is not limited to a mentor from the host culture. It is also performed by other expatriate Americans, experienced international residents of various nationalities, a career mentor back at headquarters, or by social or commercial networks—international schools, churches, social-athletic clubs, and business associations such as the chamber of commerce.

Recall Carl, the engineer introduced in Chapter Three who studied and worked with researchers in a German university. He and his family were totally on their own, and the initial months were fairly difficult for them. His advice to other expatriates is to locate a cultural mentor in the expatriate community and to rely on God.

• • • • • • •

I would say to probably find somebody who has been there previously in that particular country, or city especially, if you can. Find
some contacts—expatriates who are in the country that you can
talk to and lean on really for support and for help in getting
through the initial bureaucracy. And all the small things, I mean,
the shopping. Where do you go for this and where do you go for
that? Who do you see for this? Things like that. They are going to
have a lot of questions. I think they need someone there who has
been through it. . . . For myself, it was important to have a good
special foundation. Because I found, to me that helps me, that I
can lean on God and get through things. So I got Him—I got no
problems. I try to deal that way here in the United States as well;
it is not just peculiar to over there [in Europe].

• • • • • • •

For believers, God is the ultimate magical friend who provides
protection, dispenses wisdom, and helps us rise to a higher level of
spirituality or consciousness. Overseas churches are also seen by
many expatriates as communities that extend a warm welcome to
newcomers. Carl described the role his church played:

• • • • • • •

This was an English-speaking Catholic group, and we just kind of
stumbled on them and we found them to be very helpful. They
had all been there, all been through the same things we were
going through, so they just passed their wisdom on to us. And we
in turn passed ours on to new people who arrived, as soon as we
could be helpful. But that was really a steadying influence in our
stay over there.

• • • • • • •

Expatriates make similar comments about other U.S. groups
abroad: international school "PTA's" and such groups as the

chamber of commerce are familiar social systems and safety zones to which expatriates can turn. If expatriates are not careful, however, these same groups can also function as threshold guardians that prevent expatriates from venturing deeper into the local culture. Indrei Ratiu (1983) states that the "most international" expatriates he studied went back and forth from "safety zones," such as the organizations just mentioned or individual retreats, to greater involvement in the local culture. The less adjusted expatriates spent more time in the safety zones with people from their own culture.

For many expatriates, cultural mentoring takes place in social situations. This explains why some expatriates describe the way they socialized abroad as an evolutionary process. In the beginning, they sought out Americans because they had common interests and desperately needed answers to logistical questions, such as, "Where can I buy good peanut butter?" In some cases, inability to speak the local language forced the expatriates to restrict their socializing to their compatriots. As time went on, they socialized more with other nationalities, either locals or long-term third-country expatriates. When questioned about this transition, they stated that they wanted to avoid "grumblers" in the American community or were interested in learning about other cultures.

Harry, a flamboyant engineer in his forties, was promoted to the position of director of a high-profile international division headquartered in Great Britain. Many American expatriates who also worked for his company lived in the town in which he worked. He purposefully chose, however, to live in a neighborhood peopled by British subjects rather than by American expatriates. Thus, it was his neighbors who taught him about British culture and tried to protect him from opportunistic countrymen.

• • • • • • •

Our neighbors . . . would explain why things were done that way and how it's done and the significance of it. See, like, you've heard the rhyme, "You ride a cock horse to Barberry Cross?" Well, Bar-

berry Cross is the geographic center of England. . . . So you get
into the nursery rhymes and the significance of the nobility. . . .
Our neighbor would take us shopping and say, "Let me bid at the
auction because they'll hear your voice and they will send the
price up."

* * * * * * *

V. S. Naipaul writes in his book *A Bend in the River* that Africans
see everyone as either prey or predator. Foreigners, be they expatriates, tourists, or even immigrants, are seen as prey in many parts of
the world. Predators see them as gullible, wealthy targets who
deserve to be fleeced. Therefore, protecting expatriates from predators is common for magical friends. Some of my own favorite cultural mentors were the house servants who worked for us. In
addition to explaining all manner of things (the young Peruvian
maids taught me how to do the salsa so I could wiggle my shoulders
and locomote simultaneously and not be an embarrassment at the
office party), they would also warn me by a lift of an eyebrow when
vendors were overcharging or when beggars or employees were
lying.

While some expatriates seek enlightenment about logistical and
cultural issues, others are more concerned about their relationship
with headquarters. For them, the more important magical friend is
a mentor or advocate back at U.S. headquarters who provides support and ensures that they are not forgotten.

Regardless of who they are, cultural mentors are likely to share
three characteristics: (1) they have the ability to develop a trusting
relationship with the expatriate; (2) they have the willingness and
capacity for translating cultural meanings; and (3) they have a desire to protect the expatriate from errors or danger. How do people
find cultural mentors? Some stumble upon them (for example, language teachers or compatriots) and others deliberately seek out people who appear to be both approachable and wise. Mentoring by
host-culture people almost always takes place within a relationship;

there must be a certain degree of trust before it is appropriate to ask certain questions. Mentors usually have to care about expatriates before they will protect them from their own predatory compatriots. Expatriates need all the normal skills for developing relationships—trust; a sincere concern for the other person rather than the intention of using them; listening skills; consideration; and respect. Because they are in a cross-cultural situation, expatriates must also be open-minded, willing to accept feedback on their behavior, and careful not to insult or criticize the other culture. If they do not come across as people who accept advice and are sincerely interested in learning, help will not be forthcoming.

Expatriate Learning

The learning that occurs between expatriates and cultural mentors is only one element of the frequent references to learning in expatriates' stories. Along with adventure and challenge, learning was one of the three most commonly used words in expatriates' descriptions of their lives overseas. This makes sense in light of David Kolb's (1984) contention that learning is the major process of human adaptation. An overseas experience is an unparalleled opportunity for learning because it touches upon so many different areas:

1. It increases one's understanding of another culture.

2. It adds to one's understanding of the ways of the world, including economics, politics, history, fine arts, and so forth.

3. It broadens one's business sense through exposure to areas outside one's normal job or function.

4. It supports the self-discovery that is an integral part of the hero's adventure.

A few key lessons about cultural understanding are common to most expatriates. We learn patience and respect for the other culture; we learn that people all over the world are basically "people," even though their customs and ways of thinking and perceiving may be quite different. The basic message of any book or course on cross-cultural communication should be the necessity of appreciating differences and weaning oneself from the ethnocentric perspective that "my culture is better than yours." Surely most expatriates are exposed to this message at some point before they go abroad. And yet, it seems to be a concept that must be experienced firsthand before it can be truly mastered.

The very nature of a cross-cultural experience encourages self-examination and prompts many expatriates to ask questions like, What's important in my life? and, What are the most important values for me? Thus, while abroad, expatriates often learn who they are, and, as a result of exposure to a different culture, they learn what it means to be an American, a Colombian, a Japanese, and so on. In Scotland I learned that, whereas I had a passion to make changes at work, my employers were equally passionate about tradition. In Colombia I realized that I tend to appreciate people at work for what they accomplish, whereas Colombians appreciate co-workers for who they are. In Burkina Faso and Senegal I learned how individualistic my culture is in comparison to collective cultures in which people are responsible for a large extended family. I also learned that my customs were every bit as strange to the people of these countries as some of their customs were to me. Sometimes we mistakenly assume that tolerance only goes in one direction. For example, is left-handed aerial nose-blowing in a hot country with limited paper products any more bizarre than blowing one's nose into a handkerchief and saving it in a pocket? Once someone did ask what I was planning to do with it.

All these forms of learning are so crucial to a good experience that *willingness to learn* should be one of the key criteria for selecting expatriates. The commitment and sacrifices they make to learn the language, culture, and job often distinguish successful from unsuccessful expatriates. This willingness is especially important

during the first six months abroad, which is usually a period of accelerated learning. George, the head of a European auditing department of a multinational who was introduced in Chapter Three,
describes his beginning months as "a blind panic."

· · · · · · · ·

I have to learn everything there is to learn over there. I have to
learn how to be a manager. I have to learn the European way of
living. I have to learn the European company's ways of functioning. Just everything is brand-new. And I am the one who is
expected to learn this thing. So I better learn it quickly and figure
out the right way to do it quickly.

· · · · · · · ·

While the onslaught of demands to learn lessens after a while,
most expatriates constantly come into contact with new and different behaviors or customs that keep them in a learning mode. The
initial months function like a frame-breaking or upending experience that propels expatriates into a learning mode and forces them
to be more open to learning than most people need to be at home.
Doug, a talkative, energetic man, was assigned to London in his
mid-twenties to do new product development for his bank. Listen
to how he describes his experience.

· · · · · · · ·

Living abroad is just like when you are a kid. You get all these new
adventures and every day something is new. And then you get
older and there are no new challenges. And all of a sudden you get
thrust overseas and it is like being a kid again. You know, that type
of excitement.

· · · · · · · ·

In the same way that not all expatriates enact heroism overseas,
not all expatriates open themselves up to learning. Less successful

expatriates buffer themselves from the other culture and cling tenaciously to lessons from their own culture, even though the context has changed. This behavior is a coping mechanism rather than an acculturation strategy. For those proactive expatriates who are trying to adapt to another culture and become effective at work, learning is both a necessity and a pleasure.

Lessons About the Departure Stage

Neither mythical heros nor expatriates are always assured of a receptive audience that is willing to listen to the lessons they learned during their adventures. Nevertheless, I want to pass on the wisdom about the departure stage that I have gleaned from other expatriates and from my own experiences, in the hope that others may find it useful. Alexander Solzhenitsyn, one of this century's most famous expatriates, is said to have offered this advice: "Own only what you can always carry with you; know language, know countries, know people. Let your memory be your travel bag." Various advice books for expatriates are available, but the advice contained in these books seldom takes into consideration that the expatriate is about to take off on an adventure, an oversight that the expatriates I interviewed did not make.

Who Should Go Abroad?

An overseas experience admittedly is not for everyone, so how can people decide whether or not it's something they should do? The final chapter of this book contains a more complete discussion of selection criteria for companies, but the following questions may give prospective expatriates and their spouses something to ponder as they make their own decisions about pursuing an overseas assignment.

First, is working abroad something they would find extremely exciting and attractive—not the same level of excitement they might feel about going on vacation to a foreign country, but a deep, gut-level response to the idea? They will need this strong motivation to go abroad to help them over the trials and hardships that are part of all overseas experiences.

Second, are they at a point in their lives where they are ready for an adventure? Do they understand that it will be not only challenging but, if they are willing to see it in such a light, a very enriching, personal experience? An overseas assignment does not automatically pay off in terms of one's career or financial situation; this is determined by company policies for expatriates and, of course, by the expatriate's performance. Given the current emphasis on global business, it is hard to see how international experience would not be an advantage. Yet, in companies whose HR policies have not caught up with their international strategies, going abroad still constitutes a career risk. In the case of the person considering such a move, does the chance for a valuable personal experience outweigh the career uncertainty that might result? This is another way of asking if they would be satisfied with the intrinsic rewards of the experience if the extrinsic rewards failed to come through.

Third, are the prospective expatriates relatively flexible, adaptable, and open-minded? Can they see things from various perspectives other than their own? People who are uncomfortable with ambiguous situations, who insist on having things a certain way, and who have great difficulty tolerating and accepting people and customs that are different from their own are less likely to enjoy the expatriate experience. The same is true for people who tend to be constant complainers or people who have difficulty thinking well of others; a positive attitude seems to be an important prerequisite for adapting overseas.

Fourth, do prospective expatriates have good interpersonal skills that allow them to easily form relationships with people? In particular, do they get along well with people from different backgrounds, social classes, and ethnic groups? Creating a network of social support abroad is essential for adjustment, and good work relationships help expatriates be more effective on the job.

Fifth, how do they manage stress and conflict? Do they have a fairly high tolerance for delays and snafus or do things like this send them into a tizzy? Or do they have the initiative and skills to resolve stress or conflict situations? Do they have a history of negative coping mechanisms, such as brooding or turning to alcohol? Have they responded positively to challenges, hardship, and frustrations in the past? Have they shown both initiative and tenacity? Do they have a stable personality and strong sense of identity?

Finally, if they are married, are their marriages solid and characterized by consideration and good communication? Do their spouses also possess the characteristics mentioned here? If children are involved, have they been raised to be flexible and make the best with what they have, or do they expect a certain lifestyle that may not be possible in another country? Are they at a good age to be moved? It becomes more difficult, though not impossible, as they get older. If the children have special educational or medical needs, can these needs be readily met in a foreign country?

Advice to People Who Are Going Abroad

When the expatriates in my study were asked to take on the role of magical friend, the advice they gave prospective expatriates fell into the following categories: attitude, preparation, arrival, acculturation tips, and how to be effective at work.

Attitude

The element most commonly emphasized by these experienced expatriates is the importance of one's attitude toward the experience. Expatriates should not expect life abroad to be like life at home or business as usual. Instead, it is a golden opportunity to have an adventure and experience something different that can enrich the person's life. Over and over again, expatriates talk about how important it is to take full advantage of the overseas experience by learning the language, involving oneself in the other culture, and seeing what there is to see. Jack, an experienced international lawyer who was introduced in Chapter Two, regularly gives the following advice to the prospective expatriates who consult him:

· · · · · · ·

> I don't know anybody who's moved under any package who thinks they didn't lose money. So relax, you're going to lose money. Look to the other side of it. The overriding advice is, "take advantage of it for what it is." It's maybe for you a once-in-a-lifetime opportunity to live in a different place in a different culture. Yeah, there will be different things that will be hard to get adjusted to. Yeah, you may need the security blanket of the American community as a transition period, but try to get over that as soon as you can. You can meet Americans anyplace, anytime, but how many chances will you have to meet other people? Take advantage of it and learn the language. By all means, learn the language. Don't come back unless you speak the language fluently.

· · · · · · ·

Not all expatriates agree with Jack's opinion that expatriates always lose money overseas; it depends on the company compensation package, location, and individual spending habits. But his advice to look beyond the tangible benefits of money to the incalculable, intangible benefits of experiencing another culture, learning another language, and developing oneself is very sound.

One's attitude toward a cross-cultural experience is closely related to one's expectations. Some of the worst cases of culture shock occur in England, where a common language and heritage lulls American expatriates into assuming that they will readily feel at home there. When the inevitable cultural differences surface, some expatriates are unprepared and struggle to adjust their expectations. Lou is a project engineer for an oil company who went to England with his wife when she was pregnant with their first child. He expected that England would be different from the United States. Other than the initial difficulties of enrolling his wife in the British health care system, he thinks they adjusted very well abroad and attributes this to their attitude.

． ． ． ． ． ． ．

I think you also have to take a laid-back attitude towards the
whole thing and realize there are going to be differences, and
when there are differences, just accept them for what they are.
You're not really going to change anything. And if you go into it
that way, you're going to be in pretty good shape because there are
a lot of nuisances that Americans could find if they wanted to.

． ． ． ． ． ． ．

The truism that is passed down from expatriate to expatriate is,
"Take advantage of the good points and try to overlook the
bad points of where you are going." Lou took advantage of the good
points by touring all over Great Britain, even with a brand new
baby. In his words, "Every weekend was an adventure." He also
worked with a highly skilled counterpart—the host-country
co-worker who performs the same job as the expatriate assigned to
work with him or her—who taught him much more than he could
have learned in his U.S. job. When he returned home, he felt that
his life had been enriched, both professionally and personally. In
contrast, Dan (introduced in Chapter Three) was very successful in
his Brazilian assignment as operations manager, but looking back,
he regretted not having been more adventurous.

． ． ． ． ． ． ．

For selection criteria, I'd look for a person with a sense of adventure. I think that is something that maybe we did not have enough
of, or me personally. And I think that if we went someplace again,
we would force ourselves. It would not come naturally. You know,
we knew people where it became natural. They would get in their
car and go. They'd get stuck because they were driving from here
to there and there was no road. "What did you do that for? You
might be late for work on Monday.". . . But we don't get some of
those experiences that are unique and that make it worthwhile
going. We are a little bit too reserved. So there is not so much to

look forward to down there if you are not taking these little adventures and seeing things.

Preparation

As with any move or new job, the more realistic one's expectations, the less likely one is to be disillusioned. On an expatriate assignment, one can't overlook the road of trials that is part of any adventure. People should therefore obtain a realistic job preview and, if possible, visit the other country before accepting the assignment. Some expatriates try to reduce the uncertainty and the possibility of misunderstanding as much as possible by getting everything in writing—salary, job description, benefits, housing, school allowance, visits to home, and what kind of position they can expect upon repatriation. Nevertheless, there are often surprises or unforeseen complications. The period prior to departure should be one of information gathering about the job, the country, and its culture, and a time for both the expatriate and his or her family to begin learning the foreign language and cultural customs.

Expatriates should always ask several people who have lived in the country for which they are headed what they should pack to bring to that particular country. Solzhenitsyn's advice to take only what you can always carry with you, though extreme, has some merit. My advice would be to give priority to the belongings that make one's house feel like home—the paintings and "pretties" that you treasure—and the objects that enrich your life (such as music, books, games, or sports equipment), ahead of furniture, which may not fit a different climate or lifestyle. Belongings always require time and attention; in some countries, they are more trouble than they are worth.

Arrival

The first few days in a foreign country often are overwhelming. One prudent expatriate recommends that people get adequate sleep in order to deal with the onslaught of overstimulation that is a by-product of entering a new culture. One way of easing the initial period of adjustment is to take time to get the family settled before diving into a consuming job. Too often, expatriates make a beeline from the airport to the office. Married expatriates seldom endear themselves to spouses who are solely responsible for an overwhelming deluge of settling-in tasks. Unmarried expatriates who do this may not unpack for months and, as a result, may take that much longer to feel at home in the country. This stalling can set off a vicious cycle in which they work all the time because they have nothing to go home to and they have no other life because they work all the time. It makes more sense to let people get the home front organized so they have at least an illusion of control over one aspect of their overseas life.

The choice of neighborhood often determines the type of cultural experience an expatriate will have. For example, living in a Golden Ghetto populated by affluent Americans and foreigners reduces one's exposure to the local culture and, since such neighborhoods are often targets for thieves, may encourage a fortress mentality that colors attitudes toward the local population. A London-based expatriate complained that everyone in his well-heeled neighborhood owned country homes, so the street was deserted on weekends when he had time to be neighborly. Some areas are friendlier to foreigners than others, so it is important to talk with people to determine the character of different neighborhoods before making a choice that can affect your social life and feeling of belonging.

Affluence can be an unwitting barrier to getting to know the local culture. There is more contact when riding local buses, doing one's own shopping and errands, and living in a middle- or working-class neighborhood. Servants, chauffeurs, and messengers save time (and may even become cultural mentors), but they also buffer the expatriate from the daily contacts that can add up to greater cultural understanding.

No matter how much research I have done ahead of time, there have always been things about the other culture that surprised me. For example, when we returned to West Africa, I was expecting the same type of relationships and the traditional village social structure we had enjoyed and admired on a previous assignment. Instead, we found ourselves in a city that was unique in its strong anti-white sentiment. The city had experienced an apartheid-like style of discrimination during the colonial era. Adult Africans were never rude to white people, but they did not intervene when children and teenagers harassed whites verbally and sometimes physically in the streets. It was hard for me to reconcile my previous experience in Africa with this situation. Yet I had to accept it and look for the many positive things in that culture so I could be content living there. Expatriates have to move as quickly as possible beyond both failed expectations and the negative experiences that sometimes occur in the beginning of an assignment.

Parents should be careful in what they say about the other culture in front of their children. Children usually take their attitudes from their parents, at least in the beginning of an assignment. If parents complain openly and at great length about the local people, children may lose the will to adapt or, later on, have difficulty figuring out their own loyalties. Parents should teach children that all cultures, including their own, have both pros and cons.

Acculturation Tips

Although expatriates undergo varying degrees of culture shock, some difficulty should be expected during the first six months. Culture shock is defined as the confusion, disorientation, and emotional upheaval caused by being immersed in a new culture (Oberg, 1960). It is preceded by a honeymoon phase, which is followed by a period of frustration, depression, and confusion that often is triggered by a crisis involving petty cultural differences. This phase is succeeded by a recovery stage characterized by increased adjustment and satisfaction. According to Robert Kohls (1984), there is a second dip later on, the timing of which depends on the length of the expatriate's sojourn. Upon returning home, the expatriate experiences another honeymoon period followed by a readjustment crisis. Eventually, the expatriate recovers and adjusts to being home. It is usually very helpful to talk with someone who has already experienced and resolved these crises. One should not expect to feel comfortable in the other culture until late in the first year. Most long-term expatriates become skilled at entering new cultures and experience a greatly abbreviated form of culture shock.

It is hard to predict how individual family members might react in a new culture. The safest expectation is that, in addition to some exhilarating moments, the first year will be arduous in different ways for different members of the family. The only certainty here is that both spouses need to devote time and effort to helping the entire family adjust. Everyone requires both support and patience during this period. Expatriates risk being forced to request an early transfer home if their spouse or children have not adjusted, so the time and effort spent on helping them to adapt is well worth it.

Unmarried expatriates often develop a close social network that serves the same function as a supportive, caring family. Experienced expatriates advise all new arrivals to find friends and get involved in activities as soon as possible. They warn expatriates against isolating themselves, because friends who provide support, different perspectives, and advice can greatly reduce the discomfort of culture shock.

One way of easing into another culture is to utilize the resources of the expatriate community (church groups, women's clubs, the PTA, the chamber of commerce) in the beginning of one's assignment. As discussed earlier, these groups can be a wonderful source of information, advice, and quick friendships. It is dangerous, however, to limit oneself to this community and allow it to assume the role of a threshold guardian.

One of the most valuable pieces of advice for expatriates is to get involved in the local culture. Extracurricular activities and hobbies are excellent vehicles for gaining more contact with the other culture. Neil, the banker introduced in Chapter Three who was assigned to Japan, carefully constructed a well-rounded life overseas that ensured his involvement in Japanese culture.

* * * * * * *

I became a very avid potter. . . . I joined a Japanese pottery school as the only American, and this required a certain amount of language proficiency. I used to go at least two times . . . three times a week to the school. And then we collected Japanese pottery from all over the country . . . on weekends and vacations. That was my contribution to the nonworking part of our lives.

* * * * * * *

Other expatriates learn to substitute their usual activities with local approximations. Some play local sports, such as rugby in Great Britain or jai alai in Latin America, or became local-history buffs. I tried to keep up my music habit by learning local instruments; some of my fondest memories of Scotland are the bagpipe lessons I took from a crusty old piper. He couldn't get around much, but that didn't prevent him from trying to teach me how to do Scottish dances, using two fingers on the arm of his stuffed chair. Another unforgettable extracurricular experience that leaps to mind is the aerobics class I took in Senegal that regularly came to a screeching halt whenever the French participants felt a need to swap fattening recipes.

As this chapter has elaborated, given the proven benefits of having a cultural mentor, expatriates should try to find someone or several people knowledgeable about the local culture and willing to answer their questions. When foreigners demonstrate a genuine interest in and respect for the other culture, most host-country nationals are pleased to explain their culture. Often, the people who are most capable of doing so are those who have learned to see their own culture from a foreign perspective.

Culture provides us with ready-made solutions to basic human issues. For example, old age and dying represent an inescapable problem for all societies, but the manner of approaching and resolving this problem depends upon each culture's values and beliefs, such as attitudes toward the elderly, beliefs about the afterlife, and economic values. Each culture has its own internal logic; if that logic is understood, then norms and behavior make sense within that context. Being cross-culturally effective means taking on the perspective of the other culture and seeing the world from that viewpoint. As stated before, cultural mentors teach expatriates the foreign point of view and provide both advice and reassurance. Understanding why people behave as they do in the local culture and understanding one's own culture are prerequisites for acculturation.

All cultures are also ethnocentric. Expatriates must work hard at keeping their natural ethnocentrism under control by avoiding criticism of the local culture and unflattering comparisons with their own culture. They should strive to appreciate the other culture and its artifacts for what they are rather than focus on what they are not. Ethnocentric attitudes lie distressingly close to the surface of people's minds. If I enter a post office in a foreign country and am forced to wait a long time while the employees poke around and conduct personal business, I may be tempted to say, "Ah, these (insert the name of the nationality in question), how slow and lazy they are!" However, if the same thing occurs in a post office in my own country, I don't leap to the same conclusion. If I am moved to make any observation at all, I may mutter about civil servants (another unwarranted stereotype) or inefficient individuals, but I would not make negative attributions about my fellow citizens as a whole because I have enough different experiences with them to make such stereotyping laughable.

Nipping negative attributions in the bud and trying not to complain about the other culture helps the adaptation process along and makes for a good "foreign guest." Almost everyone grumbles or giggles occasionally about the foibles of another culture, but, as with gossip, one should indulge in such talk in a limited fashion and carefully consider who should be the repository of one's confidences. Having negative feelings about the other culture is a normal part of the adjustment process. However, there is a world of difference between the occasional carping that helps one cope, and the obsessive complaining that indicates that a person has either gotten trapped somewhere in the adjustment process or is a victim of permanent negative affect (the "glass is half empty" approach to life). The first rule of expatriate etiquette is, "Never complain about another culture to the members of that culture even if they themselves are complaining." This rule is transgressed far too often and is a major contributor to the Ugly American, Ugly Dutchman, Ugly Whatever Nationality syndrome.

Expatriates repeatedly mention the need for a positive attitude in connection with overall adjustment, especially when they compare themselves to other expatriates. Adam actively sought out an international assignment and was sent to Venezuela by a large accounting firm.

. . . .

I think that I probably adapted easier to it [living in Venezuela] than a number of individuals I heard about. . . . I think the experiences [we encountered] were all the same. How they were handled, or not handled, was different. . . . The people who handled them well enjoyed it [the overseas experience] and made something of it. And the people who didn't, complained and are still complaining. The large number of people that I became friends with were long-term overseas people . . . from the U.S. or elsewhere. So those people don't tend to have problems with moving from one site to another. The other people I am talking about were like I was, who were just shipped in for a couple of years, but they never got past [certain paradoxes of overseas life.] Some part of [the reasons why these two groups were different] is probably maturity. The other part is just an openness to new situations and a willingness to try things.

. . . .

There is undoubtedly a range of difficulty and hardship in expatriate assignments and living situations. For example, occasionally an expatriate is set up for failure by an organization that gives him or her a truly impossible assignment. Other times, expatriates may be sabotaged by their host-country counterparts or co-workers. Nevertheless, most expatriates attribute the unhappiness of other expatriates to their negative attitude and lack of acculturation effort. Other factors may well play an important role, but it is a difference in attitude that is most striking when well-adjusted expatriates compare themselves to unhappy expatriates. This is the conclusion that Stan, the director of international operations introduced in Chapter Three, came to when he reflected on other expatriates:

• • • • • • •

I would guess that on the whole, of the expatriates that we saw [in nineteen years overseas, some] . . . may not have had as pleasant a time as we did. I think they made . . . problems of their own. . . . They didn't seem to look at it as an opportunity. . . . The major complaint was, "We can't get this and we can't get that," rather than taking advantage of things they could get, even if they were different. . . . There were those people that just made themselves . . . unhappy.

• • • • • • •

I heartily agree with these expatriates that a positive attitude is crucial. Over the years, one of the conversations I learned to avoid was the "Yes, but" dialogue with bored, unhappy expatriates. In one variation, the person starts off by complaining that there is "nothing to do in this country." An expatriate with a more positive attitude may fall into the trap and, in a spasm of misbegotten helpfulness, suggest some activity the bored expatriate could do. The latter then replies, "Yes, but . . ." and goes on to name the myriad reasons that prevent him or her from doing much of anything. Another variation of this dialogue plays out when unhappy expatriates criticize the host country locals (sometimes in their presence) and refuse to acknowledge that there is anything positive about the other culture. Occasionally you can help unhappy expatriates look at their situation from a different perspective, or you can modify their job or living situation so that it is more pleasant. But if their basic attitude toward the experience and the other culture is negative, they seldom stay abroad for long, or if inertia or a bad job market keep them there, they seldom flourish or do an effective job. My advice to newly arrived expatriates is to avoid bored, unhappy expatriates because their negativism can be contagious and color a newcomer's first impressions.

Being Effective at Work

It is especially important in new international assignments to listen carefully and figure out what is going on, and why, before making major changes. Because expatriates are usually not experts on the local culture or business scene in the beginning of an assignment, they are often obliged to develop a flexible and fairly participative management style in order to be effective. An autocratic management style is risky when you do not yet fully understand the situation. Expatriates frequently need to modify their management style to suit the particular circumstance.

I was only twenty-three when I first became a supervisor in Tumaco, Colombia. I phrased "orders" as they were given in my family—"Would you please . . ." and "Would you mind . . ." My subordinates, accustomed to an autocratic style, did not recognize this particular verb tense in Spanish as an order when it came from me; sometimes they opted for "no." It also made them uncomfortable if I asked the group for their opinion on certain matters, because I was supposed to be the expert. I quickly realized that I needed to look and sound more like a Colombian boss, but since I was both new and inexperienced, I could not always make good decisions in a unilateral fashion. Therefore, I resorted to a faux autocratic style. Whenever the issue was so simple that any idiot would have recognized the correct decision, I would take a firm stance, pound my fist on the table, and say, "This is what we're going to do." When the issue was complex and required a more participative decision-making process, I would go to each of my subordinates and ask them privately what they thought we should do. After assimilating their suggestions, I would resume my autocratic mantle in the next staff meeting, pound my little fist and say, "This is what we're going to do." I also learned to use the imperative verb form (direct orders) without flinching. Once I had gained their respect and trust, I gradually became more openly participative in meetings, and eventually we became a real team. This transition to a different style was possible only because in the beginning of our relationship I matched their expectations about how managers should act.

Succeeding abroad often depends on adapting your behavior to local expectations about how things get done. Particularly in more traditional cultures, people get things done as a result of their relationships with others. There is more emphasis on in-group/out-group relationships in many of these countries, which means in-group members are treated more favorably than out-group members. Until one develops the relationships that make one seem more of an in-group member and cause people to feel a personal sense of loyalty, things move very slowly, if at all. It is important, therefore, to take time to greet people daily and to take a genuine interest in their families and jobs. In numerous overseas offices, focusing solely on one's work without greeting others and exchanging small talk is perceived as boorish behavior. Being helpful to other people (such as translating, editing their English, bringing back from a trip something they cannot obtain in their own country, mentoring them at work) is another way to establish the ties of reciprocity that are so important in many cultures.

Another related cultural difference that expatriates metaphorically bump into concerns personal boundaries. In the dominant U.S. culture, it is relatively easy to penetrate an individual's outer shell (they will readily tell you a good deal of personal information and establish a quick friendship). Kurt Lewin (1948) described this phenomenon as a small degree of social distance in the "peripheral regions" of the personality. It is more difficult, however, to get beyond the inner boundary that protects the central regions of the personality. As a result, Americans make friends easily, but are sometimes accused of superficiality by other nationalities. In some other cultures, the outer shell is more impermeable and takes longer to penetrate. However, once the person has "been approved" and gets beyond the outer boundary, it is easier to penetrate the boundary around the inner core of the personality. Therefore, relationships take longer to develop, but they are more permanent and involve greater claims upon both parties. A cultural difference of this nature means that one has to adjust one's expectations about how to form relationships with other people and how long that process should take. The ability to form good relationships with people from another culture—and with cultural mentors, in particular—makes it easier to travel the road of trials, the next stage in the hero's adventure.

. . . .

5

The Road of Trials

Learning to Live with Paradox

*The test of a first-rate intelligence is the ability to hold
two opposed ideas in mind at the same time and still
retain the ability to function.*
—F. Scott Fitzgerald, *The Crack-Up*

The second stage of the hero's adventure myth is initiation. It
begins with "the road of trials," on which heroes are confronted
with numerous obstacles and tests. "A hero ventures forth from the
world of common day into a region of supernatural wonder: fabu-
lous forces are there encountered and a decisive victory is won"
(Campbell, 1968, p. 30). Mythical heroes slay dragons, elude monsters, and brave the dangers of the underworld in order to pass the
test and win their prize, "the ultimate boon" (p. 36).

Psyche, a beautiful princess, disobeyed her husband, Cupid, and
could not find him. After a useless search, she humbled herself and
begged her jealous mother-in-law, Venus, to help her find Cupid.
Venus ordered Psyche to sort a pile of grains before nightfall. An
army of ants helped Psyche complete this otherwise impossible task.
Next, Venus sent Psyche to gather wool from poisonous sheep; a
green reed told Psyche not to give in to despair, but to wait until
nightfall and gather the wool from sharp briars. Venus then sent her
to bring back water from the river Styx. It was impossible for a
human to approach the river, but an eagle filled Psyche's flask for

her. Finally, Venus sent Psyche to the underworld to find a box of supernatural beauty. This time Psyche's magical friend was a tower that told her how to cross the threshold of the underworld and get beyond the threshold guardians, Caron and Cerberus. With a little help from Cupid, Psyche successfully passed this final test. She was rewarded for her trials by being transformed into an immortal god so she could live forever with Cupid, effectively ending her mother-in-law problems.

Joseph Campbell describes the initiation stage as follows:

* * * * * * *

> Once having traversed the threshold, the hero moves in a dream landscape of curiously fluid, ambiguous forms, where he must survive a succession of trials. This is a favorite phase of the myth-adventure. It has produced a world literature of miraculous tests and ordeals. The hero is covertly aided by the advice, amulets, and secret agents of the supernatural helper whom he met before his entrance into this region. Or it may be that he here discovers for the first time that there is a benign power everywhere supporting him in his superhuman passage [1968, p. 97].

* * * * * * *

There is no question that expatriates also traverse a road of trials. I have already described some of the common obstacles and hardships, such as logistical, acculturation, and language difficulties, that occur in the beginning of an assignment when expatriates cross the first threshold. Smooth, flawless moves, transitions, and sojourns are fairly rare. Even experienced expatriates who have lived in several countries find that there are always some problems and obstacles beyond their control. The only thing they can control, or at least attempt to control, is their attitude toward these obstacles. Maladjusted expatriates with an unrelenting negative attitude often perceive the normal expatriate hardships as a personal insult or affront that justifies their dislike of a country and its people. In contrast, those who perceive and frame hardships as a normal part of the expatriate hero's adventure can deal with them more effectively. Developing patience, a positive attitude, and a sense of humor is crucial to withstanding the testing process that all heroes undergo.

A Peace Corps volunteer named Liz had a good attitude about her own unique road of trials. She was not fond of insects in general, but she had such a severe phobia about spiders that she underwent desensitization therapy before entering the Peace Corps. On her application form, she wrote she was willing to go anywhere that did not have spiders. When she arrived in Burkina Faso, Liz discovered that, "Yes, Liz, there are spiders in Burkina Faso" in the form of the *chevalier du scorpion*, a giant spider that signals the presence of scorpions in the vicinity. If you stand your hand up on your fingertips, you will have an idea of the size of these hair-raising beasts that are harmless to humans but deadly to scorpions. Whenever I saw one in our house, I never knew whether to be sad because it meant a scorpion was lurking nearby or happy because the chevalier was on the job, hunting it down. Liz saw these giant spiders as a huge joke on herself.

Liz's next challenge began when she rented a one-room, recently built house, only to discover that it was a superhighway for army ants who did not intend to let a small construction alter their travel plans. Periodically, the ants marched up her outer wall and down the living room wall, across the living room floor, up the other wall and, to Liz's relief, down the outer wall to continue their singleminded journey. Although new houses usually have fewer insects in residence, Liz's house was the exception. Rather than curse the fates, she laughed at her situation, learned to cohabit with the insects, and took pride in overcoming her fear of spiders.

Talk to almost any expatriate and they will produce similar stories, a litany of challenges or hardships they recollect from their time overseas. This chapter will focus on another form of obstacles that constitutes a different challenge to the expatriate—the paradoxes and contradictions inherent in the expatriate context. These trials are seldom articulated, much less studied or written about.

Expatriate Paradoxes

Paradox can be defined as "a situation involving the presence of contradictory, mutually exclusive elements that operate equally at the same time" (Quinn and Cameron, 1988). Paradox is a strong theme in Campbell's interpretation of mythology. For example, mentors and threshold guardians are both positive and negative figures, helpful to some, harmful to others. Paradox is also present in the "master of two worlds" stage, discussed in Chapter Seven, in which mythical heroes wrestle with the complexities of a higher consciousness. According to Campbell, paradoxes in mythology represent the polarities that exist within our own subconscious.

Expatriates experience paradoxes because they live in a cross-cultural setting. These paradoxes are obstacles either to their effectiveness at work or to their coexistence with the other culture. I had both experienced and heard about so many paradoxes in expatriate stories that I wanted to measure whether business expatriates grappled with the same paradoxes I had observed. Asbjorn and I developed the list of nine paradoxes that appears in Table 5.1. When I presented this list to the expatriates I interviewed, their reactions to the paradoxes ranged from polite interest to enthusiasm. Several people commented that they had never put these paradoxes into words, although they had certainly experienced them. Some were excited to see their experiences, which they had thought to be unique, conceptualized in this way, saying, "That's it! That's exactly the way it was." I found that business expatriates do indeed experience paradoxes in varying forms and to varying degrees, and that the paradoxes tend to fall into four categories: social acuity, marginality, mediation, and identity values. (See the statistical information on paradoxes in the appendix at the end of the book.)

Social Acuity Paradoxes

In general, these paradoxes occur in the expatriate's relationships with individual people and in situations that require cultural under-

Table 5.1.   Expatriate Paradoxes.

Social Acuity Paradoxes

1. Possessing a great deal of power as a result of one's role, but downplaying it in order to gain necessary input and cooperation.

2. Seeing as valid the general stereotype about the local culture, but also realizing that many host-country nationals do not fit that stereotype.

Marginality Paradoxes

3. Generally thinking well of the host-country nationals while at the same time being very savvy about being taken advantage of by them.

4. Feeling at ease anywhere but belonging nowhere.

Mediation Paradoxes

5. Feeling caught between the contradictory demands of headquarters on the one hand and the demands of the host-country nationals and the local situation on the other.

6. Trying to represent one's company as best one can in order to succeed, but also realizing that the "ideal" values one acts out abroad may not exist back at headquarters.

7. Being freed from many of one's own cultural rules and even from some of the host culture's norms, but not being free at all from certain host-country customs that one must observe to be effective.

Identity Values Paradoxes

8. Giving up some of one's American cultural ideas and behaviors in order to be accepted and successful in the other culture while at the same time finding some of one's core American values becoming even stronger as a result of exposure to another culture.

9. Becoming more and more "world-minded" as a result of exposure to different values and conflicting loyalties, but becoming more idiosyncratic in putting together one's own value system and views on life.

standing. One such paradox is that expatriates are at the same time both *powerful* and *powerless*. They possess a good deal of power as a result of their role at work, more power than they experienced in the United States. Yet this power is paradoxical because it is not without constraints. Expatriates, more than other managers, are extremely dependent upon subordinates for their knowledge of the local culture. Because expatriates are less certain of how subordinates of another culture think and behave, they are compelled to be more participative and concerned about gaining commitment. They feel they must downplay their power in order to gain from their subordinates the input and cooperation they need to do a good job. Even in cultures where the autocratic use of power is acceptable, the same behavior by an American may be perceived as neocolonialism. In cultures where managers are expected to be omniscient experts who make all the decisions, expatriate managers struggle with the need to look autocratic while being painfully aware that they do not have all the answers. One expatriate refers to this managerial style, which many overseas managers feel compelled to adopt in order to be effective, as "managed powerlessness."

Glenn's company, a large manufacturing concern, was expanding, so he was sent abroad as the vice president of European operations. Glenn is an expansive man in his forties who had worked for the same company for more than twenty years, yet this high-level position was his first overseas assignment. He was quick to perceive cultural differences.

· · · · · · ·

Here [in the United States], say you want to get something done and . . . you start the mechanical thinking. Okay, if we do this, here are the consequences. And logistically, here is how we get it done. In Europe, the first thing you think about is, "What impact is this going to have?" . . . It is sometimes more important how your approach is than executing it. Because without question, if the nationals did not accept it, I don't care if you are God, you are going to have an awful time getting it done. . . . I have seen very few times that a European has ever disagreed with me. When they disagree they'll say, "We will take a look at that and we will send you a little report and let you know what we can do." And of course, you are not going to get a report. In the U.S., they just more or less disagree with you and you know when someone has a little bit different idea. But there you have to sort it out. If you are inexperienced, you will walk out of that room saying, "I did well. This is wonderful!" You walk out of that room and that will be it. Nothing will happen!

♦ ♦ ♦ ♦ ♦ ♦ ♦

Harry was introduced in Chapter Four as the flamboyant director of a high-profile international division. Like Glenn, he was based in England but oversaw operations in many different countries. In spite of his high-level position, what he learned abroad were the limits of power.

♦ ♦ ♦ ♦ ♦ ♦ ♦

The Lilliputians would let Gulliver be the power as long as he didn't threaten them. But as soon as he threatened them, they nailed him down. I was Gulliver, though it didn't end the same way. They never nailed me down, but . . . they taught me the limits of power. Here in the U.S., everybody is trying to take power. And [in England] that isn't really the way it works. It's, You are given power by the consent of the governed. Because without that, there is no power, because you have no influence over there. You only have influence with people if they let you have influence.

♦ ♦ ♦ ♦ ♦ ♦ ♦

With the possible exception of staff positions and technical adviser jobs, expatriate managers often wield a great deal of power in their role. This power is the result of various factors: their technical ability, their role as representatives of headquarters, their hierarchical position, and the degree of autonomy they enjoy. American expatriates who work in cultures characterized by large power distance—the degree to which a society accepts the fact that power in institutions and organizations is distributed unequally (Hofstede, 1980)—are treated with a deference not necessarily found within their own culture. The United States is below average in its acceptance of power discrepancies in the workplace. That explains why subordinates usually call their supervisors by their first names and tend to think of themselves as equals to them. That is also why employees become disgruntled or disillusioned when bosses take advantage of their position for personal gain. In countries characterized by large power distance, bosses are expected to be inaccessible, addressed with great formality, and entitled to special privileges.

Acclimating oneself to status differentials is one of the largest hurdles for many Americans working in Latin America. It is hard to grasp that people will unconsciously make large adjustments in their behavior and their speech in accordance with the status of the person they are dealing with. People in all cultures do this to some degree, but the differences in how people are treated are noticeably greater in Latin cultures than they are in the United States.

Twenty years ago, my husband and I were lowly Peace Corps volunteers in Cartagena, Colombia, working for the Institute of Social Welfare. A major part of my job was coordinating the speakers in a training program on nutrition and child care that took place in "my" barrio. I would sign up well in advance for the office jeep to take the speakers to the barrio, only to discover when it was time to go that someone else had requisitioned the jeep at the last minute. The "someone else" was anyone who had more power or status, or who had longer relationships with the chauffeurs than I— in other words, just about anybody in the entire office building. My stomach would churn when I thought of tromping all over the barrio to drum up interest in this meeting only to end up with a no-show. My husband, Asbjorn, had similar experiences. For instance, he was ordered to inform a remote community of farmers that they would be given free fruit trees. He hiked from farm to farm for several days, giving them the news. Then he made several more circuits on foot to make sure their three-foot holes were dug correctly in preparation for planting the trees. To his dismay, the trees were donated to someone else for political reasons. So much for the credibility of the community development workers, although I suspect it bothered us more than it bothered the Colombians because they were more accustomed to broken promises. Because of our status as volunteers and foreigners, we were fairly powerless in such situations. We had to learn to work around these "trials."

Asbjorn eventually accepted a position as head of a development agency in an isolated, poverty-stricken town in Colombia where his organization was the largest employer. In addition to the power to hire and fire, he now had many resources to fund community development projects, so we were perceived by the local people as "power objects." Immediately, we became "Don Asbjorn, *el patron*" and "Doña Joyce" (even though I continued working for the Peace Corps), and these honorifics indicated our status. We were treated with far more respect than our callow youth warranted, but I must admit we adjusted to deference, and even ingratiation, remarkably fast. I went from fighting for a chauffeur to fighting off obsequious chauffeurs who were more than willing to make other employees wait if the boss's wife needed the car. This was a textbook case of status whiplash—we had not changed a bit inside, but our assigned roles determined that others would treat us in a very different manner; and because this promotion occurred in a country characterized by large power distance, the leap from volunteer to director, or even to director's wife, felt enormous.

Even though expatriate managers may have higher status abroad and wield more power than at home, they have less confidence about how to "push" within a foreign culture. Glenn explains why he thinks some expatriate managers are more participative:

· · · · · · ·

I guess when you are here in the States, you feel like you are going to be around here much longer. . . . If you go and force something a little bit here, you have a better feel that it is going to work with the people all the way down to the bottom of the pyramid. But in Europe, you are not sure. You know how it might work a couple of levels down, but you are never sure of how it might touch the bottom . . . or how it might be perceived . . . further down in the organization. And here you know it so well, but there you are dealing with different people and cultures. You are not real sure, you know intuition-wise, that it is right and you should go ahead and do it. So you really give them a little bit more of a chance to participate in decisions.

* * * * * * *

What leads many expatriates to a more participative approach is their status as an outsider and their desire to be effective. Because the crisp, clear lens of one's own culture is absent, more tentativeness and reliance upon others is required. Nevertheless, the trick in cross-cultural management is one of balance—knowing when and when not to use your power. If you are too participative, people may not respect you and will make their own power plays; this is especially true in cultures with a history of authoritarian leadership. But if you go overboard with your own power, they may sabotage you. Thus many good expatriate managers describe their management style as trying to get input from local employees and allowing them to participate in decision making whenever that is feasible; they don't hesitate, however, to display their power at the right moment.

Ron, introduced in Chapter Two, managed the European marketing office for a large multinational that sells chemicals. As stated earlier, he is a down-to-earth fast-track manager with good managerial experience in both the United States and Europe. His description of the following incident illustrates both sides of the power distance paradox:

* * * * * * *

We had changed the operation when I went over. And I had certain guidelines to run the business from my boss. The guy I was replacing had reported to the head of the sales company that was in Europe. . . . Now, in the new organization, I reported to a guy back in the States . . . but I only reported to him for specific things. The other guy [a Dutch predecessor] had to report to him on everything. So I came waltzing in, and one of the issues that sticks in my mind was that up until that point . . . the branch manager in the manufacturing plant had a limit on what he could spend, a typical Dutch system. He could spend $500 without anyone approving it. . . . When I first heard that, I said, "Good God, you can't even buy a dial for that!" He agreed and said it took three months to get everybody's signature and all kinds of justification. In the States, I could spend $45,000 on my own signature as a production manager. . . . So I told him, "My authority level is $50,000. I am going to give you $25,000. You can buy anything you want up to that amount without approval as long as it is within the budget." It was like Christmas. . . . And it wasn't sixteen hours later that the financial guy said, "Whoa, by whose authority are you doing this?" I said, "My own." He said, "Well, it's never been done before. . . . I think we need to verify this." I said, "Fine, go ahead." So a little bit later, he said, "It's okay." Now that felt *"Wow!"* . . . I knew that had to be done right at the start. . . . I was willing to cooperate, but I wanted to make it damned clear where the boundary was on the power. . . . There were two or three little tests like that the first month."

* * * * * * *

Ron let people know he was the boss at the same time that he empowered subordinates so they could be more effective.

Another type of social acuity paradox has to do with *stereotypes* and *individual differences* of the local people. Expatriates may believe that some of the general stereotypes about their host culture are valid, but they will also see considerable exceptions to these stereotypes. As they become increasingly sensitive to the individual differences in the people in their host culture, they also become increasingly uncomfortable with the set of perceptions they either brought with them from their native country or developed during the beginning of their overseas assignment.

This paradox acknowledges the validity of both stereotypes and individual differences, by recognizing both the truth that is at the root of cultural stereotypes and the importance of seeing beyond those stereotypes to the individual differences that abound within cultures. In fact, in any culture, there is more variety in personality than in the observance of social customs in that culture (Feshback and Weiner, 1982). Nevertheless, the seed of truth in ethnic stereotypes may at times help the expatriate predict behavior and avoid making cultural gaffes. Robert Detweiler (1975) found that well-adjusted expatriates make less rigid evaluations to explain the behavior of others and are more likely to modify their impressions in the light of new data. Like good scientists, they keep formulating, testing, and rejecting hypotheses about the behavior of members of the other culture. The more one is exposed to and becomes familiar with another culture, the easier it becomes to see the differences between individual members of that culture or ethnic group. The same phenomenon is at work in perceptions of physical difference—all people of a different race look alike until we have spent enough time with them to learn to distinguish their features.

A recently arrived white expatriate in West Africa mistakenly hired two chauffeurs one day because he assumed he was talking to the same person on two different occasions. Months later, he could not even see a resemblance between the two men. He felt marginally better about his mistake after several Africans informed him that all white men look alike.

Neil, introduced in Chapter Three, spent six successful years working in a bank branch in Japan. He had numerous Japanese friends and was well integrated into the culture. Neil believes that foreigners' perceptions about the Japanese depend on how much time they live in Japan. He believes, "You've kind of graduated from regarding your experience as being an experience with a foreign people in a foreign culture to being an experience involving a very specific job with a very specific group of people in a neighborhood, in a community. . . . The cultural aspects of it, the foreign aspects of it, begin to break down and it becomes much more personal."

This paradox of seeing both cultural stereotypes and individual differences also occurs with our own culture when we are abroad. Expatriates are often forced to acknowledge and consider the stereotypes about their own nationality. This occurred with Mitch, who was only twenty-six when he went abroad and ran into a variety of situations that forced him to mature more rapidly than he might have done otherwise. He worked for an international bank, developing new products, and was promoted toward the end of his assignment to a position of vice president.

. . . .

The values that I demonstrated or hoped to show in England were shared by the people I had a lot of dealings with in Chicago and my friends back here. But in the background, I knew that many of the stereotypes that were said about Americans were valid. That Joe Steelworker sitting in his living room in Gary, Indiana didn't give a damn about what was happening in England. And when he picked up a newspaper, all he read was the sports page and the funnies. And I became very sensitive to that . . . a sort of contradiction. I'd want to tell Brits that, "Hey listen, Americans are different from that." But at the same time, I was realizing for myself that many of these stereotypes were true.

. . . .

For many expatriates, working abroad is their first experience of being a minority and being stereotyped. It is not always comfortable. In particular, several of the expatriates I interviewed who were assigned to Europe encountered unflattering stereotypes about Americans.

Marginality Paradoxes

Typically, marginality paradoxes pertain to the expatriates' perception of and relationship with the other culture as a whole. One paradox in this category has to do with feeling both *positive regard* and *caution* about the local people. Expatriates may generally think well of the host-country nationals, but at the same time they may also be very savvy about being taken advantage of by them.

Bruce, introduced in Chapter Two, experienced this paradox while working for a U.S. bank in Hong Kong. He was involved in a joint venture with a local bank and trained eighty Chinese employees.

• • • • • • •

> This is especially the case in China. I generally liked the people, but I know they're out to move ahead faster and they will step on people to get their way. The turnover rate, for instance, in Hong Kong—people skipping from job to job—is incredible. . . . The people of Hong Kong live under the threat of 1997 when the Communists take over . . . and they are worried about their own freedoms. . . . Some of them sense that they have to get ahead in a hurry because time is running out for them. And so, as an employer, you sometimes felt that you were hiring people who were just abusing you, because you were going to pay them a little bit more, but they were only going to stay around long enough [to] find the next job to pay them a little bit more.

• • • • • • •

The first truth in this paradox, positive regard, means "thinking well of the local culture." It has been identified as one of the competencies possessed by effective U.S. information agency officials working abroad (McClelland and Dailey, 1973). Positive regard for one's employees has also been found to be a competency of successful managers in the United States (Boyatzis, 1982). The other side of this paradox, being savvy about being taken advantage of by members of the local culture, is usually more apparent to expatriates living in countries whose cultural attitudes toward honesty and manipulation differ from such attitudes in the United States.

Another factor that affects whether expatriates experience this paradox is their perceptual system. Some people are innately suspicious of ethnic groups they do not understand. For them, being wary about being taken advantage of may be rooted in ignorance or ethnocentrism rather than in experience. (Conversely, sometimes locals really are trying to exploit expatriates who are unwilling to see it.) The inability to perceive the positive regard/caution paradox may also indicate a lack of cultural understanding.

The second of the marginality paradoxes has to do with expatriates' *feeling at ease anywhere but belonging nowhere*. Becoming comfortable in other countries often means sacrificing an unconscious sense of fit within one's own culture. Peter Adler (1974) describes "multicultural man" as being neither part of nor totally apart from his culture, but living on the boundary between the two. This theme, heard repeatedly among bicultural people, is in a sense the price one sometimes pays for leaving home and adapting to another culture. "I have become a queer mixture of the east and the west, out of place everywhere, at home nowhere. . . . I am a stranger and alien in the West. I cannot be of it. But in my own country also, sometimes, I have an exile's feeling" ("Nehru," 1964). Almost half the expatriates I interviewed experienced feeling at ease anywhere but belonging nowhere. Those who did not report this paradox felt they belonged everywhere.

Elliot, an articulate, sophisticated man in his forties, is a good example of a bicultural expatriate. He was transferred to France with a Big Six accounting firm when he and his wife were in their twenties, and they both fell in love with Paris. They became very well acculturated and took advantage of their seventeen years abroad. The first time they returned to the United States, they experienced some difficulty readjusting, partly because they had been exposed to different perspectives and partly because they felt out of step.

* * * * * * *

I remember experiencing this paradox when we came back home the first time and realized that we were not really in the mainstream of what people were thinking about and doing. . . . We were natives and we lived there and worked there and talked like them, but weren't necessarily feeling like them, part of the community. . . . We spent a weekend with a couple [who] were among our best friends . . . and felt out of it, I guess because we had evolved in different ways. I am not being critical of what they did and they weren't critical of what we did, but it just wasn't meshed. . . . I had a very hard time understanding the average American point of view on Vietnam, after having looked at it from a couple of different directions. . . . It is not that we were bad guys and those little guys were good guys. There were no good guys over there. . . . It was naive to be there in the first place . . . and the Watergate thing, too. . . . I guess we were looking at it from a distance, from a more detached point of view than the person who was living here the whole time. So I think that experiences like that show you that, Yes, I am here, I can understand it, . . . I can discuss it, but I don't belong . . . in this particular environment.

◆ ◆ ◆ ◆ ◆ ◆ ◆

There is a flavor of Thomas Wolfe's famous phrase, "You can't go home again," to Elliot's story. One does not have to leave the country to experience this; one can simply move from a small town to a city. The difference with expatriates is that they usually do not feel a sense of total belonging in other cultures, no matter how well acculturated they become. As Elliot commented:

◆ ◆ ◆ ◆ ◆ ◆ ◆

When we go to France, we can chat with some of the old waiters that I have known from the cafes for 20 years, and go to the club and see friends. And I can live in France for three hundred years and still not be French. I am very at home there, but I wouldn't want to spend the rest of my life in France. And if someone had told me in France, at the best of times, that I had to make the choice today of staying in France forever or leaving, it would be no question—I'm going; I'm out of here!

◆ ◆ ◆ ◆ ◆ ◆ ◆

One would expect that feeling at ease anywhere and belonging nowhere would be more common with long-term expatriates, like Elliot, who have spent most of their adult life outside their own culture. However, people who had lived abroad for fairly short periods also experienced this paradox.

Sam and his wife, introduced in Chapter Two, spent only two years in South Africa. On the way to and from this assignment, they traveled all over the world. They returned to a U.S. city where they had both friends and family, and Sam resumed the same job in the same office in which he had worked for five years before going abroad. Nevertheless, he reported that he and his wife had felt very comfortable when they were traveling but were not at all sure if they really belonged back home.

Belonging nowhere is one way to describe marginality. Marginal people feel like they live on the periphery rather than at the center of a group or community. Some expatriates may have experienced this marginality within their own culture before they ever went abroad. An unknown percentage of expatriates have always marched to a different drummer, or they were raised in a bicultural or immigrant home, both of which make it somewhat easier to slip out of the bonds that tie people to their homeland. Virtually all expatriates, however, experience some degree of marginality when they live within another culture. One expatriate described living in Luxembourg as "being on the outside looking in" until she became more acculturated.

There are limits to how well integrated foreigners can ever become in another country. Some cultures are more open and welcoming than others, but most expatriates would not say they were totally integrated abroad, no matter how fluent or acculturated they became and no matter how many years they resided in another country. Long-term expatriates sometimes run into a glass ceiling of acculturation (Osland, 1993), because they have higher expectations than newly arrived expatriates about what it means to be accepted by the other culture. As Elliot said, he could live in France for three hundred years and still not be French. Unless they marry into the local culture, most expatriates always remain a kind of outsider and perceive themselves as marginal.

When asked whether it was easy for Americans to be accepted by the Japanese, Neil answered that he found it impossible. As related earlier, he and his wife felt at home in Tokyo and had close Japanese friends, but they always had a nagging feeling that they didn't belong. They longed for their own country. And yet, when they returned to the States, they mourned for their life abroad and did not feel totally at home in the United States either.

Mediation Paradoxes

These paradoxes are related to the conflicting demands that expatriates often experience in their roles as mediators, boundary spanners, and goodwill ambassadors for company and country. The first of the mediation paradoxes is that expatriates feel *caught between the contradictory demands of headquarters and the demands of host-country nationals and the local situation*. This paradox is characterized by role conflict and the difficulty of mediating between two organizations.

Expatriates have multiple loyalties to satisfy, as seen in the following example. Art, a reserved man in his forties, did not want to go abroad; he accepted the call only because he was afraid his career would be "plateaued." His mission was to investigate and turn around the management of an ailing subsidiary based in Europe, but he was not assigned the general manager's (GM) position. As executive vice president of operations, his role in the hierarchy was unclear. Therefore, he had to work hard to gain acceptance by the local management and employees. In addition, his largest problem was the disparity between the goals of headquarters and those of the subsidiary. In Art's words, "The subsidiary could care less what corporate wanted, and it was my role to focus the business so it benefited the corporation." This particular type of assignment has built-in role conflicts that can make the expatriate job a sort of "mission impossible."

Role conflict also occurs when headquarters and the subsidiary have different ways of operating and do not understand each other's culture. Headquarters often ask expatriates to do things that are not acceptable in the other culture. This was the case with Carl, first introduced in Chapter Three, who was researching a new technology at a German university.

* * * * * * *

It was more a cultural way of doing things that was in conflict. Once [the company] was looking for some information. And they said, "Well, why don't you just see what you can find out. Give them part of the information and then try to get some back from them." "Well," I said, "they don't deal that way. They are straightforward, honest, just call a spade a spade and that's that.". . . The company wasn't asking me to do anything deceitful; it was just a different way of doing things. I think some people feel, "Well, this is the way we do it, you know, so just do it!" And they don't do it that way over in Germany.

* * * * * * *

Michael went overseas when he was in his late thirties. Like many expatriates, he described his time abroad as the personal and professional highlight of his life. His current office was decorated with pictures of his house and neighborhood in England. He had been the European tax director for a large multinational and had served as both troubleshooter and technical advisor. Since his job had been new, employees in some countries had resented his involvement in decisions they had previously made by themselves. Michael described his inclination in dealing with the situation as "treading lightly," a strategy that was not shared by his boss.

* * * * * * *

I proceeded according to the boss [at corporate headquarters] and did what he said. Although that was perhaps not the best way to go about it. I would have been more tactful and worked with the local people. When you're there, you begin to appreciate the local problems and you see it's not just black and white. When your boss wants to react in a particular way, it's not necessarily the best way. I didn't have any particular problem with my co-workers. You have to walk that fine line between what the boss and the local people think. There's actually three viewpoints—the local management, U.S. management, and the expatriate himself.

* * * * * * *

Half the expatriates in my study experienced this paradox; most of the others stated that their companies supported them while they were abroad, or at least stayed out of their way and allowed them to be productive.

Organizations create role conflict for their expatriates with policies that reflect their own lack of sensitivity and understanding about the local setting. Refusal to compromise or understand the position of the local office is an organizational constraint that affects expatriate effectiveness (Newman, Bhatt, and Gutteridge, 1976). Some headquarters are blatantly xenophobic and fear that expatriate managers will "go native" and give more weight to local concerns than to corporate concerns. For this reason, headquarters may transfer people more rapidly and be quick to point out what it perceives as "disloyalty." In doing so, it functions as a threshold guardian.

Expatriates can deal proactively with admittedly difficult situations by learning to be good boundary spanners. Proactive expatriates employ a variety of tactics to reduce role conflict. For example, they discern the critical factors that cannot be overlooked for both headquarters and the local facility. In other words, they figure out what headquarters absolutely has to have from the field (information, profit, and so forth), and do the same for the local office. They are diligent about meeting the needs of both organizations and thereby gain the trust of both of them. Over time, proactive expatriates may develop a scheme for indexing priorities when conflicts

arise, or they may learn to look for common ground and try to negotiate solutions that are acceptable to both organizations. They also
make an effort to educate both the local office and headquarters
about the other's needs and attitudes. Finally, they pick their fights
wisely.

Edward, an assistant chief engineer who worked at an R&D center in Europe, did a very good job of educating both the local office
and the headquarters. He was a boundary spanner between two
regional divisions of the business that were independent except for
shared product-development programs.

. . . .

> I had to coordinate with headquarters so that we were doing
> development in an integrated fashion. We had our usual hassles,
> and it is a difficult thing to do. . . . I think the fact that I was there
> helped [us] make some steps that would not have been made had I
> not been there, because I had been at headquarters and I could
> explain to them why headquarters was doing what they were
> doing. And I could communicate to headquarters what the Euro-
> pean technical center was doing and why . . . because I under-
> stood. I could interpret for them because I knew the "whys."
> Otherwise, they don't understand the "whys." They make things
> up, they think the worst. Both of the organizations do that. They
> think the worst unless [they] understand the "whys." And if you
> work both places, you know why people are doing what they
> are doing, and there are usually darned good reasons why they are
> doing them. It is just that they don't always get communicated on
> both sides.

. . . .

Edward's words illustrate the valuable role expatriates play in
keeping far-flung multinationals integrated. Misunderstandings and
a "we-they" attitude can develop whenever a branch is geographi-
cally separated from headquarters. In the international setting, this
distance is exacerbated by cultural differences and worry caused by

the "out of sight, out of mind" syndrome: the fact that senior managers tend to overlook expatriates and promote headquarters employees, who are more visible and close at hand.

Ron, the savvy expatriate European marketing manager introduced in Chapter Two, was very careful to avoid conflicting demands and distance problems.

• • • • • • •

> You can only do so much by telex and reports and an occasional phone call. On some issues, you have to sit down [around] a table and talk them through. You can't do that efficiently when you are four thousand miles apart. . . . Tensions develop over four to five months. . . . I negotiated for a trip back to the States every three to four months for a week . . . to have some time with the GM here, some time with manufacturing, and R&D and marketing. . . . At one point, a couple of years later we tried to extend it to six months, but that was too long. Because I could tell the frictions were building up [between] my own people [and] the U.S. There would be good communication for a while and then gradually slip apart after three to four months and you start getting nasty telexes back and forth. . . . So whenever I went to the States, I said, "Okay, what are the problems?". . . and I'd dispense all of this information to my group in Holland. But I don't think it was so much a cultural problem as just the physical separation of people [who] have to work together.

• • • • • • •

Another mediation paradox occurs when expatriates are *representing both ideal and real values*. Expatriates feel they are trying to represent their company as best as they can in order to succeed, but they also realize that the "ideal" values they act out abroad may not exist back at headquarters. Part of being the sole overseas representative for one's company means broadening one's focus and taking on a different role. One expatriate confided that when he was called upon overseas to speak for the company, he thought to himself, "What would I say here if I were the CEO?" By doing this, he forced himself to look at issues from a broader perspective. Good employees are conscious that they represent their companies at all times, but this feeling is even stronger abroad, where an individual or small handful of expatriates may believe that the fate of the company in that country or region rests solely within their hands. Yet, as they feel this loyalty to the company, they are also aware that the ideal they may be presenting to the locals is not always reality back at headquarters.

Rick is a geologist, a solid-citizen type who was sent to London in his mid twenties. It is easy to imagine him doing field work, which is what he expected to be doing until his career took an international turn. Rick was the sole representative for his company and ran their sales office in Europe. He experienced the ideal-versus-real paradox in his dealings with customers.

• • • • • • •

> I think that you like every customer to feel as though he or she is number one on your list . . . but certainly there are customers who are higher in the pecking order. We are part-owned by American companies . . . and they are [each] paying to be that number one priority. Therefore, all of the European customers that I had . . . abroad come somewhere in the second order.

• • • • • • •

Andrew, a former Peace Corps volunteer, worked in the field of international development. He is a hard-working soul with an outrageous sense of humor and an uncanny ability to strike up good relationships with people from all walks of life. In addition, he is a very talented cross-cultural manager; he set up a string of successful new offices in different countries around the world. Because he was the only person from his organization the locals had ever seen, he *was* the organization in the eyes of both the employees and their clients. This was a tremendous responsibility, and Andrew worked hard to establish the trust and credibility that were necessary for a new organization to succeed. His headquarters, however, did not always act with as much integrity as Andrew. Occasionally their decisions were dictated more by political expediencies than by their stated mission. Andrew never let on, even to employees, that these discrepancies existed, because he wanted to protect both the company's reputation and his own credibility.

Expatriates experience a variation of this paradox when they feel they are representing their country overseas. One expatriate referred to this as being "on a UN peace mission." In his study of Swedish expatriates, Ingemar Torbiorn (1982) called this the "ambassadorial feeling." Many expatriates instinctively assume this role of goodwill ambassador; they want other cultures to think well of their country, regardless of the expatriates' personal criticisms or discomfort with their country's foreign policy or domestic conditions. In other cases, the host culture forces expatriates to assume this role by questioning them about their homeland and their government. Because of the United States' active role in foreign affairs, Americans are frequently asked to explain U.S. policy. Whether the response is a "party line" answer, a personal opinion, or some combination thereof probably depends in part on who asked the question and how long the person asked has been overseas. People are most compelled to defend their native country and its values in the beginning months of expatriation, when they feel most threatened by exposure to different cultural values. Later on, they have a more relaxed attitude toward the ambassadorial role and see their country from a broader, more complex perspective.

Many expatriates have a strong, constant commitment to being a good representative of their country. Ithiel Pool (1965) found that American businessmen who were abroad for many years saw themselves less as representatives of their company and more as representatives of their country. This orientation is part of being a good citizen abroad—not only do expatriates want to avoid doing anything to embarrass their own country or company, but they see

themselves as part of a chain of expatriates. For example, in Burkina Faso and Senegal, Americans are usually warmly received,
thanks to good impressions made in the past by Peace Corps volunteers. Not all nationalities are so welcome in this part of the
world. Conscientious expatriates acknowledge a debt of gratitude
to the Americans who have gone before them paving the way, and
they vow to be a good guest so that those who come after them will
also be welcome.

This attitude is apparent in Ron's description of his years in Holland as the GM of a regional office:

. . . .

> I found that I had to make decisions quickly and as accurately as I
> could and follow through on them. I felt people were watching me
> in my performance. . . . I tried to be extra certain of what I was
> doing and not drop the ball, because I didn't want to mess up on
> the next expatriate that could come. You know, try to keep that
> continuity. At work, and the same thing at home, curiously
> enough. When you go out and you're in an expatriate company, as
> soon as you open your mouth people know that you are different.
> And you feel different. There is more of a sense that you are kind
> of wearing a patch on the back of your jacket or something that
> has the American flag on it. So you feel . . . Well, gee, should I do
> this? Some of the things I might do here, I wouldn't do there.
> Because it would be disrespectful to the host country. You feel like
> you are a representative of the States. . . . My wife mentioned it
> once when she said, "Sometimes when we go out on vacation or a
> trip or something, I get the feeling that you are in a petri dish in
> the lab—that people are looking to see what grows there." You
> have a tendency to try and act like a good ambassador for your
> country. Sometimes it works, sometimes it doesn't. If you make a
> social gaffe, then people tend to allow it more because you are a
> foreigner, but they also watch out of the corner of the eye to see,
> you know, Does he pick his nose while he is eating dinner? Does
> he drop his food in his lap? How does he perform in a social

setting? How does he perform in a business setting? And they tend to classify Americans by what they see. If you are the only contact they have had with an American and you are a klutz, then they are going to think that all Americans are klutzes. You feel pressure really. After a while, two or three years, you feel, damn, I can't even go out to my backyard without being dressed right and doing the right things. That is one thing we noticed after being overseas for a while, that maybe some people don't feel, but we thought we felt a certain pressure.

* * * * * * *

The metaphor of the hero's adventure provides another slant on the representative role. Campbell (1968) states that loyalty is one of the most important characteristics of mythical heroes; they do not forget their quest even if they are momentarily distracted. According to Campbell (1988, p. 123), heroes give their lives to something bigger than themselves. For some expatriates, manifesting their loyalty to their country or company by being a good representative allows them to enact heroism. But though they try to present their company and country in the best possible light, their loyalty does not prevent them from seeing the discrepancies between the ideal they try to present abroad and the reality that exists back home.

The last of the mediation paradoxes occurs when expatriates are *both free and not free of cultural norms*. Expatriates may feel they are free from many of their own culture's rules and even from some of the host culture's norms, but they also acknowledge that they are not free at all from certain host-country customs that they must observe in order to be effective abroad. Ron alluded to this when he said earlier that "if you make a social gaffe, then people tend to allow it more because you are a foreigner," but host-country nationals also scrutinize expatriates closely for culturally inappropriate behavior.

Going abroad may feel to some like "slipping one's leash" and having no social norms to measure up to or observe. One expatriate described his reason for wanting to return abroad as, "to be a little more independent of all the social forces that tend to crowd around you once you live someplace for a period of time."

Expatriates often comment on their freedom from the expectations and customs of their extended family. Mark, introduced in Chapter One, was based in London but traveled all over the world as a member of a training team. He reveled in the absence of demands for conformity that he found abroad.

. . . .

> One of the things that sticks in my mind is an expatriate who said, "I will never go back to the States for more than four days. It is too competitive. You know, if I don't have my little alligator shirt and my bright green shorts with my Topsiders, someone thinks I don't have money or something. Whereas I can dress any way I want to over here." There is no possible way that you could be out of style or anything, or make a statement that . . . would [make someone] think you are nuts, in a city the size of London. You don't have to be a conformist, whereas at home you do have to play more by those rules, whether you like them or not. . . . I can't find the word for it to save my life, but there is an anonymity that really appeals to me. . . . Maybe it's a big city thing, and I suppose I could find that in New York where maybe it is less conformist than here . . . but there is something very appealing to me [about] not [having] to have a label on.

. . . .

Cultures allow strangers a certain latitude that is not proffered to their own members (Cateora, 1983). If one fails, however, to discern where the boundaries of that freedom end, censure or isolation results. For example, the Japanese forgive most social faux pas when foreigners appear to be well intentioned and do not speak the language. However, they do not tolerate public displays of anger or embarrassing one's superior. Expatriate managers in West Africa may not have to entertain business contacts as they would at home, but they are expected to attend all their employees' baptisms, weddings, and funerals. Every culture has some rules that are absolutes, what Cateora calls "cultural imperatives." Expatriates who perceive only freedom will invariably transgress important cultural norms, thereby inhibiting their effectiveness.

Identity Values Paradoxes

Generally, identity values paradoxes relate to identification and personal boundaries. Understanding these paradoxes helps to provide insight into what happens to expatriates' value systems when they are exposed to the values of another culture. One paradox in this category occurs when expatriates feel they are simultaneously *relinquishing and strengthening their values*. As part of the cultural assimilation process, they adopt certain values of the host culture (Berry, 1983). At the same time, they give up some of their American cultural ideas and behaviors in order to be accepted or successful in the other culture. In the process of shedding some of their peripheral cultural beliefs and values that are less acceptable to the other culture, some of their core values assume even greater importance.

This paradox captures the basic dilemma of identity and acculturation: How much of one's identity (or values) must be given up in order to be accepted by the other culture?

The concept of figure/ground in Gestalt psychology helps to illuminate this paradox. *Figure* is what we see first because it stands out from the background. Our cultural values are usually *ground*, or background. An analogy used to explain culture is that of the fish that is not aware of the surrounding water until it is removed from the ocean. In the same way, people are introduced to their own culture in the act of confronting another culture. One learns what it means to be an American by rubbing up against other nationalities. When I asked expatriates, "Were there things that surprised you about the way people thought or worked in the foreign country?" I knew their answers would reveal as much about U.S. culture as about the foreign cultures. The most striking difference for them was the work ethic, which they generally found to be weaker in Europe and stronger in Asia than in the United States. The different values of the host culture forced their own values out of the background, where they had been taken for granted, and made them figural. They could more readily articulate their values because they had something with which to compare them.

Ron and his wife came face-to-face with their own cultural value of egalitarianism.

* * * * * * *

> I moved a manager of a division between countries . . . so he was an expatriate from Holland in France. He had a small child who was three years old. The wife put him in French school. She wanted to meet the other mothers and children. She called up everyone in the class to invite them over. The first thing everyone asked was, "What does your husband do?" She didn't get one single acceptance, because he didn't work for an oil company. His position was not high enough. Even though he was a division manager . . . a pretty high-level job in our company, his status wasn't high enough to be accepted. That's something that would be almost unheard of in the United States. And it just drove my wife crazy that people would think that way. That is totally contrary to the American way of thinking. . . . You could accept it, but it doesn't mean that you like it or you relate to it. That's one bad factor about Europe. It is very, very status conscious, very class conscious.

* * * * * * *

In reality, Americans are also conscious of status, albeit in different ways and perhaps to a lesser degree. An experience like Ron's, however, can force expatriates to think about the issue and decide where they stand on it. If a person's values survive a thoughtful comparison with those of another culture, those values become stronger. In contrast, the peripheral values or cultural beliefs that are not essential to one's sense of identity are reexamined and jettisoned at this point in the quest for acceptance and effectiveness.

Ron described what values he gave up during his sojourn in Holland:

* * * * * * *

It is maybe some outspokenness. You tend to be more reserved in what you say. Probably give up some informality. Americans tend to be very informal at home. And in Europe, you may be a little more formal, even going out to the market. Everybody is dressed a lot better than they are here [in the States]. And you tend to say after a while, "I don't want to stand out that much.". . . You can pick out an American four miles down the street! . . . Giving up some of your American values, you find that you change in subtle ways—the way you live, the way you act. But at the same time, reinforcing a lot of the values that we have here—the freedom of action, the creativity, the aggressiveness in a good sense, that you don't see in a lot of European nationalities.

* * * * * * *

Jay, a gregarious, insightful marketing executive, also experienced this paradox. He spent four years in Belgium as the managing director of a European manufacturing and sales division, and a year in Vietnam as an intelligence officer.

* * * * * * *

What did I give up? I never wanted to know something about French wines, but I felt that I ought to know something about them in Europe. Becoming stern and tough because this is what the German likes. I even could tell I was imitating the French guys. Noticing waving my hands because they did it. I'll do it if that's what they want. I don't normally wave my hands, but when our French salesman would come up, he would get all excited and I would do that because I felt that he liked it. And it would make the conversation go better. The American [value] that became stronger [was] my belief in individual freedom. I think I became much more of a patriot after being over there. I see the advantages to our constitutional system. I'd say that is the biggest one. I guess even going further than that, I think I have a new respect, a different feeling about religion over there, too. You know, I can see a difference between the way they look at religion and the way we do. . . . I think my religious values have become stronger after being there, and seeing the coldness of things.

* * * * * * *

Carl came face to face with different values about the environment when he lived in Germany. He was shocked to receive a pint-sized garbage can that resisted his futile attempts to cram a mountain of garbage into it—until he learned to recycle like his neighbors.

* * * * * * *

I remember . . . I tried to adapt to their ways so that I would feel more a part or have some success with them. I don't know whether it is really giving up American values. I guess giving up American values means I wasn't as wasteful. I went along. . . . "Okay, I am going to crush cans and I am going to recycle bottles." I could have just thrown them in the trash.

* * * * * * *

Expatriates indicate three reasons why they give up aspects of their own culture: to gain acceptance by the other culture, to be more effective on the job, and to avoid "standing out" and looking too much like a tourist or foreigner. Yosup Lee and Laurie Larwood (1983) found that highly satisfied American managers in Korea adopted some Korean values while retaining American values. They hypothesized that to be successful, these expatriates sought to accommodate those Korean values that did not alienate them from crucial American values. That makes sense, but for many expatriates, their core values—patriotism, capitalism, individual freedom, initiative, egalitarianism, and religious values—also become stronger as a result of the exposure to a different culture. As one expatriate said, "I became more American while I was there. Even though I accepted the way things are there, it made me realize how American I really am."

Many expatriates reportedly became more patriotic while living overseas. Neil, the banker who had such a good experience in Japan, described it in the following terms:

* * * * * * *

Now I was going to talk about a personal paradox. And that is, becoming more aware of your inherent patriotism, which I think most people take for granted until they live overseas. . . . My wife and I graduated from college in the early 1970s, which means we participated in the strike, we protested vigorously against the war in Vietnam, the bombing in Cambodia, the draft. . . . So I never thought of myself as . . . having strongly patriotic inclinations, but . . . I found that when . . . [I lived] in a foreign country, . . . I became almost a sloppily emotional patriot—the type of person who would break down in tears when he heard "The Star Spangled Banner," who resented any criticism of the United States. And these were aspects of my character that I never would have anticipated before going to Japan.

* * * * * * *

Why do so many Americans become more patriotic abroad? Several explanations come to mind. First, running into stereotypes and criticism of their country and feeling forced to defend its actions is likely to elicit patriotism. Whenever the United States makes a bold gesture, expatriates feel the ripple effect in a very personal way. Glenn, the London-based vice president of European operations introduced earlier, reported that his children did not have a patriotic bone in their body until they lived through the bombing of Libya and the Falklands crisis. The degree of anti-American sentiment that surrounded these incidents in the media and in their school had two effects. It made them feel like a minority, and they learned to appreciate their country more.

Second, the adjustment to another culture is so difficult and anxiety-provoking that patriotism may be necessary to help maintain one's identity; for some, national pride may well serve as an organizing principle that helps maintain the personality structure.

Third, some people become more patriotic as a result of having their consciousness raised about the advantages of their own country. Free speech, free markets, freedom of religion, freedom of the press, and a relatively functional justice system look very good in comparison with less favorable conditions in other countries.

Finally, an idealization of their own culture occurs for many expatriates when they are abroad. Harry Triandis (1967), an insightful cross-cultural psychologist, discovered that Americans in Greece thought more highly of Americans than did Americans in Illinois. Some expatriates forget the negative aspects and wax poetic about the wonderful attributes of their country (until they are repatriated and begin to idealize their time abroad).

Another paradox in the identity values category concerns the *macro/micro perspective* that expatriates experience. At the same time that they feel themselves becoming more and more "world-minded" as a result of exposure to different values and conflicting loyalties, they also become more idiosyncratic in putting together their own value system and views on life. Peter Adler (1974) alluded to this paradox involving personal boundaries when he wrote, "Where the configuration of loyalties and identification is constantly in flux and where boundaries are never secure, multicultural man [and presumably woman] lays himself open to any and all kind of stimuli. In the face of messages which are confusing, contradictory, or overwhelming, the individual is thrown back on his own subjectivity with which he must integrate and sort out what he allows himself to take in" (p. 373).

The expatriates I interviewed ranked this paradox as the most significant. Hugh is the unmarried expatriate introduced in Chapter Two who spent two years in Venezuela working for a Big Six accounting firm. During that time, he made a point of traveling extensively and exposing himself to other cultures. His description of how he changed abroad is an example of the macro/macro perspective paradox.

• • • • • • •

> I have changed as a result of the experience in that I am more understanding of a wide range of people. . . . Definitely more interested in experiencing different situations and cultures than I was when I went, although that is what drove me to want to do it. More of a need to go and do things other than just staying at home and being content. . . . And of course, I am much more independent than I was before. . . . And probably that idiosyncratic question, I think I have changed in that way. I have sort of created somebody. Not intentionally, I don't think, but I think that is what happened.

• • • • • • •

How do expatriates "create somebody?" Long-term expatriates speak of adopting values or practices from other cultures that they find lacking in their own. As one expatriate says, "You find you start picking parts of different cultures that you like and saying, Gee, I wish we could have all of these together." An example is the person who forms a unique religious belief that, while still containing the basic core of Christian beliefs, also incorporates "the best parts" of other religions to which the person has been exposed. For each of the countries where I have lived, I can identify values that I admired and worked to acquire or emulate.

Hugh's recent story, in addition to illustrating how one takes on new beliefs and attitudes, also brings to mind something that was written by an expert on heroism. In his book *The Denial of Death*, Ernest Becker (1973) described people who throw off their "cultural lendings." This term refers to the beliefs that we inherit unquestioningly from our native culture. Becker states that people discard this "borrowed self" in order to embrace a more authentic self. This idea fits with Campbell's suggestion that modern-day heroes are those who are not content to imitate others but who journey inward to find themselves. Perhaps this growth is why the expatriates in my study ranked this paradox as the most significant. It represents a "coming of age" and a liberation from a prior conception of both the self and the world.

Understanding and Dealing with Expatriate Paradoxes

I was curious about whether or not there are factors that affect the perception and experience of these nine paradoxes. When I analyzed my findings I arrived at two conclusions. First, the more involved expatriates are with the foreign culture (involvement is determined by such factors as language fluency, having local friends and co-workers and/or staff, and a job that forces one to interact closely with the foreign culture), the more likely they are to perceive these paradoxes or contradictions. In other words, a certain threshold level of acculturation is necessary before expatriates become aware of these paradoxes.

Second, the paradoxes were only problematic when first confronted; once resolved, they no longer constituted an obstacle. Mastering them or learning to live with them seems to require an even higher level of acculturation than simply being aware of them. This brings to mind Alfred North Whitehead's observation that "In formal logic, a contradiction is the sign of defeat: but in the evolution of real knowledge it marks the first step in progress towards a victory" (1925, p. 267). In Gestalt terminology, the perception of paradox appears to change from ground to figure to ground as the expatriate's level of acculturation evolves, which raises the question of why these paradoxes originate in the first place.

Paradoxes occur abroad because expatriates are mediating between two cultures and two organizations, and they have fewer anchors and accepted forms of etiquette to guide them. Uncertainty about how to proceed is often exacerbated by language barriers. As a result, the trust, social cues, and implicit understanding taken for granted within one's own culture and organization have to be developed consciously abroad. Paradox is the shadow of the ubiquitous ambiguity and uncertainty in the expatriate experience. As such, paradoxes represent complexity frozen in time and the inability to index priorities outside one's own culture. For expatriates, paradox may well be "the muddle" before new sets of contingencies are both accepted and clarified. Knowing which truth to choose in a paradoxical situation appears to be dependent on both cultural sensitivity, which is a form of acculturation, and a concern for effectiveness.

There seem to be three common ways of dealing with paradox. People can accept both truths, reframe the situation, or look for a higher unifying principle (Quinn, 1988; Quinn and Cameron, 1988; Smith and Berg, 1987). The higher unifying principle for expatriates seems to be effectiveness; they choose the side of the paradox that furthers their work goals and preserves their work relationships. Bertrand Russell (1913) resolved the famous Liar Paradox ("All Cretans are liars; I never tell the truth") by accepting both truths and reframing the paradox as two statements having different levels of reference that are not paradoxical when kept separate. For example, in certain circumstances all Cretans are liars and in other circumstances I never tell the truth, so the two sentences do not necessarily cancel each other out. Expatriates accept both sides of the paradoxes and eventually learn under what circumstances a particular side is true. Expatriates resolve paradoxes by learning to take a contingency approach, once they have developed the cognitive maps that include both contradictory truths as well as the cues that tell them which truth is most closely aligned with effectiveness; that is, managers learn to judge a situation and figure out when they need, for example, to manifest their power and when they need to empower others, based on what would be most effective in the particular situation.

I asked expatriates to tell me about a critical incident that involved a paradox they handled overseas and then compiled the following list of common approaches they used:

1. They looked for reasons to explain the situation so they could understand why the other culture behaved as it did—so they could understand the "foreign" side of the paradox.

2. They determined what their role was in the particular situation and gauged whether they could influence or change the situation and whether or not they had the right, as an expatriate, to do so.

3. They weighed the contingencies of the situation: What would happen if they chose to act on either side of the paradox?

4. They discerned the critical factors (either norms or actions) in the situation that were absolutely essential for effectiveness or success.

5. They "picked their battles" in conflicts between headquarters and the local company and avoided those conflicts they could not win.

6. They accepted what they could not change. For example, the typical response when dealing with a paradox involving differing cultural values was, "Once I realized I couldn't change it, I just accepted it. There was no other alternative."

7. They learned from the experience and applied it to the next paradoxical situation.

One of the great payoffs of the overseas assignment is that it is a good training ground for developing the ability to perceive paradoxes and for learning to deal with them. This understanding leads to the next phase in the hero's adventure: "the ultimate boon."

The Ultimate Boon

Transforming and Enriching Ourselves

All nice people, like us, are We
And everyone else is They:
But if you cross over the sea,
Instead of over the way,
You may end by (think of it!) looking on We
As only a sort of They!
　　　　　　　—Rudyard Kipling, "We and They"

Once mythical heroes have proved themselves on the road of trials, they arrive at the final step of the initiation stage—the ultimate boon. At this point, the heroes penetrate to a source of power and receive a boon as their reward, which in many myths is meant to be shared with the heroes' world when they return. For example, Moses answered God's call and went to the mountain, where God gave him the Ten Commandments, a boon to all Jews, and eventually to Christians, although they have not always heeded these commandments. Nevertheless, Moses was transformed by his relationship with God.

In myths, penetrating to a source of power involves a transformation to a higher consciousness by means of a death and rebirth. The death symbolizes the submission of the ego, giving oneself over to a higher good or "putting aside" a former life and way of looking at the world. The rebirth lies in seeing the world through different eyes or taking on a different role. The heroes' consciousness is transformed either by the trials themselves or by illuminating revelations. According to Joseph Campbell (1988, p. 126):

. . . .

> If you realize what the real problem is—losing yourself, giving yourself to some higher end, or to another—you realize that this itself is the ultimate trial. When we quit thinking primarily about ourselves and our own self-preservation, we undergo a truly heroic transformation of consciousness. And what all the myths have to deal with is transformation of consciousness of one kind or another. You have been thinking one way, you now have to think a different way.

. . . .

Transformation is one of the most frequently heard themes in expatriate stories. Carl, introduced in Chapter Three, reflected on the two years he spent doing research at a German university. He echoes a common refrain:

. . . .

> Anyone who lives abroad has to change. They have to be more open to the different situations and . . . that makes them a more open person. I think you tend to be a little less impulsive and a little more willing to sit and listen to the other side first rather than just making a snap decision, saying, we have always done it this way.

. . . .

Three aspects of mythical transformation help to elucidate the expatriate experience: (1) the need for sacrifice, (2) the move from dependence to independence, and (3) the heroes' discovery of a universal power within them.

The need for sacrifice. Campbell (1968, p. 108) describes the hero as a person of self-achieved submission who "must put aside his pride, his virtue, beauty, and life, and bow or submit to the absolutely intolerable." Although such extravagant demands are seldom required of them, expatriates are no strangers to sacrifice. Their stories are full of references to doing difficult things "for the good of the company" or for their family. Many of them make sacrifices to accomplish difficult tasks abroad and to be effective and accepted in the other culture. Furthermore, some expatriates sacrifice their values, normal ways of behavior and perception, their extended family, and, in certain instances, their comfort.

Mack, the introverted program manager introduced in Chapter Three who worked for an oil company in London, felt that he sacrificed his free time in order to help his family adjust. They had a very rocky, homesick beginning, and during that time his biggest challenge was keeping his family happy. Although he prefers to relax at home, he took his wife and two children sight-seeing every weekend so they would not mope at home. He felt he owed them that, because they were overseas due to his job. Nevertheless, he stated, "I did things I would definitely never do in the U.S., for the good of the family."

The move from dependence to independence. The move from dependence to independence is a common mythological theme that also involves a form of sacrifice. It means leaving behind a former way of life, a former consciousness. This transformation is the basis for many initiation rites found throughout the world. Most cultures use such rites to formally mark the end of childhood (dependence) and the beginning of adulthood (independence). As discussed in Chapter Four, on magical friends, expatriates often experience a sense of dependency during the beginning months of their assignment. They have left behind many of their cultural and personal anchors. In many respects, they are starting over again, like a child, learning a new culture and a new language. Once the code of the new culture has been broken, with or without the help of a cultural mentor, they can function independently once more. This move from dependence to independence is a proud moment and one that many expatriates can pinpoint as the specific time when they began to feel comfortable in the culture or effective on the job.

Discovery of a universal power within. Mythical heroes, like expatriates, find that the adventure evokes qualities of their characters they did not know they possessed. Heroes learn that the power or ability to accomplish something lay within them all the time— Prince Five-Weapons's knowledge, Luke Skywalker's "force," and Dorothy's ability to leave the Land of Oz are examples. As Campbell (1968, p. 39) states: "The perilous journey is not labor of attainment but reattainment, not discovery but rediscovery. . . . Godly powers were within the heart of the hero all the time. . . . The hero is symbolical of that divine creative and redemptive image which is hidden within us all, only waiting to be known and rendered into life."

Most modern societies have fewer rites of passage and opportunities to test oneself. For many expatriates, life in the States is not as challenging as it was overseas, because they are not called upon to use all their talents or to rise to the occasion in the way that is demanded by an international assignment. I don't mean to imply that one cannot be challenged within one's own culture. However, the sheer novelty and uncertainty of entering another culture can throw expatriates off-balance. As a result, they often become aware of hidden resources and skills that were not needed within their own culture but that are essential for coping abroad. This pattern confirms David Szanton's (1966) belief that in the effort to understand another culture, one comes to know oneself. As Campbell (1968, p. 25) writes, "By traveling outward, we come to the center of our own existence."

In addition to a different level of consciousness about themselves, expatriates may acquire a new way of perceiving the world. Because the balance of their lives is disrupted and their normal routines are left at home, expatriates are usually more open to new experiences and new perceptions. Expatriates will say that they sometimes become calloused in their own culture by predictability, routine, and even materialism. Finding novelty at home requires a special effort. Once the familiar frame is broken by entering a new culture, people are freed to look at their surroundings with a more childlike appreciation. Novelty and learning emerged as major themes in my interviews of expatriates, and these are two of the factors they missed most when they returned home.

In myth, consciousness is transformed by exposure to trials or illuminating revelations. For expatriates, consciousness is transformed by exposure to cultural differences, to trials, and to paradox, sometimes with the help of the magical friend who provides explanations. Making sense of different cultures and their beliefs is a challenge. In the process, the expatriates' own views change and they acquire a different consciousness, a bicultural or multicultural perspective. This is the change in consciousness most frequently described by expatriates—the acquisition of a more cognitively complex perspective that also includes an appreciation of paradox. Becoming a citizen of the world, acknowledging the similarities and differences among cultures, and learning to see one's own culture through the eyes of another are other examples of their new consciousness.

American businesspeople generally live in an objective and empirical world in which reality is measured in terms of profit and goal attainment. The expatriate often finds that the world overseas is not operationalized in the same way. This opens the door for the expatriate to achieve a different way of looking at life. Jack, the respected international lawyer introduced in Chapter Two, lived in Europe for seven years and still travels there frequently. When he compares himself with people who have not lived abroad, he finds the following difference:

* * * * * * *

I pay a lot more attention to my personal life than most of my colleagues do. Vacation is sacrosanct to me. If I have a vacation that's planned, there's nothing that can keep me from my vacation. I think I have a much different perspective on the importance of work. I guess to put it in a nutshell, at the extremes, when I went to Europe I was probably more of a "live to work" person, and when I came back, I was much more of a "work to live" person, and I continue more along that line than the former.

The Nature of the Expatriate Transformation

The basic theme of the hero's adventure is a separation from the world, a penetration to some source of power, and a life-enhancing return. The source of power for the expatriate is a bicultural perspective, increased self-awareness, and the knowledge that he or she had the inner resources to master a difficult situation. These are some of the ways that expatriates change overseas. The nature of the changes depends on the individual expatriate and the type of adventure he or she sought. Nevertheless, the transformation process expatriates describe seems fairly universal. A thorough understanding of this process helps to provide an understanding of why repatriation can be just as difficult as going abroad.

• • • • • • • •

For mythical heroes, the process of transformation involves a dying and a birth. But whether small or great, and no matter what the stage or grade of life, the call rings up the curtain, always, on a mystery of transfiguration—a rite, or moment, of spiritual passage, which, when complete, amounts to a dying and a birth. The familiar life horizon has been outgrown; the old concepts, ideals, and emotional patterns no longer fit; the time for the passing of a threshold is at hand [Campbell, 1968, p. 51].

Letting Go and Taking On

The death and rebirth of the transformation process that expatriates describe takes the form of a "letting go" (death) and a "taking on" (rebirth). The various factors involved in this process are presented in Table 6.1.

Table 6.1. The Transformation Process.

Letting Go	Taking On
Cultural certainty	Internalized perceptions of the other culture; increased patriotism
Unquestioned acceptance of basic assumptions	Internalized values of the other culture
Personal frames of reference	New or broader schemas so that differences are accepted without a need to compare
Unexamined life	Constructed life
Accustomed role or status	Role assigned by the other culture or one's job
Social reinforcement knowledge	Accepting and learning the other culture's social norms and behavior
Accustomed habits and activities	Substituting functional equivalents
Known routines	Addiction to novelty and learning

During their sojourn, expatriates relinquish the following factors: (1) cultural certainty, (2) unquestioned acceptance of basic assumptions, (3) personal frames of reference, (4) the unexamined life, (5) accustomed role and status, (6) knowledge of social reinforcement, (7) accustomed habits and activities, and (8) known routines. The first four factors are either cognitive or attitudinal; they relate to the mental maps that undergo extensive redefinition as a result of a cross-cultural experience. In Campbell's (1968, p. 51) terms, they are "the old concepts, ideals, and emotional patterns" that no longer fit. The other factors are concerned with social relationships and outside activities.

Letting Go of Cultural Certainty: Internalizing Perceptions of the Other Culture

Cultural certainty is the implicit faith and pride people have in their own country. For example, many Americans have an image of the United States as a superpower that generously comes to the aid of other nations; if they stop to consider this image at all, they usually assume that other countries are very grateful for U.S. help and for the role the United States plays in international affairs. International politics are not that simple, however, and rightly or wrongly, the image of the United States abroad is not always favorable.

Expatriates, regardless of their nationality, often find themselves on the firing line, forced to defend their country's foreign policy and domestic conditions. To their chagrin, they are not always defensible. Furthermore, expatriates discover that other countries have some advantages that are lacking at home. They are therefore forced to relinquish the certainty that their country is always "right" and "better" than other nations. Doug, introduced in Chapter Four, "let go" of his own cultural certainty while working in the banking industry in England.

* * * * * * *

> I became aware of my nationality. I became aware of the kind of stereotypes that exist about Americans overseas. I became aware and sensitive to the perception of Americans overseas. That, to summarize in very broad terms, was . . . that all Americans were loud, ignorant of world events and politics . . . ruder than the European environment . . . and that Americans had a tendency to be short-sighted.

* * * * * * *

Neil, the banker who worked in Japan, described the gradual movement he made in this area.

. . . .

I think eventually you have to give up your instinctive emotional
reaction to any criticism about the United States. . . . After a
while, you realize that . . . there was another way of looking at the
United States. . . . At that point you became receptive to criticism
as long as it was presented in a positive, constructive way, which
in Japan it almost always was. . . . I think you have to be prepared
to accept criticism of your country by an outsider. When I first
arrived, I wouldn't accept it. . . . That is probably part of the arro-
gance for which Americans are so famous overseas.

. . . .

The process of letting go of cultural certainty is hastened by bold
U.S. foreign policy moves that are debated endlessly in the overseas
press. While this exposure to different and often critical external
views of their country often forces expatriates to acknowledge its
flaws, they do not necessarily become less patriotic. In many cases,
the opposite effect occurs, and they become even more patriotic.
At the same time, however, they "take on" some of the views the
other culture holds about Americans, so they return with a more
cognitively complex view of their country. This usually means they
have a clearer idea of their homeland's positive and negative points.

Lou, introduced in Chapter Four, described how he came to
internalize the different perspectives to which he was exposed during his two years in England as a project engineer:

. . . .

We used to get into these discussions and I think it did change me
a lot, how I look at things and realizing that the Europeans do
have a whole different way of looking at things than we do and
they're not necessarily wrong. And I still have the option of dis-
agreeing with them, but it gave me a way of looking at things differently, for example, when the Libyan crisis came up. To me, after

living with the English for a year, it wasn't surprising to me that
there would be a lot of anti-American sentiment and also a lot of
hostility about the bombing. And I'm really amazed that the State
Department would be taken aback by that, and I thought to
myself, What do those dumb bastards [diplomats] do in this country? Don't they ever talk to the people? Don't they ever read the
papers and get a feel for it? . . . I've learned to look at things from
a bigger picture and I did have a hard time adjusting to that a
little bit.

Letting Go of Unquestioned Acceptance of Basic Assumptions: Internalizing the Values of the Other Culture

This category, like the preceding one, forces expatriates to consider factors that were previously taken for granted. Edgar Schein
(1988) wrote about the basic assumptions that form a hard-to-
excavate layer of cultural notions—the implicit cognitive maps that
people inherit from their cultures. Coming into contact with other
cultures makes these assumptions visible and forces expatriates to
question their validity. At the same time, they may be "taking on"
values of the other culture. (This paradoxical activity was discussed
fully in Chapter Five.)

Rick, introduced in Chapter Five, lived in England and traveled
throughout Europe representing his company. He was in his twenties at the time and described himself as fairly conservative.
Although he did not always agree with the different perspectives he
encountered, he made an effort to understand and respect them.

◆ ◆ ◆ ◆ ◆ ◆

I think I was introduced to a lot of different thought processes, a
lot of different backgrounds—democracies—socialism being one
. . . major difference. And I certainly learned to try to evaluate
people who acted differently and came from a different background than I did from that person's perspective. Now whether I
do that well or not, I don't know, but I certainly learned to do it a
bit better.

* * * * * * *

During his stint in Germany, Carl was surprised by the smaller appliances used by Europeans and the German attitude toward conservation.

* * * * * * *

My wife and I used to put them (the Germans) somewhere in the 1950s in terms of where their appliances were and their way of liv-ing. In some ways, they were superior to us. The one thing I guess we really came away with, overall, was that we began to see that they were a very conscious society . . . conscious of their limited raw materials, and didn't waste a lot. They used everything to the fullest. And we quickly began to see ourselves as the throwaway society. . . . It really made us look at ourselves and see how waste-ful we are in the United States.

* * * * * * *

When expatriates return home, many become aware of the val-ues they have internalized abroad. After spending almost six years in West African countries where women do not expose their legs (breasts are a different story), I stopped dead in my tracks when I saw women in short shorts in a U.S. grocery store. It took me a moment to remember where I was and to recall that I had once worn shorts like that, albeit in a long-gone, pre-varicose-vein era. I was amazed to see how deeply and quickly I had unconsciously internalized a proscription from another culture.

Geert Hofstede (1980) defines culture as collective mental pro-gramming. We who live abroad realize that our particular cultural software is not the only one that functions, nor is it necessarily the best one. We find ourselves pondering certain questions—Why do Americans always start conversations by asking strangers what kind of work they do? Why is voluntarism so strong in the United States and so weak in many other cultures? Eventually, we begin to see that all cultures have advantages and disadvantages when considered objectively and that cultures can be viewed in terms of trade-offs. Traditional cultures with clear norms may be more confining and slower to change, but their members usually possess a strong sense of identity and belonging. Creativity and adaptability are often identified as by-products of American culture; however, the price we pay for allowing people the freedom to go their own way in our polyglot and highly mobile society is insecurity and rootlessness.

Jay, introduced in Chapter Five, listed some of the pros and cons he perceived after living abroad for seven years:

* * * * * * *

> It makes me more appreciative of what I have here [in the States]. The educational opportunities, the job opportunities, the idea that you can go as far as you want is more applicable to the U.S. than to Europe. . . . On the other hand, I see in Europe closer-knit family groups. . . . You get a person from a certain village. I bet you my paycheck that they have parents there, or a brother, or a sister, or an aunt, uncle, niece all living within two kilometers, and they see each other once a week. Good God, . . . I haven't seen one of my brothers for five years! That is almost unheard of in Europe. . . . I think their care of the elderly and the sick under the socialist-type principles is much better than our approach. But I would not want to see our structure go to where somebody who works hard has to pay 70 percent of their income to taxes either.

Letting Go of Frames of Reference: Adopting New and Broader Schemas

When we first go abroad, we are intrigued by the differences we observe; as time goes on, it is the similarities that capture our attention. But in the beginning, we inevitably compare what we see to what we know at home, which is our frame of reference. Over time, we relinquish this frame of reference as a basis for "judging" the other culture. Well-adapted expatriates learn to accept the other culture "as it is," without feeling a need to compare it to home-country standards.

Social cognition theory (Fiske and Taylor, 1984) provides one possible explanation for this phenomenon. According to this theory, people organize their perceptions into schemas, or mental maps of various concepts, events, or types of stimuli. For example, people have somewhat unique schemas for the concept of "mother" that include the attributes they think mothers have (caring, helpful, kind, strict, permissive, and so on), based on their own experiences with mothers. Once a schema has been established, it affects how people handle future information or stimuli because it determines what they pay attention to and remember. When they see a mother behaving in a way that is not included in their schema for mothers, they pay attention and are often moved to comment on it. Generally speaking, expatriates either "take on" and develop new schemas (Peruvian mothers become a separate category and have their own specific list of characteristics) or they expand their own schema of mothers to include mothers of more than one nationality (American mothers and Peruvian mothers). Eventually, they stop noticing things that do not fit their original schema.

Acculturated expatriates commonly complain about others who cannot cease making comparisons. Eric, introduced in Chapter Three, who spent almost five years in Japan and Korea, sees these comparisons as a characteristic of "Ugly Americans."

. . . .

Ugly Americans think everything is better in the United States than it is [elsewhere] in the world. . . . One of the things I try to do is appreciate people for their own culture and their own situation, as opposed to trying to ask, how do they stack up to Americans? But most other cultures look at Americans conversely as, how do they stack up compared to the Asian culture?

Letting Go of the Unexamined Life: Constructing a Life

As Socrates noted, the unexamined life is not worth living. For many expatriates, the experience of living overseas triggers an examination of their life. When they leave their normal context, the surprises, changes, and contrasts (Louis, 1980) confronted in a new culture lead to introspection. Spouses in particular have to construct a new life for themselves (Adler, 1986), and, in doing so, evaluate their lives to determine what should and should not be included. Several expatriates echoed one expatriate's observation, "My wife had nothing. I mean, she woke up and had no structure to her day. She really had to construct her life, and fortunately [she] did it."

Constructing a life is one of the skills I honed overseas, out of necessity. When my children were young, they took precedence over my career. During this era, we moved to a new country about every two years. I spent the first three to six months getting the children settled in, which often meant sitting on the floor as they played with the neighbor kids, unobtrusively translating for them so they could learn a new language. Since Asbjorn's employer did not ship household goods, I usually had to locate and buy everything we needed for the house anew—no mean feat in the remote areas where we usually lived. In countries where furniture is not sold "off the rack," I designed most of our furniture. If the country was West African, the next step involved daily visits to the carpenter to make sure my place in the queue had not been supplanted by a more persuasive customer. By the time we had been in the country six months, our personal belongings had usually arrived and we had a semblance of a home filled with fairly happy campers and friends. At this point, I had to sit down and create a life for myself. I began by taking stock of what I enjoyed and had missed in recent years and by questioning the contribution I was making. Piece by piece, I put together the professional and non-work-related activities I needed to feel fulfilled. Challenging, part-time work opportunities miraculously emerged, often through social contacts. Had I not moved and been forced to start from scratch, I would not have taken the time to evaluate and change my life so frequently. I suspect I might have chosen a rut and plowed through it for much longer than was healthy.

Expatriates usually live under a time sentence. Except for those who settle permanently in another country, we think in terms of the length of our assignment. This pushes us to "take advantage" of whatever a foreign country has to offer or to get certain goals accomplished at work. These deadlines encourage us to take a closer look at our lives and to live them more fully. Thus, many of us let go of an unexamined life and take on a carefully considered, constructed life.

Letting Go of Accustomed Role and Status: Taking On the Roles Assigned by the Other Culture or by One's Job

An expatriate assignment usually involves some type of role change, either at work or in one's personal life. Such changes may involve both higher and lower status, although the former is most likely the case with expatriates in terms of their work roles. Some find themselves hobnobbing with ambassadors and business magnates, playing the figurehead role for their company.

All expatriates assume the role of the stranger, an unknown commodity, once they leave the borders of their own country. If they cannot speak the local language, they may even be treated as if they were morons, a humbling shock to one's self-concept. An even greater shock is to find oneself stereotyped in an unflattering role. Europeans often describe Americans as "cowboys" who take action without pausing to consider all the options or consequences.

Paul and his family, introduced in Chapter Three, lived in Mexico where many people dealt with them as "gringos" rather than as individuals.

. . . .

I think they approached us with initial trepidation or prejudice. We tried to treat people like people, and those people who took the trouble to get to know us and judge us on our merit would arrive at the conclusions that they liked or didn't like us for our opinions on things or our way of behavior and not simply because we were gringos.

. . . .

Expatriates have only limited control over the particular roles they are assigned in another culture. My husband and I went from being *los padrinos* in Colombia (godparents responsible for the welfare of the community) to "capitalist, imperialist pigs" in the eyes of a Communist labor union in Peru. Neither role described us accurately, but we had to work around these attributions. Expatriates "take on" the roles that are assigned them by the particular foreign culture/office and, in the case of effective expatriates, whatever other roles are necessary for them to get the job done. Some expatriates also have to take on such roles as figurehead, troubleshooter, controller, and cheerleader for global programs or policies. Relinquishing accustomed roles and assuming assigned roles can be threatening to one's sense of self. Maintaining one's own identity and not buying into someone else's mistaken perception, be it overly positive or overly negative, is a challenge.

Letting Go of Social Reinforcement Knowledge: Accepting and Learning the Norms of Another Culture

Lack of knowledge about the social cues of another culture is the principle definition of expatriate culture shock (Oberg, 1960). Expatriates quickly discover that their accustomed social behavior does not yield the expected results, for example, "I didn't know how to get business done or . . . buy meat, for that matter!" To function effectively, expatriates give up some of their habitual behavior and decode and "take on" the social norms and behavior of the other culture. Art, introduced in Chapter Five as the vice president of operations for a European subsidiary, had to adapt to various cultures.

•   •   •   •   •   •   •

Well, I had to do business with a great number of different people. And dealing with the Italians, who were very vocal and very expressive . . . [is] a lot different than doing business with the Germans, who are very stoic and very methodical. All are very, very competent in what they do and the way they do it if you understand why they are doing it or why they are reacting the way they do. So, you have to look beyond that.

* * * * * * *

Dan, who spoke a unique version of pidgin Portuguese that his closest Brazilian employee obligingly adopted, struggled with communication barriers:

* * * * * * *

I went through four controllers in five and a half years. . . . I probably should have been a little bit more sensitive. They wanted to please me and they wanted to tell me what they thought I wanted to hear. I went through about three personnel people, too. [I'd ask them,] "Can we work overtime? What is the law?" The underlying current is, I need to work overtime. And I would get the answer that I could work overtime. It was against the law. . . . I guess they were bending over backwards trying to make sure [that] what I wanted to have happen, happened. And all I wanted to know is, What is the law? . . . Looking back on it, I am not sure with the differences we had that I gave them enough instruction so that we could work together. I think that was part of the language problem. . . . [Eventually I learned that] certain things mean different things to different people. You have to be more specific.

Letting Go of Accustomed Habits and Activities: Substituting Functional Equivalents

It is not always possible to carry out one's usual activities abroad. This sounds obvious and yet it is surprising how many expatriates never accept this fact. Rather than bemoan this loss, successfully acculturated expatriates "take on" replacements and substitutions that serve the same function. Instead of playing with a rock band, for instance, they learn how to play flamenco guitar or the sitar. Instead of complaining that there are no good hamburgers in West Africa, they learn to eat *chawarma*, a close relative of the Greek gyro sandwich. Instead of playing handball, they play rugby, soccer, or *fronton*. These substitute activities also bring them into closer contact with the local people.

Letting Go of Known Routines: Becoming Addicted to Novelty and Learning

When expatriates accept the call, they leave behind their known world. Many of them grow to thrive on the learning and novelty that is part of an overseas experience. Some travel constantly to perpetuate the novelty and learning. Hugh, for example, the auditor with a Big Six firm, spent two years in Venezuela picking up as much Spanish as possible and traveling all over South America.

. . . .

In the beginning you get there and it is all exciting. But see, I was picking that up throughout the entire tour by going someplace else. . . . Every long weekend I was gone somewhere on an airplane. . . . [I came back] definitely more interested in experiencing different situations and cultures than I was when I went, although that is what drove me to want to do it. Now I have more of a need to go and do things other than just staying here at home and being content.

. . . .

Harry, introduced in Chapter Four, the international director of a division for a large manufacturing company, reflected on his choice between living in a neighborhood with the other Americans working for his company or in a British neighborhood. He opted for the novelty of a different culture.

. . . .

I decided to live with the Brits, and it was a good move, because I knew Americans but I didn't know Brits. I got to meet a lot of good Brits; it was a lot of fun. The interesting things you learn. We lived across the street from my doctor, who is a Scot. . . . We would be invited to his New Year's party. Everyone would be invited for 8:00, but we were invited for 7:00 and we only lived across the street. So every year, we would come over there and he would welcome my wife, a redhead, and she would enter first and nobody would be there. . . . We didn't understand this. . . . It turns out there is a Scottish legend or tradition that if an auburn-haired person is the first to cross your threshold on the New Year's Eve, you have good luck for the year. So he always had this little hidden agenda. And you have to work hard to figure it out because you don't know what the cultural ways are. So you are constantly wondering what the intrigue is. You would not have that in an American community.

* * * * * * *

Known routines and people provide a sense of security and comfort. But for people with a taste for adventure, the pleasure of learning about different cultures is worth sacrificing the known for the unknown.

The Impetus Behind Transformation

What is the impetus behind the transformational process that occurs with most expatriates? Very simply, it is their desire to become acculturated, to fit into another culture, and to be effective at work. They talk about transformation in terms of letting go of things, which sometimes involved sacrifices or adjustments that not all expatriates were willing to make. Their stories are full of comparisons with unsuccessful expatriates who were not flexible enough or not committed enough to let go. Many expatriates carry a clear picture in their minds of the Ugly American they do not want to be. For example, one expatriate commented that he tried very hard not to be a "typical American," which he defined as "brash, obnoxious, always saying that what America does is right." Such efforts represent yet another sacrifice expatriates make to be successful overseas. It is not a simple matter to give up things as fundamental as cultural certainty, basic cultural assumptions, or accustomed roles. It takes courage to examine oneself and one's culture in this way and to step outside the bounds of conformity. But only by sacrificing these things can the expatriate be "reborn" in Campbell's terms and move to a higher consciousness—a bicultural perspective. Expatriate transformation promotes the type of self-knowledge that characterizes Campbell's definition of modern day heroes—people who discover "the inward thing you really are," rather than merely imitating others. As one expatriate stated with obvious satisfaction, "I have a better idea of how I tick." This is one of the boons he brought home.

Expatriate Boons

Virtually all expatriates acknowledge that they have changed overseas in a positive way. These changes constitute the personal boons they bring back with them, and include (1) positive changes in self, (2) changed attitudes, (3) improved work skills, (4) increased knowledge, and (5) closer family relationships.

Positive changes in self. Among the positive changes expatriates noticed in themselves are increased tolerance, patience, confidence, respectfulness, maturity, open-mindedness, competitiveness, adaptability, independence, sensitivity, and decreased impulsiveness. Some expatriates simply felt they were better people for having lived overseas. Even expatriates who did not completely enjoy the experience felt that it was a form of personal development. All expatriates see the experience as one that helps them to mature and build their character.

Changed attitudes. Some of the commonly reported changed attitudes that expatriates bring home are (1) a broader perspective on the world, (2) greater appreciation of cultural differences, (3) increased realization of how fortunate Americans are, (4) different attitudes toward work, and (5) a feeling that life is more interesting now than before.

Improved work skills. A particularly important boon for companies are the improved work skills expatriates bring home, including (1) improved communication skills in general and increased listening skills in particular, (2) an improved management style, (3) a better understanding of power, (4) the ability to do higher-quality work, and (5) broadened exposure to business. Improved interpersonal skills are mentioned most frequently.

A common fear among prospective expatriates is that they will fall behind technologically if they go overseas. Sometimes this is the case, but it depends on the particular technology and on the assignment.

Lou, the engaging young chemical engineer introduced in Chapter Four, had a great time during the two years he worked as a project engineer in England. He and his wife toured the country every weekend and developed close friendships in their neighborhood. Lou's British counterpart at work not only gave him an education in leftist politics but was also a magical friend who took the time to mentor Lou.

* * * * * * *

In addition to gaining a wider viewpoint, another way I've changed is careerwise. My overall way of looking at work things has also been exposed to a higher level. I learned a lot of tricks of the trade I wouldn't have learned otherwise. And because of that, I can address problems better here. Peter, my counterpart, had thirty years in the boiler business, and he used to teach me all kinds of things to look for. He'd drag me up and down stairs in plants to look at boilers that were even outside the scope of our work, just to show me how they run. My technical scope was really broadened.

* * * * * * *

Increased knowledge. I've mentioned repeatedly that expatriates see their time abroad as a period of accelerated learning. Much of that learning naturally centers around other countries—their language, history, culture, politics, economics, and art. American expatriates often report that they learned about the "finer things" in life while they were abroad. Furthermore, their friends from all over the world continue to educate them about the issues that are important in their countries. In many respects, an overseas assignment is like a good liberal arts education.

Closer family relationships. Common wisdom holds that an overseas experience either brings a family, and in particular, a marriage, closer together, or it breaks it apart (Komarovsky, 1968; Lanier, 1975; Torbiorn, 1982). When expatriate couples leave behind the extended family, and long-time friends and activities, they discover whether their relationship can stand on its own and whether there are family problems that require attention. This was the most important thing Sam learned in his first six months in South Africa.

* * * * * * *

I came to appreciate that it was a time that my wife and I never before had together. We were finally alone. . . . We have learned to appreciate each other's company. Because if you can't get along with your spouse, that's not the place for it to show, because there's only the two of you. You don't have a lot of friends at first and a lot of people to turn to. And you don't have family to run to and things like that. . . . So we were able to travel and take time and spend time together. Most of the time was our time, not everybody else's time. So I think our relationship strengthened. . . . We would plan a lot of trips and do things and it was just so much fun. We worked as a team.

* * * * * * *

Edward, the assistant chief engineer at a European R&D center introduced in Chapter Five, found the work transition to be fairly easy. Getting his family settled in was more challenging.

* * * * * * *

Personally, I think it was a difficult time for our family. There [are] a lot of adjustments . . . when you relocate into an area where you

don't speak the language. There is a lot your family goes through
where you find out, it kind of encloses you, and you find out that
you have a lot of areas that you have to work on in your relationships as a family. And I think it was a difficult time for us. A time
of change but a time of growth, too. I think we came back a better
family because of it. Because we had to work on things that we
could have easily avoided working on in our relationships here
because we each had our own things to do. So it kind of forced us
to develop as a family. I think that is a positive aspect. For my kids,
it was very worthwhile to be in an international school. I think it
helped them to see things from a little bigger perspective and realize that everybody doesn't have to be from the same area. They
have friends who are from all over the world. . . . From their perspective it was a good opportunity and they were old enough to
enjoy it. They were eight and ten . . . and I think they were old
enough to remember the things we did and remember the experience and remember friends, and they still communicate with some
of the kids they went to school or church with while they were
there. It was positive.

* * * * * * *

It is common for families to draw closer overseas, particularly
during the initial culture shock phase when the need for psychological support is greatest (Torbiorn, 1982). Some expatriates talk
about this time as "circling the wagons" in response to an external
threat. For other families, it is not so much adjustment difficulties
that draw them together as having more time available for the family. There are usually fewer organized activities for children overseas, and many adults are also less involved in outside activities.
Stay-at-home spouses are common because of laws that prohibit
them from working locally. The "work to live, not live to work"
credo found in many other cultures affects how much time expatriates are expected to spend at the office, and living in countries
where servants are easily affordable also allows parents to have
much more time for their children. Finally, families may be drawn
together by their common experience of a new and novel culture.

They are more likely to take off exploring together rather than pursuing individual interests, which seems more common at home.

Stan, the director of international operations at his multinational introduced in Chapter Three, lived abroad with his family for nineteen years in six different countries. They became experts at entering and adjusting to different cultures. His four children, now grown, are especially good friends. They are all married, but they still talk once a week and vacation together. Stan thinks this is a result of living abroad and frequent transfers. Because they were uprooted and lost friendships, they learned to rely on each other.

Expatriates seldom identify negative changes in themselves that occur overseas. However, I did run into two expatriates who reported both positive and negative changes in themselves. The negative changes they noticed had to do with becoming too sensitive to the viewpoints of other people, experiencing decreased confidence because the time abroad highlighted the weaknesses of the expatriate's work style, and becoming more of a loner.

While virtually all expatriates report experiencing some personal change as a result of working abroad, the particular type of transformation depends on the individual. As Campbell (1968) warns, the hero gets the particular adventure for which he or she is ready, and the "journey inward" that is an integral part of the hero's adventure will, by definition, produce unique learnings and boons. The deeper expatriates throw themselves into the belly of the whale, the more likely they are to experience personal change.

Lessons from the Initiation Stage

The initiation stage consists of the road of trials, which was discussed in Chapter Five, and the ultimate boon, explored in this chapter. As with the departure stage, much of the expatriate advice concerning this portion of the hero's adventure has to do with attitudes and expectations.

Expatriates should expect that hardships and trials are a normal part of the overseas experience. There may be a tinge of masochism here, but these trials are responsible for the positive changes expatriates see in themselves and for the sense of mastery and self-efficacy they bring home. A cross-cultural experience would not be so significant if it were not a major challenge. Expatriates should approach trials with a positive attitude and figure out how to overcome them or, at least, learn to accept them. Patience and the ability to laugh at oneself and one's condition are prerequisites for dealing with trials.

Expatriates should be forewarned about the paradoxes they may encounter. The more acculturated they become, the greater complexity they perceive. There are numerous situations abroad, like the paradoxes described in Chapter Five, that are not at all black and white. Instead, they require a tolerance for ambiguity and the ability to understand multiple perspectives simultaneously. Greater cognitive complexity comes about automatically for many expatriates as they mediate between two cultures and organizations. However, the process can be facilitated by relinquishing an ethnocentric attitude and the belief that there can only be one truth, and then by learning to see other perspectives by continually asking people from the other culture to explain their views and by seeking ever-greater cultural understanding. Many expatriates report that they became better listeners overseas. Some of this is due to the increased concentration required by a foreign language, but it is usually because it is so important to understand exactly what people mean when there is no shared cultural context to the conversation. Active listening skills—paraphrasing, reflecting underlying feelings and implications, and being nonevaluative—are crucial in intercultural communication.

In addition to active listening, cultural understanding requires the self-discipline to look for a cognitive understanding of what is occurring. Craig Storti (1990, pp. 61–62) compiled descriptions of the expatriate experience from literature. He suggests that people expect others to be like themselves, but they are not. Thus, when a cultural incident occurs, it provokes a strong reaction, such as fear or anger. This encounter becomes a choice point. People either withdraw from the other culture, a negative coping reaction, or they make an effort to put aside their emotional reaction and think about the incident cognitively—"What's going on here?" In doing so, they become aware of their reaction and look for its cause, which in turn usually makes the reaction subside. This allows them to observe the situation and develop culturally appropriate expectations. Doing so means acknowledging that their own cultural scripts do not explain behavior in another culture.

Let me provide an example of how this model works. When I gave seminars throughout Latin America, a chauffeur for my organization would deliver large boxes of didactic material to the airport. He would leave them piled up by the counter of whatever airline I was flying. On one occasion, there was a huge crowd waiting in several lines. When I reached the counter, the agent suggested I go to the agent closest to my boxes so that I would not have to move them. I did as he suggested, waiting until the agent in question was done with his customer. When I explained to him (politely, mind you) why I was there, he yelled at me for butting into line and waved me off to "wait my turn." He called to me after serving two more people and processed my ticket. I was offended, angry, and humiliated at being treated this way in front of hordes of curious spectators. Since I teach customer service, I am probably less tolerant of bad service than the average person. I did, however, restrain myself from launching into my "the customer is always right" lecture.

As I waited, I tried to figure out exactly why this incident bothered me so much. First and most important, I was offended because the agent questioned my word, as if I were a liar and had really done something dishonorable or unethical. Next, I felt I had not been treated fairly, since I had done my share of waiting and was only following orders. Also, if I am polite to others, I don't expect to be spoken to rudely in return, especially if I am a customer. And finally, I disliked being the center of attention. It may be paradoxical, but while expatriates like being "special," they also like to blend in.

Once I identified these emotions, my anger subsided. I realized that my feelings in the incident were indicative of both me as a person and my cultural background. One cultural difference that existed in this situation was my need to be perceived and trusted as an honest person, which conflicted with the lower degree of trust that characterizes most Latin cultures. This does not mean that Latins are untrustworthy, but that they have less trust in their fellow humans than Americans do. Expatriates working in Latin America run into many organizational policies and procedures, such as elaborate control systems, that have their roots in this mistrust. Mistrust is also reserved for out-group members (Triandis and others, 1988), which I probably was in the eyes of the agent.

If I go further and try to put myself into the shoes of this agent, I might hypothesize that he was overwhelmed by the cast of thousands waiting to be served and that he had previous incidents with honest-to-goodness line-jumpers. He might have felt obliged to look strict so that others were not tempted to break out. Another characteristic of Latin culture is that people often do try to get around the rules, seeking personal exceptions in their case. This has its roots in a legal system that had many rules on the books that were not enforced. In the colonial era, people petitioned the governors for personal exemptions, and this cultural practice still exists in Latin America to a larger degree than is seen in U.S. culture. Perhaps the agent interpreted my behavior in this light; how was he to know I was raised with a quasi-Germanic respect for order and obedience?

So what did I learn from this experience? The primary lessons are not to take it personally if someone acts as if they do not trust me, and to realize the other culture might have a different form of queuing behavior and crowd control.

Once expatriates have gained an understanding of different perspectives, they often need to pass on this understanding and educate people both at headquarters and in the local office. This communication is particularly important when expatriates find themselves in tricky situations because of corporate decisions or local pressures. Expatriates who are good boundary spanners mediate between headquarters and the local office, advocating for both when necessary, in a way that should gain the trust of both sides.

Greater cultural understanding, which is facilitated by cultural involvement, reading about the other culture, and learning the native language, leads naturally to transformation and personal development. Expatriates should expect to be transformed by their sojourn, unless they wall themselves off from all contact with the other culture. Expatriates should expect to experience new emotions and perhaps find sides of themselves that have not emerged previously. An open attitude toward the experience and the willingness to question basic cultural values and assumptions and to reassess aspects of one's life all contribute to personal development.

Thinking of their assignment as temporary encourages expatriates to take advantage of what there is to do and see, and helps some expatriates withstand difficult conditions. However, there is also a danger in "just passing through." Expatriates are more likely to enjoy their sojourn if they act as if they are there for the duration and make the effort to put down some roots, create a fulfilling life, and become a member of the community.

The initiation stage has a strong impact upon the family. The mutual dependency that normally exists within families often becomes more pronounced as family members support each other through trials and tribulations. Children's attitudes are usually cued by their parents; if the parents have a positive attitude toward the local culture and the hardships that arise, children will too.

Sometimes the personal growth that occurs during this stage is threatening to family members. Parents may worry about their children "going native." Spouses who dislike the local culture may be appalled to find their partners not only happily integrating into that culture but also uncovering disconcerting new sides to themselves. Like everyone else, spouses will undoubtedly have different hero's journeys (indeed some may not be at all interested in a hero's adventure) and different reactions to the local culture. If spouses can share and respect each other's different experiences and perceptions, they can still help each other try to make sense of the experience. It never hurts to have a spouse who, like a magical friend, provides assurance that you will succeed on a difficult quest.

It is reassuring that most expatriates see themselves changing in positive ways during their sojourn. Even though they have grown and learned a great deal in their overseas assignments, there is no guarantee that their company is prepared to deal with these changes or to use the boons expatriates bring back. This is one of the key problems of the repatriation stage, described in the next chapter.

The Return

Making Meaning of the Experience

*So the journey is over and I am back again where I
started, richer by much experience and poorer by
many exploded convictions, many perished certainties. For convictions and certainties are too often the
concomitants of ignorance. Those who like to feel
they are always right and who attach a high importance to their own opinions should stay at home.
When one is travelling, convictions are mislaid as easily as spectacles; but unlike spectacles, they are not
easily replaced.*

—Aldous Huxley, *Jesting Pilate*

The return is the third and final phase of the hero's adventure
and, according to Joseph Campbell, perhaps the most difficult
phase of all. It is characterized by three substages: (1) the hero's
refusal to return, (2) the crossing of the return threshold, and (3)
the hero as master of two worlds. The theme of the first substage is
the reluctance some heroes feel to leave the mystic realm and return
to their former life. The second substage is characterized by the difficulty heroes have, once they have returned, in sharing the illumination they have gained with people back home who have not
undergone the same life-changing experience. In the third substage,
heroes experience themselves as "master of two worlds" because of

the higher consciousness they have attained during their journey and the ability they now have to function in both the known and the unknown world.

Refusal of the Return and Rescue from Without

Some mythical heroes were reluctant to return home. One example is Muchukunda, a Hindu warrior who helped the gods win an important battle against demons. As a reward, they promised him whatever boon he desired. Exhausted, he chose to sleep endlessly; whoever awoke him would be burned. He awakened many years later in the presence of Vishnu, Lord of the World. Rather than return to earthly pleasures and interests, Muchukunda retreated even further from the world by going to the mountains and becoming an ascetic.

While most mythical heroes and expatriates do return home sooner or later, there are some expatriates who, like Muchukunda, refuse to return. Categorizing the reasons for their refusal is no simple task. There is a unique flavor to the stories resident expatriates tell about why they chose to remain abroad. The reasons they mention include business opportunities, better weather, great beaches or mountains, escape of some sort, feeling more at home in the foreign culture than in their own, and marrying into the local culture. The metaphor of the hero's adventure does not always describe the experience of resident expatriates who settle down and spend the majority of their lives in another country. When a foreign country becomes the "known," it is no longer an adventure but simply a more exotic address.

Some expatriates are like the mythical heroes who must be "rescued from without" (Campbell, 1968, p. 207). This was the case with Amaterasu, the sun goddess in a Japanese Shinto myth. In one of the more outrageous examples of sibling conflict, her brother the storm god was so annoying that Amaterasu barricaded herself inside a heavenly cave, taking the sunlight with her and unleashing all sorts of havoc. The eight million gods assembled and assigned a deity named Thought-Includer to create a plan to lure her back to the world. Their laughter at a dance by a young goddess aroused Amaterasu's curiosity. Once she opened the door, she was enticed outside by a mirror. When she left her cave, a god tied a rope of straw across the entrance and forbade her to pass beyond it. Thus, the sun returned to the land; but like humans, Amaterasu was allowed to retreat at night to refresh herself, taking the sunlight with her.

The expatriates I spoke with who were rescued from without, usually by their companies, were called back to the States before their tour of duty had expired or before their projects were completed. Most of them expected to be abroad for approximately three years. Instead, they returned after eighteen to twenty-four months, just when they felt they were becoming acculturated and/or effective. When they talked about repatriation, it sounded as if they had gone through a period of grieving.

Carl, introduced in Chapter Three, was called back before he had completed his research work at a German university.

* * * * * * *

> For me, it was difficult [to come back] because I did not feel that we were ready to close it down at that point. I didn't think I could do as good a job from this side as being directly there, . . . so I had some resistance, let's say, within myself. I was a little hurt that I had to come back and not be able to finish up what I had started. It took some adjustment. . . . I didn't like it, but I went along with it. . . . I had been reading up on expatriates . . . how they become so far out of the mainstream that they are totally forgotten. So, on the other side of it, I thought maybe I should get myself back there. . . . I did not want to be left out in the cold.

* * * * * * *

Paul, also introduced in Chapter Three, was forced to request an early return from Mexico because his children were not doing well in the local school. He also thought his wife missed her mother too much to live so far away.

* * * * * * *

I'd call the last months [of my time abroad] the autumn months, although it's a little sad. By the end, I was quite able to get along, and at that point it was all cut off and [I came] back here. . . . I felt a little cheated. . . . I don't feel that I did as much professionally as I wanted to, because it took me so long to become acclimated, to assess reactions to directives, and so forth. That I would have a little bit better idea of how to accomplish more and have a better, more personal identification. . . . One of the reasons I didn't like leaving Mexico was . . . leaving without the feeling of accomplishment that I would have wanted. Maybe no one ever does, but I would have liked to have been able to stay around longer . . . to see some major projects through. And it has nothing to do with credit . . . but you have to harvest the fruit as well as plant it.

* * * * * * *

There are several possible explanations for the severe disappointment of these early returnees. First, expatriates in this group mentioned repeatedly that they expected to be abroad for a longer time and it was difficult to readjust their thinking. Expatriates set their goals, both personal and professional, in accordance with the amount of time they think they will have overseas. They find it irritating and frustrating to have their plans disrupted and their expectations unmet.

Stewart and his family, introduced in Chapter Three, expected to spend three years in Japan, but he was transferred back after only eighteen months.

* * * * * * *

Well, there were some things that we were happy to be back to, but I think, on balance, the feeling was one of, we weren't ready yet. We weren't finished. And that did not have anything to do

with just coming home. It was the fact that when we went, the
expectation was that we would be there for a longer period of
time. So we didn't plan to come home as soon as we did. If somebody [had] said, "You are going to be there eighteen months" when
I left, I would have come back with a different attitude. It was an
indefinite assignment, but we had a three-year visa and we had a
two-year lease on the apartment and, as I said, we came back in a
year and a half. . . . None of us had really learned the language to
the extent that we had committed . . . giving up the house [in the
United States] and going through the trauma of moving and doing
all of that. . . . One thing that we were looking forward to was
being able to speak Japanese . . . which would have made me more
effective and a better contributor to the company. But that is a
small thing. But it was disappointing to come home so soon. . . . I
think the only thing that would prevent it [going abroad again] is
we have made sort of a commitment to this house which, in a
sense, was the therapy for coming back—that we built this and it
was a neat project.

* * * * * * *

   Several of the expatriates who were forced to return early mentioned that their remedy for coping with this disappointment was
to buy or build a new house and throw themselves into fixing it
up—a nest-building reaction that may well be the extreme opposite of their adventurous touring abroad.

   Stewart's thoughts reveal another reason for the disappointment
of those expatriates who were rescued from without. Acculturation
requires commitment, energy, and sacrifice. Almost all expatriates
pass through a common adjustment process that includes euphoria,
discomfort, settling in, and finally, functioning well and feeling
adapted. To be called home before reaching the last stage where one
can be productive and experience a sense of mastery is frustrating.
Expatriates like to realize the benefits of their efforts and gain clo-
sure on the experience—to, in Paul's words, "harvest the fruit as
well as plant it." Unlike the mythical heroes' adventures, their's
were interrupted in mid-journey.

The third reason for the difficulties this group experienced comes from what we know about crossing cultural thresholds. The difficulty of crossing either the initial or the return threshold is made easier by a strong desire to do so. Those expatriates whose assignments were cut short did not have a strong desire to return; therefore, crossing the return threshold of their own country was problematic in a way that those who returned according to schedule did not experience.

The Crossing of the Return Threshold

Regardless of why or when mythical heroes and expatriates return home, they all face the problem of crossing the return threshold. In a fairy tale motif found in various cultures, the hero comes out of the forest with gold and it turns to ashes. This story symbolizes the great difficulty mythical heroes have in successfully transporting their boons across the return threshold. Both mythical heroes and expatriates also face the possibility that they might not be received as heroes in their own land.

The first challenge of the returning hero is to reconcile the profound experience of expatriation with the reality of life at home— "the passing joys and sorrows, banalities and noisy obscenities of life" (Campbell, 1968, p. 218). Why bother trying to share a spiritual experience with people consumed by everyday passions whose reaction is most likely to be "reasonable queries, hard resentment, and good people at a loss to comprehend" (Campbell, 1968, p. 216)? In addition, as one expatriate commented, "It's hard to hold onto the experience. You get back here and fall into a rut."

More than half of the expatriates I interviewed said that repatriation was difficult. Some said that coming home was even more difficult than going abroad. The themes expressed in the stories of expatriates who sang the repatriation blues can be summarized as follows:

1. "You can't go home again"

2. "Little fish in a big pond"

3. Readjustment to decreased autonomy

4. Uncertainty about the job or the move

5. Others' lack of interest in their experiences

6. Idealization and false expectations

7. The testing period

8. Missing life abroad

You Can't Go Home Again

Virtually all expatriates report some form of personal change abroad; many perceive their time abroad as a life-changing experience. They return home no longer the same person they were when they left, and they sometimes find that they have outgrown parts of their previous lives.

Returned expatriates often discover that they have little in common with friends from the past because "it's just not like it used to be." In my own experience, this distancing never occurs with true bosom buddies. However, superficial relationships that owe more to propinquity sometimes fall by the wayside.

Mark, introduced in Chapter One, who spent two years traveling around the world implementing a new training program, is a prime example of an expatriate who can't go home again.

◆ ◆ ◆ ◆ ◆ ◆ ◆

Funnily enough, the repatriation was and probably still is to a large extent much more traumatic than going the other way. Because now, being back, some of the things that you see in your lifestyle are not as easy to buy into. . . . Sometimes I think I gave up a lot in coming home. . . . I also realize that when I left in 1985, I severed a lot [of relationships]. And although it takes time to build up relationships, it is something very different now. I don't really fit, not just at work but socially. I tend not to belong . . . even though we are great friends. I kind of sit [observing everything], like I did in England. . . . And when I think about who can I really confide in [about] how I am feeling, I [just] have my wife. I cannot explain my feelings to anyone who hasn't traveled. . . . [Out of] three thousand managers, there were only fifty-five applicants for nineteen positions [abroad]. I found that mind-boggling, that it just doesn't interest a lot of people. They say, "I'm in the U.S. of A." They raise the flag and this is it. That's fair enough. In a lot of ways, they are probably happier than I will ever be from here on in. You know, you see the other side and [things are not the same]. I'm not sure what it would take to make me happy now.

• • • • • • •

Not all expatriates feel as strongly about this as Mark does, but his ambivalence about being home is not uncommon.

Much of the "you can't go home again" syndrome has to do with changes in the expatriate and the difficulty of "keeping them down on the farm" after they've seen more of the world. Yet, sometimes the former life has changed as well while the expatriate has been away. For example, long-term expatriates are often out of sync with changes in their own culture; for them, "the record gets stuck." One can peruse other expatriates' bookshelves or music collections and listen to their expressions and hazard a guess at the year they went abroad. Although expatriates may assimilate values from the host culture, they retain many of the dominant values, customs, and tastes that were dominant in their homeland when they left; but while they are overseas, their home cultures continue to evolve. Cable TV and the Internet now allow expatriates to maintain a closer link with this evolution; but before these options were available, for many U.S. expatriates *Time* magazine and the *International Herald Tribune* were the primary vehicles for keeping abreast with new happenings on the home front. It is not surprising, then, that when career expatriates return home, they find themselves out of step with a culture that has moved on in their absence. If their image of their company, friends, or community has remained static, they may experience a reverse form of culture shock when they run up against reality during repatriation.

The companies that expatriates return to also may have changed radically during their absence. Carl experienced being out of step after only two years abroad in Germany.

* * * * * * *

> Life went on here and all of our friends moved right along for those two years. I mean, they still accept us as their friends, but it's like we are starting over again. It is a different relationship . . . even here within work . . . [after all the years] I have been with the company. . . . You are taken a little bit differently.

Little Fish in a Big Pond

This is a well-known phenomenon that pertains to the fact that some expatriates play a more prestigious role abroad than they played, and will play, in the States, and to the power they enjoy in smaller overseas offices. Jay, the insightful head of European operations for four years in Belgium who was introduced in Chapter Five, described this phenomenon best:

* * * * * * *

> There are big shocks to coming back. . . . I found it at work. The first day I was back, the boss wasn't even there to meet me. Here I am, the managing director! He wrote a nice note apologizing . . . but you are no longer the expatriate, the important, glamorous, "our man in Cairo" sort of image. . . . You're just Joe Schmo again here in the company. When I would come back from Belgium, it was very dramatic. I would come in and be "Our Man in Belgium." It's like the officer coming back from the front lines. "How's the war going out on the front lines?" And everybody is listening to what you have to say and you tell your little funny stories about how life is and [about] dealing with the Belgians. Well, suddenly you are back in a regular, mundane, routine job in an assignment

somewhere. . . . And that is a tremendous shock. I don't think many people can deal well with that. I think it is a big problem for a lot of people, unless you are moving into a bigger new assign-ment. . . . I notice that most of the people that I know don't stay with the company when they come back. They go on to some other company because they can't adapt and the company can't adapt to them and it becomes an estrangement. You sort of become estranged while you are overseas, and trying to fit back into the company again is hard. Like me—the guys who had sent me over there were gone when I returned.

• • • • • • •

Finding oneself with fewer friends in high places is a common repatriation complaint in companies with high turnover in the executive ranks. Rather than riding the wave of a job well done overseas, some expatriates feel the need to prove themselves all over again to new bosses and to compete with people who see their return as a threat to their own career progression. Adjusting to being a small fish in a big pond is even more difficult when expa-triates perceive their new job assignment at home as a demotion, or when there is no set job assignment. Although it is hard to believe, occasionally companies bring back high-level expatriates without determining their next work assignment. "You come from such an exciting job where you're running the whole operation. But when you return to headquarters and have to come into work every Monday to find they still don't know what they're going to do with you, that's tough."

Readjusting to Decreased Autonomy

The decreased autonomy that many expatriates describe when they are repatriated is best understood as a differentiation-integration problem. Paul Lawrence and Jay Lorsch (1969), who developed this concept, explain that departments and sometimes individuals become specialized or differentiated from the rest of an organization because of the different environmental demands they face. The effectiveness of the overall organization, however, depends upon its ability to integrate the various differentiated parts. Some expatriates become differentiated abroad in ways that do not fit with the home office organization. For example, the relatively autonomous role that some expatriates perform abroad, especially in smaller facilities, lies in sharp contrast to what is expected of them in their large, hierarchical bureaucracies back home. In order to succeed abroad, they have to make decisions on their own and not wait for others to take the initiative to make things happen. Once they become accustomed to working in this fashion, it is more difficult to integrate them back into the corporate fold when they return home, because their work style is more suited to a different setting. Expatriates do readapt to working in the United States, but not without at least some initial discomfort adjusting to reduced autonomy.

George, introduced in Chapter Three, was in charge of the entire European auditing function for a large multinational. He talked about his repatriation after almost two years in England.

. . . .

It was very nice to come back and see the people and get settled into the house. Of course, those would be the high points. But all of a sudden, I went from this position of being a manager and having virtually complete control of what I did and what the people did who worked for me, to being just one of the people here again—having a director sitting twenty feet away and two managers sitting even closer to me. I was answerable to all three after almost having no boss at all. . . . When I am doing something related to Europe or am in Europe, I am happier from a work standpoint. I just feel that what I am doing makes more of a difference in Europe than here.

. . . .

George not only had greater autonomy overseas; he also appreciated the greater impact he felt he had working abroad.

As the general manager for a European subsidiary, Ron also
enjoyed a great deal of autonomy.

* * * * * * *

> In Europe, we had maybe two meetings a week; we made about a
> dozen decisions every day. Here I have seventeen meetings a week;
> we make two decisions a day. It is the bureaucracy, the having to
> work through nine other different organizations. . . . Over there, I
> could say, "Hey, what are you going to do about this price?" Leave
> it, explain it, make a decision and run with it. You didn't have to
> go to that other power. . . . Subordinates would come to me and
> ask for a decision about certain things. That's a nice feeling. You
> could go overboard with that, too. There are some people in the
> operation that I think may have trouble coming back because they
> may have fallen in love with themselves over there. I tried to
> downplay that because you know you have to come back here
> sometime.

Uncertainty About the Job or the Move

Coming back to an unspecified job not only reinforces the message
that one is no longer a big fish in a little overseas pond; it also highlights the uncertainty that can surround the whole repatriation
process, which begins even before expatriates leave for home. In
some countries, the process of leaving introduces new, last-minute
trials in the form of red tape, such as affidavits swearing that one is
not leaving behind unpaid bills or spiriting off children without the
consent of the other parent. In many countries, the only certainty
involved in the endeavor to obtain final utility bills is that it will
be arduous and involve more trips than one has predicted. An
unscrupulous landlord who knows that the expatriates are leaving
the country may keep them on tenterhooks, wondering whether or
not the damage deposit will be refunded. When expatriates finally
return home, the arrangements that await them often include

uncertainty about housing, schooling, changes at work, and, in some unfortunate cases, the returned expatriate's job assignment.

Others' Lack of Interest in Their Experiences

A common complaint of returned expatriates is that no one at home really wants to listen to them talk about their experiences. As the poet Ralph Waldo Emerson wrote in "Uses of Great Men," "Every hero becomes a bore at last" (1983). Richard Brislin, an expert on cross-cultural relations, wrote the following description of returned expatriates:

* * * * * * *

> Sojourners are excited about sharing their experiences, but none of their old friends or family members want to hear about them. As one businessman put it, others would rather talk about Uncle Charlie's roses.
>
> They realize they have changed but cannot explain how and why. Further, their friends sense a change and are likely to make trait attributions ("irritable," "mixed-up") rather than situational attributions based on the sojourner's recent experiences. Because of their disorientation and the reactions of others, returning sojourners are often rather unpleasant, feisty, and lacking in social graces [1981, p. 131].

* * * * * * *

Several of the expatriates I interviewed joked about the brief amount of time they were allotted by people at home to hold forth on their overseas experiences. Paul, for instance, really enjoyed his assignment in Mexico and was grateful to be interviewed. "I feel that many, many times I bore people that I am with when they ask how it was. . . . They want your minute and a half and that's all. And everything that happens reminds me of something and I have to bite my tongue."

Mack, introduced in Chapter Three, reported that his assignment as a program manager in England had its ups and downs, so his family was very happy to go home. Still, they didn't foresee the reaction that others would have when they tried to talk about their time abroad.

. . . .

> We were so anxious to get home and it was wonderful . . . but frustrating, too. They don't want to hear about it though you think you've gone through something unique. They'll listen for thirty seconds and tell you what the [pro football team] did in your absence. The feeling is that you can't hold their interest long enough to talk about it. . . . They think two years in England was like a vacation, so don't tell them about any problems because they're convinced you were really on vacation. And don't tell them any good things because that's boring, too. That goes for family too—they're just more polite about it.

. . . .

Not being allowed to talk is further complicated for expatriates because they believe that, like mythical heroes, they have undergone a highly significant experience. In addition, the same process that occurred when they first went overseas—the continuous comparisons with their native culture—is taking place in reverse fashion. Spotting differences and making comparisons is a natural cognitive process, but it is not always tolerated by listeners who are more interested in their own situation or who may resent such comparisons. The same phenomenon can be seen on a domestic level when people move to a different part of the country or change jobs. The new person at work who comments too often that "Back at so-and-so, we did it like this" is often an object of scorn and eye rolling. Rather than be perceived as either a bore or a braggart, many expatriates quickly learn to save their stories for other returned expatriates.

Jay and his family spent four years in Belgium. When it was time to return, his wife read up on repatriation problems and, as a result, they were very careful not to frighten off potential friends when they were transferred to a rural area of the United States.

· · · · · · ·

Most expatriates tell all of these marvelous stories about how [they] have been all over Switzerland, all over France, all over Spain . . . but they fail to realize that for most people here . . . a little of that goes a long way. And in fact, it is no big thing to them that you went to Spain seven times. They are either jealous or don't care. . . . So we are very careful. . . . I don't tell people I have been to Belgium. . . . It helps you make friends easier. If they find it out and draw it out of you, that's okay, rather than bragging that you have been to Belgium or worked four years in Europe. People here have their own stories to tell. They might not be as glamorous, but how are you going to find some basis to communicate if all of your stuff is about Europe and all of their stuff is about Austin, Texas?

Idealization and False Expectations

Expatriates often idealize home when they are abroad, which results in unmet expectations and disillusionment upon reentry. I could hazard a guess that idealization occurs more frequently with expatriates who are unhappy abroad, but I would not be surprised to find that it occurs with all expatriates to a certain degree. When something goes wrong overseas, it is tempting to think, "That wouldn't happen back home."

Dan had such thoughts during his assignment as an operations manager in Brazil.

· · · · · · ·

If I would have had the right job, I would have stayed there. . . . The only problem we had was that we were at that stage in life when you wonder what's next. . . . You feel like you don't have anything where you are. Actually you have more than you thought! But you think everything is better in the States than it was there. You just know it is—which was a real shocker when we came back. That was the hardest part. . . . It took us two years to get comfortable here . . . because we had built it up so much. . . .

People don't show up on time down there [in Brazil]. But we bought a house here and had some work done on it. People never would show up. They would not return phone calls. Workmanship was shoddy and it was just a complete shock.

* * * * * * *

Americans abroad sometimes develop a nostalgic image of the great service and efficiency back home. This image may not survive their initial dealings back in the States with, for example, the laid-back workmen they contract with to work on their homes. As a result of this and other disillusionments, expatriates may also undergo a grieving period for their life abroad and perceive their life at home as less exciting.

As I have noted, expectations play a crucial role with expatriates. It is harder to adjust overseas if the assignment or the country does not pan out as expected, and it is difficult to return home when one's assignment is terminated prematurely; but expectations also play a role in scheduled reentry.

Harry held a very high-level position in Europe but felt that he was demoted upon his return.

* * * * * * *

They [the expatriates] are thinking they've done a kindness, or a service to the company and they're thinking they are going to get some remuneration for that. In fact, it's more likely that they'll be demoted. . . . On line and block charts, everybody reports to somebody, right? Now if you're in a corporate headquarters like here, the line and block charts are pretty well defined. And when you are out there, you are not on this chart. . . . I wouldn't see why this would be any different in any company for the simple reason of "out of sight, out of mind."

* * * * * * *

Not all companies treat their returned expatriates in this fashion, but all expatriates return with some kind of expectations. Many feel they have accomplished a difficult task that required sacrifice. When this sacrifice is not rewarded, they feel like the fairy tale hero whose gold turned to ashes once he left the forest.

The Testing Period

The testing period is usually experienced when the expatriate goes abroad and crosses the first threshold. At that time, particularly in cultures that have impermeable outer boundaries and strong in-group/out-group orientations, it is not uncommon for host-country nationals to keep expatriates at arm's length until they have proven themselves trustworthy. This same testing phenomenon can, however, also occur when expatriates return to their own countries.

Luke, the bank vice president introduced in Chapter Three who spent two years in England, described the testing period he underwent.

* * * * * * *

> It was more difficult to come back than I thought it would be. Even in a couple of years, a lot of things change. There was an underlying attitude that no one vocalized here. There was a testing period among my peers and supervisors to see what this experience had done to change me. You could feel it. Nobody would verbalize it, but you could feel that it was there. You could pick up on it in subtleties and comments, which was a little disturbing. The first time I went to a meeting . . . the most senior of the committee remarked on the English suit I was wearing. I don't know why. Maybe some jealousy. There's certainly a lack of understanding. . . . There's a perception here that Britain is a little America and there's not a lot of difference. The person shouldn't change at all.

* * * * * *

Michael, the tax lawyer introduced in Chapter Five who worked in England, also noted that one had to prove that one had not changed overseas, which is, of course, precisely what expatriates do.

⋅ ⋅ ⋅ ⋅ ⋅ ⋅ ⋅

It's difficult to fit back in after three and a half years. There's a period of adjustment, especially when you've been in a creative job that you set up. When you come back, there's some resentment and jealousy—you have to get to know them again. It was a different situation in Europe and it's a matter of their accepting you again. . . . You have to show them you haven't changed at all.

⋅ ⋅ ⋅ ⋅ ⋅ ⋅ ⋅

Returned expatriates may be forced to demonstrate that they have not changed in ways that are threatening to colleagues and friends—for instance, that they have not "gone native" or developed aristocratic airs—and that they can also succeed in the domestic arena. Americans, by the way, are not the only ones to be wary of returned expatriates. When Minoru Makihara was appointed president of Mitsubishi in 1992, the Japanese were concerned that he had become too "foreign" during his twenty-plus years as an expatriate manager for the company (Sanger, 1992).

Jack, the international lawyer introduced in Chapter Two who deals with many international companies and expatriates, attributes the testing period to parochialism.

⋅ ⋅ ⋅ ⋅ ⋅ ⋅ ⋅

That's why I say the more difficult transition is coming back. I think the testing period is in part a function of the American mentality about international business generally. That it's great over there, but it's over there after all, and that's not as important as what happens in Keokuk, Iowa. . . . I think people's minds on that subject are changing. [There are] even quite a number of companies that I do work for now that bring over foreign nationals to work for the corporate headquarters, a thought unheard of a decade ago. So I think the patterns are breaking down, but historically it's been, "Well, it's nice that he's been there and we'll take advantage of it from time to time, but basically the way you're successful is being successful here."

⋅ ⋅ ⋅ ⋅ ⋅ ⋅ ⋅

Expatriates returning home with a sense of mastery and self-efficacy often resent being tested yet again. A wise expatriate counseled returning expatriates to "be humble. Your experience may be good, but your peers don't put a lot of value on that experience. You can't act like you're better than anyone else, and you're not."

Not all expatriates experience this testing period when they return. But for those who do, the return may be merely the beginning of yet another challenge to prove themselves.

Missing Life Abroad

Returning home made the expatriates I interviewed aware of what they liked about life overseas. This is the reverse of the same phenomenon that occurred when they first went abroad. They missed tangible things, like people, places, food, and a particular lifestyle. But they also missed intangible things, such as the challenge and excitement of living abroad, the adventure, the novelty and learning, the feeling of being more alive and special—all the things that are the essence of the expatriate experience.

Art, introduced in Chapter Five as the executive vice president of operations for a European subsidiary, mentioned that when they returned to the States, he and his wife missed the cultural differences they saw in Europe, and that in the United States, "everything seems to be the same, all flat. You have to look for things. It doesn't hit you in the face."

This is how Doug, the London banker introduced in Chapter Four, talked about repatriation:

• • • • • • •

When you are overseas, you know you are in a learning environment. Everything is exciting. You feel as though you are growing. When you move back, you feel as though, "Here I am at square one.". . . It is a very depressing situation to be in. You feel you are not growing anymore. And that's even further compounded if from a career viewpoint, you don't perceive your job as a growing opportunity.

* * * * * * *

If expatriates have successfully integrated themselves overseas and been effective at work, they give up quite a bit when they come home. In the arduous, initial days of repatriation, it is only human nature to wonder whether coming home was the right decision.

When expatriates complain about repatriation, some or all of these eight themes are mentioned. Not everyone finds repatriation difficult, and research has not yet demonstrated why people are different in this regard. We can see from the expatriate stories, however, that returning to a challenging job and having realistic expectations help prevent repatriation problems.

Long-term expatriates who have returned home more than once seldom find their subsequent repatriations as difficult as the first, because they know what to expect. For example, they don't expect to fit in as well as they did before they left. They don't expect most people to show much interest in their overseas experiences. They see their native land, as they see other cultures, in terms of trade-offs—some things are better there, but other things are worse. So they focus on the positive and try to ignore the negative, just as they did when they lived abroad. Returning home, like living abroad, requires certain skills that can be acquired. The career expatriates who do not find repatriation difficult use the same skills and attitudes coming home that they use to enter any culture. Thus, they look at repatriation not so much as "going home" but as entering another culture, albeit one that is much more familiar and held in greater affection than others. As one expatriate said, coming home "was just another of a series of moves."

Master of Two Worlds

As the master of two worlds, mythical heroes have the ability to function in both the everyday world and the spiritual world. In myths, the heroes achieve a higher consciousness, usually a form of universalistic spiritual enlightenment. Deities reveal themselves to the heroes, who have sacrificed their own self-will to the will of the gods, but the heroes still maintain one foot in the secular world. According to Campbell, "The realm of the gods is a forgotten dimension of the world we know" (1968, p. 217). "The Cosmic Dancer, declares Nietzsche, does not rest heavily in a single spot, but gaily, lightly, turns and leaps from one position to another. It is possible to speak from only one point at a time, but that does not invalidate the insights of the rest" (p. 229).

The "Master of Two Worlds" metaphor can be applied to the biculturalism of expatriates. Their understanding of two cultures is one of the boons they bring back to their companies and to the larger society. Like a cosmic dancer, they see the world from more than one cultural perspective and lightly pass between them. As with spirituality, such mastery is the result of sacrifice, which involves, for expatriates, opening themselves up to the experience, relinquishing their claims to cultural superiority, and striving to learn the values of the other culture with both humility and respect. Once this occurs, they will never again look at life through a monocultural lens. Nor will they see the people of other cultures as a completely separate group; instead they return home armed with a universal truth—that people are basically the same underneath their unique customs and individual differences.

A Hero's Welcome

As Campbell wrote, when mythical heroes return to their homeland, some of them are honored and welcomed as heroes; others are not. Some are esteemed for the boons they bring back from their journey, while others are unrecognized and ridiculed (1968, p. 37). The difficulty of being a prophet in one's own land is well known. The same phenomenon occurs with expatriates. Some are viewed as heroes by their companies; others are not. For expatriates who return to companies that value their experience and quickly utilize their skills, repatriation is made easier. Those who are not perceived as heroes are either demoted or put in a lateral position upon their return. They are bitter about this situation and seem to think a promotion was warranted. Certainly a promotion would be more in keeping with the mastery and heroism the expatriate experience seems to evoke in people. Those who had interpreted their "call" as a sign that they were "fast-trackers" have special difficulty making any meaning of their experience when their company does not use their expertise upon reentry.

Karen, who was introduced in Chapter Three, worked abroad almost two years in a technical research position. She was assigned the same type of job upon her return.

· · · · · · ·

It's a disappointment that I don't get to use the skills I learned abroad. I mean, it is good for people to have the experience, but nothing is ever made of it. Then it kind of seems, not pointless, because you have a broader background, but it seems to me that they could have made better use of whatever you might have learned or gained.

· · · · · · ·

The phrase, "They could have made better use of what I learned," is fairly common among expatriates. Only two-thirds of the people I interviewed reported that they use the skills they learned abroad in their domestic position. Most of the skills they still utilize are interpersonal, such as improved listening skills. Companies that do take advantage of expatriates' skills and experience make repatriation easier.

Mack, introduced in Chapter Three, worked abroad for three years as a program manager in London.

· · · · · · ·

People don't listen [to your overseas stories] even when it has to do with work. Because you were over there, what you say should be even more valid, especially in this company, but it's not. My biggest frustration is that the company hasn't used the expertise I gained abroad. Not the technical expertise, because I had that when I went over, but the social expertise. I formed a network of associates, which was necessary for you and them to do the job, and that's valuable. But if you don't use the network, it goes away. . . . Now I feel frustrated and let down. I thought people who went over and came back were put into useful jobs. Some of the [returnees] have left the company for that very reason. . . . I could be very useful in a liaison job with Britain but I doubt I would ever be considered. . . . If you got to use the skills you developed abroad, you could make sense of the experience. As it is, you're left hanging.

* * * * * * *

Obviously Mack did not feel that he received a hero's welcome. His comments highlight the importance of tying the expatriate experience into a career development plan so that the international assignment "makes sense." If companies want to retain the international talent they have developed, they should provide a hero's welcome and utilize the boons that expatriates bring back. The ability to explain the dynamics of a foreign office or market, to predict how foreign employees will react, and to call upon personal contacts to get things done in other countries are all highly valuable expatriate boons.

Edward, the chief engineer introduced in Chapter Five, described the boons he brought back to his company as follows:

* * * * * * *

[I found] my time in Luxembourg . . . professionally rewarding. I enjoyed it. I learned a lot about our products around the world. I felt it helped me to get a bigger perspective on the company that I would not have been able to get had I not gone over there. [The experience] also developed contacts from a technical context that I can use throughout my career, because now I know these people.

I have faces, they know me. And I have a much better working relationship with them than [I would have] had I not been over there. I think familiarity knocks down some walls of distrust and things like that. So when I call, they know who I am, they know why, they know where I am coming from when I ask questions, and they know and trust me more than [they would have] had I not been there. And so I think that is positive.

• • • • • • •

In addition to having an understanding of other cultures and their ways of doing business, expatriates also have a wider perspective on the world than those who have never been abroad, and often a more comprehensive exposure to business that could be helpful to the company. Those expatriates who were allowed to assume broader responsibilities overseas than they would have been given at home are naturally more well-rounded when they return and more capable of breaking out of the functional silos that hamstring many companies. Improved managerial skills and interpersonal skills are major boons that easily transfer home. The initiative most expatriates had to show abroad and the sense of mastery and self-efficacy they achieved should result in employees who are not only capable but desirous of assuming responsibility for difficult assignments.

Another boon is expatriates' ability to adapt to change. Because they have been exposed to very different ways of organizing and of doing business, they are often less wedded to tradition and the status quo in their own organization. In addition, the expatriate's ability to perceive paradox implies a degree of cognitive complexity that frequently allows returned expatriates to see issues from multiple perspectives and be more creative in thinking of alternative actions.

Lessons from Experience: Similarities Between the Return Stage and the Departure Stage

It has been known for a while that the culture shock experienced when returning home is fairly similar to the shock experienced when going abroad (Gullahorn and Gullahorn, 1963; see also Chapter

Three in this book for discussion of beginning the expatriate's journey), but the most interesting "aha!" I had while listening to expatriates talk about repatriation concerns the numerous other similarities that exist. These similarities include a strong desire to go, which is important to success in both instances. Expectations play a crucial role at both times and should be as realistic as possible. One should approach both a foreign land and one's homeland in the same manner—with appreciation and understanding, acknowledging the potential difficulties but focusing on the good points and trying to overlook the bad. The same cultural entry skills are necessary both coming and going: observe carefully, find a cultural mentor, figure out why people act as they do, resist the temptation to make negative attributions and negative comparisons between cultures, be flexible and humble, find substitutes for customary activities, get involved quickly, and, if necessary, learn to live with being somewhat marginal. Table 7.1 lists tips that these expatriates would give to both people setting off on an overseas assignment and those about to return from one.

The tendency to make comparisons between cultures is very strong in both the initial stages of living abroad and the stage of returning home. Some expatriates idealize home when they are overseas and the foreign country once they are home. The logistical arrangements that are part of settling in are burdensome at both ends, and people should try to get them taken care of before they dive into a consuming job.

Just as the new expatriate needed the help of cultural mentors (magical friends), the returned expatriate benefits from seeking out other returned expatriates with whom to talk or commiserate. Cultural mentors at work can prevent returned expatriates from making mistakes on the job, as well as guiding them through this period. Sometimes, expatriates mistakenly feel they can "really be themselves" when they return home, especially if they have consciously repressed themselves in an attempt to conform to another culture. Self-monitoring is still a necessity, perhaps nowhere more so than in a headquarters environment.

Table 7.1.　Tips for Both Beginning and Ending Overseas.

Inform yourself about the culture and office beforehand.

Find a cultural mentor.

Get eight hours of sleep in the first weeks to help you deal with stimulus overload.

Avoid negative people.

Get yourself and the family settled in before you go to work.

Choose a neighborhood that will easily accept you and where you will feel at home.

Go slow at work, and get the lay of the land before making big changes.

Expect to undergo culture shock and accept that the first six to eight months may be difficult.

Find substitutes for what you enjoyed in the previous country.

Be adaptable and flexible.

Expect a certain degree of marginality.

Don't make negative attributions about the locals.

Try to understand why people behave as they do.

Don't make negative comparisons with the previous country; accept each for what it is.

Focus on the positive and overlook the negative.

Maintain a positive attitude; try not to complain.

Take advantage of what the country has to offer.

Get involved as quickly as possible.

Be humble (neither an Ugly American nor an arrogant internationalist).

Expect a testing period before you are more fully accepted at work or in the neighborhood.

Expect logistics to be annoying in the beginning.

Beware of failed expectations; if something is not what you expected and cannot be remedied, try to get over it quickly.

Choosing a neighborhood is also as important during repatriation as it was overseas. Some returned expatriates find homogenous settings with strong norms for conformity (for example, certain suburbs or small towns) too much of a contrast with the life they enjoyed abroad. They feel more at home in diverse neighborhoods with a sense of community that most closely replicates what they experienced overseas.

Mark, who spent two years traveling all over the world doing training programs, regretted his choice of neighborhood when he returned home.

* * * * * * *

I am living in a conformist [white suburb]. [My wife] likes it there more than I do . . . but when I go out at lunchtime, I walk down [a street with an outdoor market.] For no good reason, other than they put out the little stands and they are bargaining. I don't buy anything, but it is a little hustle bustle. And it is the only hustle bustle that I find downtown. . . . There is no challenge to it, after two years of challenge and just everything new from catching the subway to finding out what time British railroads go to Dover and driving on the left. . . . I must admit I am not thrilled at all with the thought of "this is it."

* * * * * * *

Just as the expatriate overseas was helped by finding local substitutes for familiar activities, returned expatriates can suffer if they do not work at finding substitutes for the adventure, challenge, and learning they enjoyed abroad. For expatriates who lived a hero's adventure overseas, it is usually easier to come back to a demanding, challenging job that more closely matches the level of challenge experienced abroad. Returning to an old job long since mastered may be asking for disappointment if there are no new requirements for learning.

There are various other ways to maintain the learning mode and seek the novelty that some expatriates find so addicting. When we were repatriated, my family got into the habit of "exploring" every Saturday, looking to stumble upon interesting places, people, and adventures just as we had overseas. We assumed the role of foreign tourists and tried to see our own country with a different kind of appreciation. When it comes to repatriation, Marcel Proust's words come to mind: "The only real voyage of discovery, the only fountain of Youth, consists not in seeking new landscapes but in having new eyes, in seeing the hundred universes that each of them sees" (1989, p. 61).

With this chapter, we have completed the expatriates' progression through the stages of the hero's journey. The final chapter conveys lessons and advice for the companies and organizations that send expatriates abroad.

8

. . . .

Appreciating the Journey

How Companies Can Support and Learn
from Expatriate Successes

One of the funniest how-not-to-handle-repatriation anecdotes was told to me by a career expatriate, Andrew, who was returning to the United States for the first time after nine years and five countries. He had been a general manager for six years and his most recent assignments had been setting up new offices in Latin America and West Africa. Andrew described his job as pushing constantly to get things done. He arrived at his company's newly remodeled, posh headquarters building to discover that, although his transfer to the home office had been decided three months previously, he had no desk! He was told to camp out at the desks of people who were traveling. Overseas, Andrew had had spacious private offices with personal secretaries; he had overseen impressive budgets and large staffs. Yet at headquarters, he was a gypsy who wandered from cubicle to cubicle schlepping his files in a grocery cart. Abroad, he had singlehandedly furnished entire offices in countries where every desk had to be made from scratch by the local carpenter in less time than he was told it would take to obtain a desk in the United States. Andrew waited patiently for two months. He lost heart somewhat when he heard that the last person to return from abroad had waited four months for a desk. Apparently no organizational learning was taking place regarding returned expatriates. Finally, employing the initiative and drive that had made him so successful abroad, he bought a battered $15 desk at a yard sale, strapped it to the top of his car, and deposited it in a corner of the office. The executive director was upset that the desk did not match the rest of the decor, so a desk and cubicle were rapidly produced for Andrew. Lest you think this is an isolated example, another expatriate in my study had been in charge of the European auditing office for a major multinational corporation. When I went to interview him, he laughingly showed me the storage room where he had worked upon his return to corporate headquarters and the shopping cart where he had stored his files! Talk about a strong message that you are no longer a VIP, much less a hero.

Many organizations make little effort to learn from their own experiences with expatriates. As a result, their expatriate processes and policies are often haphazard and unsophisticated. Several expatriates commented that each time their company sent people abroad or repatriated them, "it was as if it was the first time it ever happened." Andrew's organization provides a handy example. The company's entire focus is international work, and they ship people all over the globe. However, no one thought to order desks until the returned expatriates physically appeared at headquarters, "as if it was the first time." In stark contrast, General Motors contracted the services of researchers who carefully studied GM's expatriates and expatriate policies (Briody and Baba, 1988). GM's program is often cited as a model because expatriates know what job they will have upon their return, and they keep in close touch with sponsors in the United States.

The lessons provided at the end of several of the previous chapters were directed to expatriates. In this chapter, the suggestions are addressed to companies that want to improve the way they handle their expatriates. The chapter is divided into the crucial areas from the expatriates' perspective: general recommendations, selection criteria, overseas assignments, human resource departments, spouses and families, communication, and repatriation.

General Recommendations

The first piece of advice for companies is that they should focus attention on the issue of expatriates and endeavor to learn not only by studying their own successes and failures but by benchmarking the practices of other organizations. Organizations that do a good job with expatriates begin with a serious international focus and a well-thought-out global strategy. They also have a strong commitment to their international employees and perceive them as valuable contributors rather than as a strange breed that is a necessary evil. When companies do not handle expatriates thoughtfully, employees naturally will be reluctant to accept international assignments.

Ferro Corporation is an example of a company with a strong global strategy that is reflected in its attitudes toward expatriates. The corporation's heroes are people who have worked abroad, and expatriates are treated with respect when they are repatriated. Top management sends a clear message that international experience is valued and has a positive impact on one's career. As a result, it is easier to make sense of an international assignment with Ferro than with other companies whose international strategy is not so clearly articulated and implemented. Companies with limited overseas business and a stronger domestic vision are more likely to overlook the contributions of expatriates and view them with suspicion when they return.

Some companies make international experience a prerequisite for promotion to high-level jobs. The HR policy reinforces the international strategy, a good example of putting your money where your mouth is when it comes to internationalizing a company. An unanticipated consequence of a policy like this is that some people feel forced to accept an international assignment they really do not want, simply to avoid derailing their career. Given the importance of the desire to go abroad and of one's attitude toward the experience, companies and researchers alike should investigate whether a blanket policy requiring all senior managers to work abroad is really in the company's best interests.

In companies that handle expatriates well, HR policies are designed to help the company achieve its global strategy. Such companies understand that there are unique aspects to international assignments that require special expertise and treatment. Their managers and international HR staff know what it's like to live and work abroad, and they try to remove company obstacles that make international assignments even more difficult than they already are. Procedures for planning and handling assignments are carefully developed and reflect an effort to integrate an overseas assignment into the employee's career development plan. An international job is not merely a blip on the screen that bears no relationship to what comes before or after.

It is not a simple matter to predict who will succeed overseas. Therefore, selection decisions should be made by people with international experience and some knowledge of the particular country and the job. In addition to the selection criteria discussed later in this chapter, many companies have special requirements that relate to their strategy or organizational culture. Those companies that do a better job than others of identifying what they are looking for in expatriates are more likely to design a selection process that yields the "right kind" of expatriate.

One interesting study of Peace Corps volunteers found that their success had less to do with their personal characteristics than with their initial hours in the foreign country. According to George Guthrie (1966), if the first day or two is a positive rather than a negative experience, the volunteers are more likely to be successful. Until I see more supporting data, I'm not about to breathe a sigh of relief and give up trying to predict what type of characteristics lead to successful assignments. However, this finding should focus attention on how companies handle both new expatriates and returnees. Many expatriates do have horror stories to tell about their first few days in a foreign country, stories that could have been avoided. Meeting people at the airport and making sure their first few days are problem free is not only common courtesy but also an attempt to ensure a successful adjustment.

The selection and training process should begin nine to twelve months in advance and should include screening for the selection criteria and interviewing, a visit to the site by the potential expatriate, area-specific briefing, language and cultural training, intercultural communication training, job orientation, and time to get personal affairs in order before the expatriate begins the overseas assignment. Stan, introduced in Chapter Three, is a career expatriate currently responsible for handling expatriates in his company. He counsels, "I think good planning ahead of time, rather than just last-minute picking someone up and then dropping them in, definitely pays benefits." People should be notified about selection decisions in a timely fashion, because numerous personal and family decisions are affected by the knowledge that an international assignment is definitely in the offing. Too often expatriates are either left hanging or not given sufficient advance notice about decisions to send them overseas or bring them home.

Unlike domestic jobs, an international assignment is more of a family affair. If the spouse or children do not adjust, the expatriate may well be distracted at work and forced to request an early termination that costs the company thousands of dollars. It makes sense, therefore, to interview the spouse and try to determine whether the rest of the family is willing to make the effort to adjust overseas. Providing the family with both cultural and language training is another investment that may increase the chances that the family will adapt and complete their tour of duty. Prospective expatriates and their spouses should make a site visit whenever possible so they have more realistic expectations about the assignment. It is a mistake to paint an unrealistically rosy picture of either the job or the living situation, because failed expectations have a negative effect on the adjustment process. Lying to prospective expatriates about hardship posts—places where few people would willingly choose to live due to inhospitable climate, armed combat, lack of amenities, or other inconveniences—never pays off in the long run. One of the best ways to communicate realistic expectations is to arrange for returned expatriates to speak with and counsel families who are considering an assignment in the same country.

Many companies cut corners on language training, which makes little sense given the link between effectiveness and fluency. Language immersion programs prior to beginning an overseas job and follow-up tutoring at the foreign post are usually the best way to learn a foreign language. In immersion programs, participants do nothing but study and speak the foreign language and learn about the culture in a setting in which their own language no longer has any currency. Critics point out that the risk with immersion programs is making an up-front investment in an expatriate family that may or may not work out in the assignment. This is a valid point, but their chances of adjustment are increased if they can speak the language. Nevertheless, many companies opt for part-time or even after-hours tutoring at the foreign post. The disadvantage of such tutoring is that expatriates who have a demanding job or one that involves frequent travel are unlikely to commit the time and energy that is necessary to master a foreign language. Unless they love languages for their own sake, most busy people will not learn another language unless they are forced to do so out of necessity. Being surrounded by bilingual people further diminishes their need to become fluent, so companies should make sure their expectations about language proficiency are realistic.

Some organizations use incentives to reward expatriates for learning foreign languages. Compensation systems for expatriates should always complement strategic goals. A surprising number of large multinationals do not have standardized expatriate compensation packages. When this is the case, prospective expatriates resort to hard-nosed negotiation. Finding out later that other expatriates received better packages can have a negative effects on their adjustment and performance.

Everyone who deals with expatriates should understand their unique problems and issues. For example, they should be aware of the paradoxes, described in Chapter Five, that confront expatriates. In particular, they should bear in mind that expatriates are boundary spanners who sometimes face conflicting demands made by corporate headquarters and the local office. Organizations create role conflict for their expatriates with policies that reflect their own lack of sensitivity and understanding about the local setting. Refusal to compromise or understand the position of the local office is an organizational constraint that affects expatriate effectiveness (Newman, Bhatt, and Gutteridge, 1976). Companies should ensure that their own demands are reasonable as well as take into consideration the needs of the foreign office.

Many of the expatriates I interviewed mentioned that someone outside their company, usually a women's club or the Foreign Service, gave them a book or a video on living abroad or coming home that was particularly helpful. With all the materials that are available today, companies could easily ensure that all their expatriates have access to good information.

Selection Criteria

Who should receive the call to adventure that an overseas assignment often represents? A quick glance at the expatriate community in any country will reveal a certain percentage of people who are both miserably unhappy and excessively negative about the local culture. It is hard to imagine how such people can be truly effective at work. Many of them go through the day offending the locals, making inappropriate decisions, and being minimally productive. Why were they chosen to go abroad, and why did they ever agree to do it? The most obvious answer lies in poor selection practices. Everyone involved with expatriates agrees that a good selection process is of paramount importance, because some expatriates never do adapt and become effective overseas. Selection mistakes are costly for companies and hard on expatriates, on their families, and on overseas offices.

Expatriates are quick to suggest that HR staff and those who select people for international jobs should have international experience. This was Mack's conclusion after his assignment in London with a multinational that has a high number of expatriates.

* * * * * * *

> I think the people who make the decisions [about who goes] are normally not in a very good position to do so, because they don't know enough about what the hell they are talking about over there. So they are picking somebody who, oh gee, this guy was great in Buffalo. He was in the Kiwanis and he has golfed well, and he knows Jack Kemp and therefore he is going to do great in Swaziland or someplace. That could be the worst possible situation. So, I think the people who are in human resources or operations, whoever these people are, have to be clued in as to what they are doing. They are not going to find this in some simple book. That's why I think international companies go for having international people around . . . so they can in turn make future judgments on some of these transfers from an intelligent point of view.

* * * * * * *

Most expatriates develop their own opinion on selection criteria, given their personal experience and observations of other expatriates who succeed or fail. Elliot's opinion on expatriate selection is the result of his seventeen years with a Big Six accounting firm in Europe.

* * * * * * *

> Well, I would look for somebody who was a little bit adventurous. I think one has got to have a little adventure and romance in one's soul to do that. Then, somebody who has flexible values. You have got to give up certain of your values . . . local sports, whether it is doing or watching things. You have to be able to give that up and

do it in a different way someplace else. You have to have flexibility, adaptability. I think being open-minded and intelligent is very important, because you have to learn a lot. And you have to learn a lot quickly. So you have got to be observant and have these things register, and learn; not everybody can do that and do their job at the same time. Somebody who is communicative. Somebody who is quiet and withdrawn I think would be a bit of a danger because you are not sure that he is reading what you are telling him, and you are not getting good feedback from him. You don't know if you are headed for a disaster or not. And then, from a corporate point of view, I would want someone who had a certain ambition within the corporation, too. Because more and more, we will all eventually realize over here that there is a global economy . . . and in order to survive and do well in it, you have to understand it well, and having lived there is a good part of the understanding. So if you are going to make this investment in this guy to go over there, you want him to not say, "Well, I really just want to go to Paris, because now I can finally hang around Shakespearean company and read Hemingway . . . and occasionally send in a report and drop out." That may be fun from a personal point of view, but I don't think the corporation really wants to pay for dropouts. They really want a guy who is going to do well, come back, go to corporate headquarters or wherever.

. . . .

Elliot's characterization of the ideal expatriate, with his references to adventure, sacrifice, transformation (through learning and being open-minded), and loyalty to the quest, reminds us yet again of the hero's adventure.

A more complete list of selection criteria identified by expatriates in my study and researchers (Black, Gregersen, and Mendenhall, 1992; Brein and David, 1971; Brewster, 1991; Church, 1982; Hammer, Gudykunst, and Wiseman, 1978; Hawes and Kealey, 1981; Mendenhall and Oddou, 1985) appears in Table 8.1. These criteria fall into five categories: (1) motivation, (2) attitude, (3) personal traits, (4) skills, and (5) background and family.

Table 8.1.   Selection Criteria.

Motivation

Has a strong desire to go
Is motivated by intrinsic rather than extrinsic reasons
Has a sense of adventure; is anxious for new experiences

Attitude

Has a positive attitude; is not a grumbler
Generally thinks well of people (positive regard)
Respects other cultures

Personal Traits

Is open-minded, not opinionated
Is tolerant; appreciates differences; is not prejudiced
Is flexible, neither a rigid personality nor a pushover
Is adaptable, not set in his or her ways
Is nonconformist
Is self-confident
Is centered or grounded (has a strong sense of self)
Is openly self-aware; doesn't let ego get in the way of work
Is inquisitive about surroundings
Is willing to learn from the experience
Is willing to try new things
Is willing to make sacrifices
Is willing to try to integrate into the host culture
Is sincere
Is honest
Is understanding
Is trustworthy and trusting
Is loyal to the company
Is ambitious within the corporation
Is goal-directed
Is persistent
Doesn't lose sight of the goal but adapts to local contingencies
Is self-reliant
Is a self-starter with initiative
Is good at completing tasks with no supervision

Table 8.1. (*continued*)

Is hardworking

Is patient

Is able to control temper

Is stable, mature

Is personable; makes a good first impression

Is sociable, extroverted (seems to learn languages and develop relationships rapidly)

Is easygoing, not abrasive

Has a good sense of humor

Possesses common sense

Is intelligent

Is cognitively complex, not a black-and-white thinker

Is a quick thinker, so he or she can respond to surprising cultural differences

Is savvy—not easily taken advantage of

Is not afraid to look like a fool at times (essential for learning a foreign language and trying out new behaviors)

Skills

Is able to learn the local language

Has good communication skills, especially listening skills

Has good interpersonal skills

Is able to develop good relationships with people, including subordinates

Makes good, quick decisions

Is qualified for the job; can make a contribution

Has participative management skills; is not a strong-willed dictator

Is able to handle stress

Is able to handle conflict

Has technical competence

Background and Family

Has had varied personal and professional experiences

Has worked successfully with different types of bosses

Has lived or traveled abroad

Has, if married, a solid relationship; spouse and children are flexible and spouse also possesses many of the characteristics on this list

Motivation

According to the expatriates I interviewed, a strong desire to go abroad is the most commonly identified selection criterion and is often mentioned in conjunction with the sense of adventure desired in prospective candidates. Having the right kind of motivation helps expatriates accept with good grace both the inevitable trials and the uncertainty about the eventual career pay-off of an international assignment. Extrinsic motivators, such as hardship pay or the chance to round out one's résumé, are seldom strong enough to motivate expatriates to make the sacrifices necessary for a successful experience. The expatriates who accept assignments in Saudi Arabia solely because the financial rewards are enormous could be an exception, but none of the expatriates I interviewed mentioned extrinsic motivation as a selection criterion. Intrinsic factors, such as the job itself and the desire for adventure, challenge, and increased responsibility and autonomy, are more important considerations in accepting expatriate positions.

Positive Attitude

Having a positive attitude about life is extremely important for expatriates. When my husband and I worked in international development, the myth that sometimes captured the essence of our jobs was the story of Sisyphus. As punishment for revealing a secret of Zeus, Sisyphus was condemned for eternity to roll a stone uphill that always rolled back down on him. Working with community groups and government bureaucrats often felt like that. In spite of numerous setbacks, we got up each morning and tried to push the stone up the hill once more. Whether or not the projects were successful in the short run, there was a certain satisfaction in knowing that we were faithfully doing our part, and a hope that this tenacity would be rewarded.

I was reminded of this experience when Doug (introduced in Chapter Four), given a difficult "turn-around assignment" intended to improve poor performance at a London bank, described what he would look for in selecting expatriates.

• • • • • • •

> How about patiently enthusiastic? One who would be understanding and would recognize the differences in culture and ways of doing things, yet would still have the enthusiasm not to be disappointed, not to be turned off. To hold a certain group of values that are important and to champion those things through adversity. . . . I think that was what was really needed in my job . . . to be willing to change colors, so to speak, but not lose that objective and that goal. Well, I was unsure [whether or not I had done that] until the very last day that I was there and a guy came up to me and said, "You know, Doug, you've changed my whole outlook on work. When you joined our office, I was nothing but a clerk, and now I am assistant product manager. You've got me excited about my career!" That made it all worthwhile for me.

• • • • • • •

In addition to the need for a positive attitude at work, expatriates mentioned this quality repeatedly in connection with overall adjustment, especially when they compared themselves to other expatriates. In many cases, expatriates attribute lack of adjustment on the part of other expatriates to a negative attitude. More research is needed to show exactly what goes wrong in failed expatriate assignments; negative attitude is probably not the only factor here but, in the opinion of expatriates, it is an extremely important one.

Personal Traits

Flexibility and adaptability are two of the most important personal traits to look for in prospective expatriates. Open-mindedness is another important criteria, since other cultures definitely have different values and customs. People with limited cognitive complexity and rigid personalities and those who are locked into a particular way of life or particular attitudes are much less likely to succeed abroad.

The same warning is true for people who lack a strong sense of self. Expatriates with a grounded, stable personality have the wherewithal to handle the normal pressures of an international assignment without "going native" or turning to destructive coping mechanisms like drugs or alcohol.

In the absence of a shared language, people rely on their intuitive trust or distrust of individuals from another culture. As one expatriate remarked, "People can sense [the] phony in people, I think. International diplomacy is built on a trust relationship." Thus, expatriates should be people who are capable of both trusting and inspiring trust.

Prospective expatriates should demonstrate a willingness to learn and to make sacrifices. Both tenacity and initiative are prerequisites for overseas work, and a sense of humor is always an advantage.

Skills

Companies often make the mistake of focusing too much on technical skills in their selection process and not enough on other factors that contribute to successful international assignments, such as interpersonal skills, cross-cultural skills, motivation to go abroad, and positive attitude. A study of fifty Fortune 500 companies revealed that 90 percent of the time, they select expatriates on the basis of their technical expertise rather than on their cross-cultural fluency (Solomon, 1994). Technical abilities should be a threshold competence that all expatriates possess. It is important that local colleagues perceive expatriates to be adding value to the organization's efforts, and their perceived competence in the technical area balances out an initial lack of expertise in other areas such as language or culture; but companies should never forget that expatriates also need interpersonal skills, communication and listening skills, cross-cultural skills, and the ability to learn foreign languages and handle stress and conflict (Black, Gregersen and Mendenhall, 1992; Tung, 1981).

Background and Family

Two indicators of the flexibility that is so important in expatriates are a background with varied experiences (both professional and personal) and the proven ability to adapt to superiors who have different management styles. Living abroad in conjunction with foreign student programs, military service, volunteer experiences, and so on, and work-related international travel may indicate both an interest in other cultures and a likelihood that the potential expatriate has a fairly realistic picture of what to expect.

If the candidate is married, the marriage should be solid and the spouse, and children if there are any, should be flexible. Companies should interview spouses to make sure that they are prepared for the adventure. A spouse's failure to adjust affects the expatriate's morale and performance and is a primary reason for early termination (Tung, 1981). Spouses are not simply excess baggage. Spouses should possess many of the same characteristics looked for in the expatriate, and they should have a plan for using their time in the foreign country if they are not allowed to work. Families that have good communication and problem-solving skills are obviously preferable to those that do not.

Historically, there have been fewer female expatriates than males. Some companies refuse to consider females on the grounds that they would have a difficult time working in cultures where women are subservient to men and seldom found in the business world. Dual-career marriages have also been used as an excuse for not sending women, although the same constraint applies to most men today. Nevertheless, research has shown that female expatriates perform as well as men overseas and after repatriation (Adler, 1987; Adler and Izraeli, 1988; Black and Gregersen, 1991). In traditional cultures, the gender of female expatriates takes a backseat to their role as a foreign business representative. Their foreign status allows them to be perceived in a different way and in a different role than the women of that culture. Even within very traditional societies where women typically work only at home, there is often a precedent of highly respected local women, usually "superwomen," who participate in male spheres. In my own work experience in cultures like this, I can remember a few chauvinistic individuals who were occasionally more difficult to deal with in the beginning of our relationship. Generally speaking, I did not find that gender hindered my effectiveness or constituted an insurmountable barrier.

Overseas Assignments

Companies can use international assignments as a vehicle for developing managers. The boons they bring home—such as improved communication, interpersonal, and management skills; greater cognitive complexity; and an international focus—are good preparation for higher-management positions. Foreign nationals should also be brought to work at corporate headquarters so there is two-way learning between headquarters and subsidiaries, and less chance of a glass ceiling for foreign nationals.

Given all the uncertainty that characterizes a cross-cultural experience, expatriates appreciate clear job definitions with specific objectives. Jay eventually figured out what he should be doing in his European assignment as a managing director, but the lack of company objectives made his job more difficult and contributed more uncertainty to the situation than was necessary.

• • • • • • •

> I think the main thing is when you go over there, you should have clearly defined objectives, which I didn't have. . . . I think [that] to be successful the company has to have written, or at least fixed, objectives, personal and businesswise. A lot of the expatriates I met when I was over there were real unhappy with their jobs because I think the company just has some slot and they said, "Good, let's have Harry do it in Belgium for three years," with no real reason to have Harry in Belgium. If you have clearly defined objectives and the guy reaches his objectives, then he comes back a success and the company knows what it wanted and it has gotten it.

• • • • • • •

Along with clearly defined objectives, it is helpful to establish how expatriates will be rewarded if they meet these objectives and where successful international assignments will lead.

It is not uncommon for expatriates to find themselves with a different job than the one they were sent abroad to do. Sometimes this occurs for reasons that no one can predict or control. Other times, companies switch jobs on expatriates with little or no thought to the consequences. In the high degree of uncertainty that surrounds crossing the first threshold, the job assignment, along with clear objectives, is like an anchor. When companies blithely change that assignment, failed expectations and a broken psychological contract result. A psychological contract is the implicit or explicit agreement on mutual expectations between employees and employers that change over time. When these contracts are broken, disillusionment, demotivation, and termination can result.

An experienced female expatriate, Louise, negotiated and signed a contract in English for an overseas job with a Latin American organization. When she arrived in country, Louise was asked to sign another contract in Spanish with a different job description that was not at all to her liking. Had she not already moved her family abroad, she would have quit at this point. Instead, she was forced to negotiate a compromise. Even though Louise had seen this happen to other expatriates, it was months before she "forgave" her bosses for their cavalier treatment.

Switching job assignments on expatriates, even when there is a valid reason, causes expatriates to distrust the company and often results in early terminations or delays in the acculturation process. Therefore, changes in job assignments should be carefully considered and discussed with the expatriate beforehand.

Changing the length of the expatriate assignment also affects expatriates' expectations and their psychological contract. Bringing people back home before their assignment is over causes problems for some expatriates, because they are not ready and have not fulfilled their expectations and goals for the assignment. Most expatriates recommend three-year assignments because it takes them two years to become really effective. When expatriates stay abroad more than five years, they run the risk of feeling "out of" the home office culture.

Human Resource Departments

Like many mythical figures, HR departments can perform the function of either a magical friend or a threshold guardian, depending upon their attitude toward expatriates. HR personnel become a key link between expatriates and the company. At times, whether they deserve it or not, they are a lightening rod for the frustration that expatriates have about the overseas experience but cannot express to their boss.

Paul was aware of how important it is for HR departments to be proficient with logistical arrangements.

* * * * * * *

The first thing that any company needs to do is to make sure they know how to handle the logistics. Getting the furniture moved. Because you have all of these little pains in the ass that take up all of your time when you are trying to deal with other things. So, many people pull their hair out and scream, and all of a sudden get the mind-set "I hate you!" [toward the company].

* * * * * * *

For this reason, it is important to have highly competent HR personnel with international experience who can warn expatriates of the pitfalls that lie ahead and who empathize with the difficulties faced by expatriates. More than one expatriate told me, "Somebody at headquarters should understand it's tough to work abroad and tough to come back home."

HR departments should respond to expatriate questions and concerns immediately. Some departments ignore requests by out-of-sight expatriates until the volume is cranked up to howls of outrage. This diminishes expatriates' loyalty to headquarters at a time when they may already be feeling somewhat cut off from the company.

HR departments can reduce the number of questions from expatriates by carefully designing and writing up procedures about the move and checklists of things to do and by providing packets of information on the specific country. Arranging for agents or a relocation service protects expatriates from some of the headaches of moving and customs. More and more companies are using transition consultants who help new expatriates with the logistical arrangements in a new post (such as housing, schooling, shopping), provide them with cultural explanations, and help plug in family members to jobs, clubs, volunteer work, and so forth. The smoother the transition for the family, the quicker the expatriate can concentrate on the job.

In their repertoire of anecdotes, many expatriates have a few horror stories about organizational stinginess that made a great impression on them. These tales often feature unreasonable scrimping on matters of great importance to expatriates such as health care, home leaves, and schooling. While there is no need to be extravagant with expatriates, it is best to take a liberal stance with budget allowances so that expatriates do not perceive the company as uncaring at a time when they may be undergoing adjustment difficulties.

Employing HR personnel with international experience helps companies avoid making numerous mistakes with expatriates. Such people understand that expatriates have differing needs. For example, we can generalize that people who are going abroad for the first time or people who are less adventurous will require more attention than people who have been abroad many times. However, the only way to know who needs extra help or attention is to call and check on their progress, both when they go abroad and when they return home. Companies should not assume that expatriates are doing well overseas simply because they have not asked to return home.

When I supervised Peace Corps volunteers back in the 1970s, I mistakenly assumed that "good" volunteers completed their two-year assignment. This was often the case, but I quickly learned that sometimes competent volunteers went home early if they had a bad job assignment where it wasn't possible to accomplish much. In contrast, some of the least productive and least acculturated volunteers stayed the full two years, chained by inertia and the fear of looking like a quitter. The same phenomenon occurs with other types of expatriates. The term that has been coined to describe expatriates who are not fully functioning is "brownout" (Black, Gregersen, and Mendenhall, 1992). Companies should maintain close enough contact with expatriates to know whether they have browned out.

Expatriate Spouses and Families

Both the company and the HR department should be very attentive to the needs of spouses for several reasons. First, spouses often play an important role abroad that is more demanding than the role they have played at home. Many spouses regularly conduct sightseeing tours and shopping excursions for visitors from headquarters and their relatives, in addition to attending numerous work-related functions. In some locations, they put up company visitors in their home. It is wise to acknowledge the unpaid effort that expatriate spouses contribute to the company.

Secondly, spouses are more likely to feel the impact of company policies abroad. At home, health care, schooling, club memberships, and housing are almost always personal decisions made by employees and their spouses. Abroad, they are usually company policy decisions that greatly affect the spouse. For example, if a child is doing poorly in a local school but the company will not pay for tuition at an international school, a spouse is likely to become resentful. If a company is being overly stingy about medical benefits overseas and the spouse is worried about the health care the family is receiving, he or she may develop a negative attitude toward the company that could eventually affect the expatriate.

When my husband was transferred to Burkina Faso, he was granted $2,000 to furnish our house; this figure was company policy, along with a rule that prevented us from shipping our own furniture. The $2,000 figure was originally calculated to allow newly assigned directors in already established posts with completely furnished houses to make some purchases more in keeping with their own taste and, as such, was a generous and considerate policy. However, the policy made no sense at all in a country where we had to set up a household from scratch and where most goods were imported and exorbitantly expensive. Most of the money went for a refrigerator and stove. We bought local furniture—for instance, chairs made from large twigs lashed together—and made do. I was always at home, either caring for a newborn or working on a research project. From time to time when I would gaze around my spartan household, my thoughts would turn to headquarters and this policy. Then I would console myself with the notion that at least we could not be accused of ostentation. Had I not worked for this organization myself and stored up enough memories of good things they had done for us in the past, I might have joined the ranks of the many expatriate wives who complain bitterly about company policies. Eventually, after a VIP from headquarters came to visit and shrieked, "My God, why are you living with a bunch of sticks?" the policy was changed.

The third reason for paying special attention to expatriate spouses is that while they are abroad, some of them identify much more strongly with the expatriate's company than they did at home, where many spouses have their own jobs and/or larger social networks. When these resources are absent, the tie to the expatriate's company assumes greater significance. Finally, although this may not be a justifiable attitude, some spouses come to feel they are doing the company a favor by living abroad. In dual-career marriages, spouses put their careers on hold when they live in countries that do not allow them to work. While some spouses come to appreciate this career hiatus as a wonderful opportunity to stay home with small children or pursue various activities, others become so frustrated and bored that they return home alone. In response, some companies are bowing to the realities of dual-career marriages and providing overseas jobs for expatriate spouses.

Companies would do well to look at expatriate couples as a team, even to the point of dealing directly with the spouse if necessary. It is a mistake to take spouses for granted when they have such a major impact on the expatriate and the rest of the family.

Companies should also be sensitive about expatriate needs regarding their extended families. Expatriates are naturally concerned about maintaining close ties with relatives. They want to ensure that their children do not miss out on getting to know either their relatives or their homeland. Middle-aged expatriates, in particular, fret about living so far away from elderly parents and having to rely on others to care for them. Home leaves are very important, therefore, and must be frequent enough so that expatriates can fulfill their family obligations and maintain their relationships and roots at home.

Not all companies appreciate how much more difficult it is for expatriates to plan get-togethers for the extended family, or how frustrating it is when these plans are thoughtlessly disrupted. One expatriate made plans months ahead of time to have his relatives come to Brazil for Christmas. Just before they arrived, he was unexpectedly called back to the States for a meeting. His boss ignored his pleas to postpone the meeting until after the holidays. Insult was added to injury when the meeting agenda was not really that urgent. This type of insensitivity promotes bitterness toward the company rather than loyalty and commitment.

Communication

In addition to ensuring that expatriates have sufficient contact with their extended family, companies also need to nurture the link between expatriates and headquarters. Ron, the general manager for a Dutch subsidiary introduced in Chapter Two, spent seven years abroad and was very proactive about the type of communication he wanted with headquarters.

• • • • • • •

> I kept contact with the head office. I think that is one of the biggest things people fear. People feel when they go overseas, "My God, three years. They have forgotten me, and when I get back there will be no job and no career." I have seen it happen in my own company. . . . So I negotiated for a week-long quarterly visit and a monthly page-long telex, now it is a fax . . . with highlights, the financials, and any exceptions to plan. . . . So that worked out pretty well.

• • • • • • •

Bill traveled internationally for years before he accepted a managing director position in Hong Kong when he was in his late forties. During his travels and visits with expatriates, he heard many complaints like, "I don't know what the hell is going on at headquarters. . . . Nobody tells me anything; we are just out here sitting." Bill avoided this problem by having weekly contact, a person in the States who reported to him, and a former secretary who looked after his affairs.

Regardless of how they decide to go about it, companies and expatriates must ensure that there is adequate communication. Glen had the following advice for companies after he returned from four years in England:

· · · · · · ·

Communication is one of the key things companies can do with the expatriate, to ensure that different levels of management are communicating with him. Not only on the company but his progress and on his situation. The worst thing that can happen to an expatriate is not to be told . . . that he's doing a good job, that someone is thinking about him and they are working with him, and they are happy he has taken that assignment.

· · · · · · ·

Given the trials and obstacles expatriates face, bosses should be understanding, supportive, and quick to praise.

Repatriation

Companies should be preparing for repatriation long before the actual move takes place. Some companies tell expatriates what job or job level they will be returning to before they ever leave the country. This eliminates one of their major sources of uncertainty. One way to ease the difficulty of slotting expatriates back into a domestic organizational chart is to assign them a career mentor at headquarters who keeps them up-to-date on opportunities. This person also serves as an advocate who ensures that expatriates are not "out of sight, out of mind" but kept in the running for jobs.

Stan, introduced in Chapter Three, is a long-term expatriate currently in charge of international operations at his company. He has given a great deal of thought to repatriation.

· · · · · · ·

A well-planned repatriation is equally as important [as the predeparture planning] . . . because as I mentioned, generally you have broadened your experiences. You come back with greater expectations than when you left. And I think you need to be able to bring these people into a challenging position back here. We have had a

couple [instances] . . . where they were just brought back and there
was no position at all for them. . . . And we lost two people for
that exact reason. They were not prepared to just sit in an office
and wait for something to come about or be put on a temporary
assignment just to have something to do. . . . I tend probably to
visit the overseas locations more than people visit me. . . . I generally try to get to overseas locations at least three times during the
year and [the expatriates] are up here at least once on home leave,
if not [for] business reasons. One reason for this much contact is to
rate them . . . but of course, in that same process, we find out what
they are looking for, what are their interests in their next assignment. If you do that and allow yourself time to do a good job of
repatriating, it pays off. That's why we tend to tell our expatriates
that it is not a fixed period of time. . . . We would prefer to make a
smooth repatriation, even if it meant keeping the individual overseas for three months longer or three months less. . . . We say generally three to four years depending on the needs of the company
and [the person's] own situation. . . . If you don't do a good job of
repatriating them, you are not going to get them to go overseas.
And that becomes known very quickly and becomes very visible,
too. So I think the more successful you are in bringing people
back, the more successful you are in getting people to go overseas.

• • • • • • •

Waiting for the right job is preferable to bringing people home
to cool their heels, hoping for a job to open up. Stan is correct in
his assumption that many expatriates find repatriation less shock-
ing and frustrating if their new domestic assignment is a challenging job that requires some of the same skills they used overseas. New
projects, turn-around assignments, and setting up new facilities are
the types of jobs that might provide returned expatriates with the
challenge and novelty they experienced abroad. Whenever possible, domestic assignments should allow returning expatriates to utilize the knowledge and skills they acquired overseas; otherwise, the
company fails to benefit from their investment in these employees.

Stan prepares his expatriates well in advance for the decreased autonomy that may occur upon repatriation, but makes it more palatable by making sure they return to challenging jobs.

* * * * * * *

When our expatriates come back, they don't have the same level of authority as they did overseas. . . . That is one of the things we tell them, even before they go. That this is an opportunity for them, but again, when you come back you are part of the big company again. And I think most people react to it very well. Of course, we have a reasonably good record on placing our expatriates. We do take it seriously . . . finding the right spot for them, not to just bring them back and not have a challenging opportunity for them.

* * * * * * *

Unless the company makes a point of telling prospective expatriates that they will return at the same level, expatriates usually expect to receive a promotion as a reward for their increased skills and their sacrifices and heroic efforts abroad.

Expatriates should also be educated about what else they can expect upon their return. They should either read or see videos that talk about not only reduced autonomy but also all the other themes that expatriates identified in Chapter Seven: the "you can't go home again" phenomenon, the "little fish in a big pond" syndrome, the high degree of uncertainty, the lack of interest in their experiences, the idealization of home and false expectations, the testing period, and what people miss about life abroad. Companies should eliminate as much uncertainty as they can about the job and the moving arrangements. The organization should question whether their returned expatriates are put through a conscious or unconscious testing period and, if so, why? Do they have to prove themselves more than people who transfer in from domestic posts? Expatriates should be informed about the reverse culture shock that can occur after repatriation and about everything else identified in Chapter Seven that would help them have more realistic expectations before they return home.

Recently returned expatriates, like brand new expatriates overseas, need a grace period at work—lower performance expectations—until they are settled in and get their feet on the ground. They should be encouraged to take care of housing and logistical arrangements before they begin their job. If that is not possible, they should have flexible hours to attend to the numerous details and errands that arise. At a bare minimum, newly returned expatriates should be kicked out of the office exactly at closing time until they get their family settled.

There are several things companies can do to ease the expatriates' transition back to a domestic office. First, they can provide them with a cultural mentor. Ideally, this would be someone who has returned from abroad within the last two years and has successfully readjusted. Cultural mentors can also be what we traditionally think of as career mentors—someone who interprets the organizational culture for protégés and provides them with valuable career advice. Since both the expatriate and the company may have changed during an overseas assignment, a cultural mentor can keep returned expatriates from making serious mistakes.

After seven years in Europe, Ron described what happens when expatriates go from a highly autonomous foreign assignment to a highly territorial headquarters job.

* * * * * * *

Good people come back, they try to utilize their international experience and nobody knows what the hell they are talking about. They were overseas making decisions that were going gung-ho. They come back and they try to do that in the head office and people start slicing them up with carving knives. "Hey, you are on my turf, man; get off!" You've got to make the cultural transition. Big companies need to realize that when you go overseas there is a cultural transition and coming back there is a cultural transition. And they need to plan for it.

* * * * * * *

When they cross the return threshold, expatriates need magical friends who are knowledgeable about both repatriation and the organizational culture.

Another way companies can ease the expatriate's transition to life back home is to provide debriefing sessions for returned expatriates so they can talk about their experiences with people who are truly interested (a rare commodity). By listening to other expatriates and having an opportunity to discuss their own experiences, expatriates are more likely to get beyond a "suitcase full of anecdotes" and make more sense of their experience.

As I mentioned in Chapter Seven, it is difficult for returning expatriates to feel like heroes when hardly anyone will listen to their adventure. One way to allow expatriates to be heroes in their own land is to have them make a formal presentation on what they learned abroad and the implications for the company. In a business environment that rewards companies who learn the fastest, it is foolish to allow expatriates to slip back into the corporate woodwork without picking their brains and jointly evaluating the experience.

Companies can also ease the expatriate transition from being a big fish in a little pond to being a little fish in a big pond by treating them with respect and using their overseas experience and skills whenever possible. Jay describes how his boss helped him make the transition from "Our man in Belgium" to "Joe Schmo."

* * * * * * *

My boss was real good about that. . . . You can overcome that a lot by giving the person access . . . whenever there is any kind of a European question about marketing or business, make a point of the fact that we are going to utilize this long-standing resource now that we have developed it and make the point that your contribution is real important. Maybe your position now might not be [important], but your skills and the stuff you have learned is going to be utilized by the company. . . . Whenever I was out with my boss the first year back, he would always play [my international experience] up to all visitors and all the customers: "Here we have the past director of our European operations who was there four years and knows a lot about this and a lot about that.". . . I think it was very smart on his part and very skillful to recognize that. I am very appreciative of that.

• • • • • • •

Organizations can both facilitate repatriation and enrich themselves by utilizing the boons expatriates bring home.

The Meaning of the Expatriate Experience

It is not uncommon for returned expatriates to resign after repatriation and accept a job with another company that presumably places a higher value on their international experience and the boons they bring back. If companies understand what the experience means to expatriates, they can select them more carefully, prepare them better beforehand, support them in a more effective manner while they are overseas, and more gracefully ease their transition home.

"Would you go abroad again?" I always ask returned expatriates this question to get an idea of what living abroad meant to them. Elliot, the seasoned seventeen-year expatriate who worked for a Big Six firm in Europe, gave me the type of answer that I have heard over and over again.

• • • • • • •

If I had a good opportunity to go to Singapore or Tokyo or Hong Kong or someplace I have never been . . . I would certainly go. . . . For one thing, I have never been there and it is an important part of our world that I am totally ignorant about. . . . So it would be professionally, intellectually interesting. But obviously there would be a lot to be learned, just as it was fun discovering foods, art, culture, whatever in Europe. . . . So if you have anything going, let me know.

* * * * * * *

The opportunity for lifelong learning is one of the principal attractions of expatriate life. Each country is a new chance to learn, whether it is the first or the tenth overseas assignment.

The other reasons expatriates give for wanting to return abroad reveal the essence of the experience—they miss the excitement, feeling "special," more alive, and more challenged, all characteristics of a hero's adventure. The metaphor of the hero's adventure contributes a deeper understanding of the common threads found in expatriate stories. I hope that many expatriates reading this book will say, "Yes, that's how it is—that's what I experienced, too." We expatriates don't call ourselves heroes, but we know that we have been on a life-changing adventure full of trials and challenges. The metaphor of the hero's adventure helps us see beyond our individual struggles to make sense of a unique experience by acknowledging ourselves as part of a long tradition of expatriates on the "hero path." Myths have always been a way of teaching unobservable realities by way of observable symbols (Lévi-Strauss, 1963). The reality of the expatriate experience is that it provides an opportunity to play a role in one of the oldest human dramas.

* * * * * * *

Furthermore, we have not even to risk the adventure alone, for the heroes of all time have gone before us. The labyrinth is thoroughly known. We have only to follow the thread of the hero path, and where we had thought to find an abomination, we shall find a god. And where we had thought to slay another, we shall slay ourselves. Where we had thought to travel outward, we will come to the center of our own existence. And where we had thought to be alone, we will be one with the world [Campbell, 1968, p. 25].

Appendix

· ·

Report on the Study of
Returned Expatriates

With the exception of the information I gained during my years as an expatriate participant-observer, this book is based on an exploratory study of returned expatriates (Osland, 1990). The portion of the study described in the book was an attempt at grounded theory building, an effort (1) to see whether the concepts of heroism and mastery, paradox, and transformation that I had observed in expatriates who worked in international development and nonprofit agencies were in fact important to expatriate businesspeople; and (2) to determine whether the myth of the hero's adventure is a useful metaphor for understanding and describing the expatriate experience. Since there were numerous references to these concepts and themes in the interviews and since the expatriates reported experiencing the explicated paradoxes, I concluded that the answer to these questions was positive.

Description of the Sample

The participants in this study were thirty-five returned U.S. businesspeople from a variety of industries. They met the following selection criteria: (1) each was a U.S. businessperson, (2) each had lived abroad for at least eighteen months, and (3) each had been repatriated within the last eight years. Although my goal was to have a mixed sample, I could only locate two women who met the selection criteria. Of the thirty-nine possible subjects, all but four agreed to participate in the study.

The participants ranged in age from 27 to 62 with a mean age of 41.2 (SD = 8.4). At the time of their overseas assignment, their average age was 35.7 years (SD = 7.9) with a range of 23 to 56 years. The great majority of the participants were married and, with one exception, to American spouses. Only three were single and two were divorced prior to the assignment. Two of the marriages broke up during the overseas assignment. Seventy-seven percent of the married couples were accompanied overseas by children. The number of children per family ranged from 1 to 4 with an average of 1.3 children.

Approximately half the participants had undergraduate degrees, while the other half also had advanced graduate degrees. The majority of their undergraduate majors were in engineering and business and accounting. The most common graduate degree was in business and economics.

The largest occupational group among these participants was general manager (37.1 percent). The other occupations that constituted the sample were engineers, chemists, auditors, bankers, accountants, and lawyers.

Prior to going abroad, the participants had worked an average of 7.9 years for their companies. The range for this previous tenure was 1 to 21 years; 6 years was the median tenure. More than half of the participants (51.4 percent) had traveled abroad extensively prior to their assignment, which reportedly facilitated their overseas adjustment. Four people had also lived abroad previously as a student or with the military.

Most of their companies sent them abroad for multiple reasons; the most common were an absence of available technical expertise (54.3 percent), a management development opportunity for the expatriate (45.7 percent), and a lack of local managerial talent (34.3 percent). Twenty percent of the participants were involved in some form of start-up activities or special nonroutine assignments (such as SWAT teams or "hatchet men"). The majority of their overseas jobs (51.4 percent) were in services (banking, accounting, and law); 34.3 percent of them worked in sales and manufacturing, while 14.3 percent were involved in research jobs.

The participants worked abroad anywhere from 18 months to 19 years. Their average length of time abroad was 3.9 years. Only two of the participants were career expatriates; they had spent 17 to 19 years abroad in five to six different assignments. Almost 90 percent of the sample had only one overseas assignment. Almost half of the participants (45.7 percent) were abroad for 18 to 24 months. Eighty percent of the participants had lived in only one foreign country. The majority (63 percent) were assigned to Europe (a little more than a third in England); others were posted in Africa, Asia, and Latin America.

With respect to language fluency, 20 percent spoke no foreign languages. Half of them spoke one foreign language and 31.5 percent spoke two or more languages. Forty percent described their fluency as low, 28.6 percent stated their fluency level was moderate, and only 8.6 percent reported their fluency was high.

Most of these expatriates (88.6 percent) lived in host-country neighborhoods rather than in expatriate ghettos, and only 8.6 percent socialized only with Americans. Most of them still correspond with non-American friends, either third-country or host-country nationals, who they met overseas, which is hypothesized as a measure of acculturation (Brein and David, 1971).

The majority (77.1 percent) were ready to return home at the end of their assignment. A third of them reported that repatriation was not difficult. Of the remaining two-thirds who found repatriation difficult, 8.6 percent claimed that it was even more difficult than going abroad.

Sixty percent of the participants would like to go abroad again, two of them would not, and the remaining third stated that a decision to go again would be contingent upon their family, career, and the location of the assignment.

Data Analysis

The participants were interviewed and also filled out various instruments (demographic survey, acculturation and effectiveness measures, awareness-of-paradox measure). The interview protocol is shown in Exhibit A.1. The paradox instrument the participants completed during the interview is shown in Exhibit A.2. The interviews were taped, transcribed, and content-analyzed by two coders. The quantitative data on the paradoxes was analyzed statistically using Pearson Product moment correlations and factor analysis. Those appear in Exhibit A.3.

Exhibit A.1.   The Interview Protocol.

Open-Ended Questions on the Overseas Assignment

Tell me about your (last) overseas assignment, from the time when you first learned about the possibility of going to _____.

What did you think when you first heard you were going to _____?

What were the first few days like?

Were there things that surprised you about the way people thought or worked?

What was your first big "aha!" about the culture?

How would you sum up your first six months?

Whom did you know at this point?

Did you have someone who could explain the local culture to you and that you could confide in?

How did people see you?

Can you describe your relationship with your co-workers?

What did you think about your job?

Can you describe your relationship with your home organization?

What was the most important thing you learned in those first six months?

What did your family/wife think about living in _____?

Stages in the Experience

Can you divide your experience into a set of stages or chapters? What would you call them? How long did each stage last and what was the biggest challenge of each one?

Expatriate Paradoxes

Can you think of any instances during this assignment when you had to deal with contradictions or paradoxes at work or in your social life? I'm defining paradox in the following way: when a person holds or sees two contradictory points of view that are both true, and he or she has to decide which point of view to act on in a particular instance.

(Administer the Paradox Instrument.)

Exhibit A.2.   The Awareness of Paradox Instrument.

Have you ever experienced the following? Please write YES or NO in the first blank. When that's completed, rank-order the paradoxes/contradictions according to the significance or importance they held for you. Assign a "1" to the paradox that was the most significant.

Yes/
No Rank

____ ____ 1. Possessing a great deal of power as a result of your role but downplaying it in order to gain necessary input and cooperation.

____ ____ 2. Generally thinking well of the host-country nationals while at the same time being very savvy about being taken advantage of by them.

____ ____ 3. Feeling caught between contradictory demands of headquarters on the one hand and the host-country nationals and the local situation on the other.

____ ____ 4. Seeing as valid the general stereotype about the culture you lived in but also realizing that many host-country nationals do not fit that stereotype.

____ ____ 5. Giving up some of your American values in order to be accepted or successful in the other culture while at the same time finding some of your core American values becoming even stronger as a result of exposure to another culture.

____ ____ 6. As a result of being abroad a long time, feeling at ease anywhere but belonging nowhere.

____ ____ 7. Becoming more and more "worldminded" as a result of exposure to different values and conflicting loyalties, but becoming more idiosyncratic as to how you put together your own value system and view on life.

____ ____ 8. Trying to represent your company as best you can in order to succeed but also realizing that the "ideal" values you act out abroad may not exist back at headquarters.

____ ____ 9. Being freed from many of your own cultural rules and even from some of the host culture's norms but not being free at all from certain host-country customs that you must observe in order to be effective.

Exhibit A.2. *(continued)*

Critical Incident Questions About a Paradox

1. Choose the paradox or contradiction that was most significant for you—
the one that represented the biggest challenge or discomfort. Either tell
me what came to mind when you filled out the questionnaire or tell me
about the time you first became aware of it. Pretend you're writing a
newspaper article on this incident and include all the "facts" so that I
will be able to describe the incident in detail afterwards.

What led up to the situation?

Who was involved?

What were you thinking?

What were you feeling?

What did you actually say?

What did you actually do?

What was the outcome of the situation?

2. So then, in your own words, the paradox or contradiction you are
describing here was what?

Did you learn to live with it? How?

Closed and Open-Ended Acculturation Questions

Do you think other Americans you saw abroad encountered or experienced difficulties of living and working in another culture that were:

___ Very similar to yours

___ Similar

___ Not similar

___ Very different

If "not similar" or "very different," describe their experience.

With whom did you generally socialize?

___ Americans

___ Host-country nationals

___ Third-country expatriates

Why?

What was the attitude of the Americans or third-country expatriates you
socialized with toward the _____ (locals)?

What adjectives would they use to describe them?

Was it easy for Americans to be accepted by the _____? Why?

Exhibit A.2. *(continued)*

Do you correspond with anyone from _____? If so, with whom?

___ American

___ Host-country nationals

___ Third-country nationals

How would you describe your living situation?

___ Lived in a compound of expatriates

___ Lived in a neighborhood composed primarily of expatriates

___ Lived in a neighborhood composed primarily of host-country nationals

What type of nonwork activities did you participate in? With whom did you do them?

How many co-workers (either above or below you in the hierarchy) did you have to deal with on an average day in order to accomplish your work objectives? And what nationality were they?

Did you feel you changed as a result of working abroad? If so, how?

Repatriation Questions

What was it like to come home?

Do you feel you get to use the skills you acquired abroad in your current job?

Would you go abroad again? Why?

HR Advice Questions

If you had to select people to work abroad, what characteristics would you look for?

What advice would you give to a friend who was on his or her way to a foreign assignment?

What advice would you give to a person ending a foreign assignment about returning to the States?

What advice would you have for HR departments about handling expatriates?

Exhibit A.3. Statistical Information on Paradoxes: Reported Awareness of Individual Paradoxes and Their Rankings.

	Percent of Expatriates	Rank in Terms of Significance to the Expatriates
1. Possessing a great deal of power as a result of your role but downplaying it in order to gain necessary input and cooperation.	68.6	4
2. Generally thinking well of the host-country nationals while at the same time being very savvy about being taken advantage of by them.	54.3	7
3. Feeling caught between contradictory demands of headquarters on the one hand and the demands of the host-country nationals and the local situation on the other.	51.4	5
4. Seeing as valid the general stereotype about the culture you lived in but also realizing that many host-country nationals do not fit that stereotype.	77.1	6
5. Giving up some of your American values in order to be accepted or successful in the other culture while at the same time finding some of your core American values becoming even stronger as a result of exposure to another culture.	60.0	3
6. As a result of being abroad a long time, feeling at ease anywhere but belonging nowhere.	45.7	2
7. Becoming more and more "world-minded" as a result of exposure to different values and conflicting loyalties, but becoming more idiosyncratic as to how you put together your own value system and views on life.	48.6	1
8. Trying to represent your company as best as you can in order to succeed but also realizing that the "ideal" values you act out abroad may not exist back at headquarters.	54.3	9
9. Being freed from many of your own cultural rules and even from some of the host culture's norms but not being free at all from certain host-country customs that you must observe in order to be effective.	62.9	8

Exhibit A.3 (*continued*)

Factor Analysis of Awareness of Paradox

Paradoxes	Mediation	Identity Values	Marginality	Social Acuity
1. Powerful/Powerless				.69
2. Positive Regard/Caution			.86	
3. HQ/HC Demands	.79			
4. Stereotype/Individual Differences				.62
5. Relinquish/Strengthen Values		.87		
6. At Ease Anywhere/Belonging Nowhere			-.47	
7. Macro/Micro Perspective		.64		
8. Ideal/Real Values	.88			
9. Free/Not Free of Norms	.63			

References

Adler, N. "Re-Entry: Managing Cross-Cultural Transitions." *Group and Organization Studies*, 1981, 6(3), 341–356.

Adler, N. *Internal Dimensions of Organizational Behavior*. Boston: Kent, 1986.

Adler, N. "Pacific Basin Managers: A Gaijin, Not a Woman." *Human Resource Management*, 1987, 26, 169–192.

Adler, N., and Izraeli, D. *Women in Management Worldwide*. Armonk, N.Y.: Sharpe, 1988.

Adler, P. "Beyond Cultural Identity: Reflections on Cultural and Multicultural Man." *Topics in Culture Learning*, 1974, 2, 23–40.

Becker, E. *The Denial of Death*. New York: Free Press, 1973.

Berry, J. W. "Acculturation: A Comparative Analysis of Alternative Forms." In R. J. Samuda and S. L. Woods (eds.), *Perspectives in Immigrant and Minority Education*. Lanham, Md.: University Press of America, 1983.

Black, J. S., and Gregersen, H. B. "When Yankee Comes Home: Factors Related to Expatriate and Spouse Repatriation Adjustment." *Journal of International Business Studies*, 1991, 22(4), 671–695.

Black, J. S., Gregersen, H. B., and Mendenhall, M. E. *Global Assignments: Successfully Expatriating and Repatriating International Managers*. San Francisco: Jossey-Bass, 1992.

Bochner, S. (ed.). *The Mediating Person: Bridges Between Cultures*. Boston: Hall, 1982.

Boyatzis, R. *The Competent Manager: A Model for Effective Performance*. New York: Wiley, 1982.

Brein, M., and David, K. "Intercultural Communication and the Adjustment of the Sojourner." *Psychological Bulletin*, 1971, 76(3), 215–230.

Brewster, C. *The Management of Expatriates*. London: Kogan Page, 1991.

Briody, E. K., and Baba, M. L. *Multiple Organizational Models and International Career Pathing at General Motors Corporation*. Detroit: General Motors Research Laboratories, 1988.

Brislin, R. *Cross Cultural Encounters*. Needham Heights, Mass.: Allyn, 1981.

Campbell, J. *Hero with a Thousand Faces*. Princeton, N.J.: Princeton University Press, [1949] 1968.

Campbell, J. *The Power of Myth*. New York: Doubleday, 1988.

Cateora, P. *International Marketing*. Homewood, Ill.: Irwin, 1983.

Chorafas, D. *Developing the International Executive*. New York: American Management Association, 1967.

Church, A. T. "Sojourner Adjustment." *Psychological Bulletin*, 1982, *91*, 540–571.

Cobb, S. "Social Support as a Moderator of Life Stress." *Psychosomatic Medicine*, 1976, *38*, 300–314.

Detweiler, R. "On Inferring the Intentions of a Person from Another Culture." *Journal of Personality*, 1975, *43*, 591–611.

Dreher, G., and Ash, R. A. "A Comparative Study of Mentoring Among Men and Women in Managerial, Professional, and Technical Positions." *Journal of Applied Psychology*, 1990, *75*(5), 539–546.

Emerson, R. W. "Uses of Great Men." In J. Porte (ed.), *Ralph Waldo Emerson: Essays and Lectures*. New York: Literary Classics of the U.S., Inc., 1983.

Fayerweather, J. *The Executive Overseas*. Syracuse, N.Y.: Syracuse University Press, 1959.

Feshback, S., and Weiner, B. *Personality*. Lexington, Mass.: Heath, 1982.

Fiske, S., and Taylor, S. *Social Cognition*. Reading, Mass.: Addison-Wesley, 1984.

Furnham, A., and Bochner, S. *Culture Shock: Psychological Reactions to Unfamiliar Environments*. New York: Methuen, 1986.

Gaylord, M. "Relocation and the Corporate Family: Unexplored Issues." *Social Work*, 1979, *24*(3), 186–191.

Gullahorn, J. T., and Gullahorn, J. E. "Extension of the U-Curve Hypothesis." *Journal of Social Issues*, 1963, *19*, 45–46.

Guthrie, G. M. "Cultural Preparation for the Philippines." In R. B. Textor (ed.), *Cultural Frontiers of the Peace Corps*. Cambridge, Mass.: MIT Press, 1966.

Hammer, M. R., Gudykunst, J. E., and Wiseman, R. L. "Dimensions of Intercultural Effectiveness: An Exploratory Study." *International Journal of Intercultural Relations*, 1978, *2*, 382–393.

Harrison, R., and Hopkins, R. L. "The Design of Cross-Cultural Training: An Alternative to the University Model." *Journal of Applied Behavioral Science*, 1967, *3*(4), 431–460.

Hawes, F., and Kealey, D. J. "An Empirical Study of Canadian Technical Assistance." *International Journal of Intercultural Relations*, 1981, *5*, 239–258.

Hofstede, G. "Motivation, Leadership, and Organization: Do American Theories Apply Abroad?" *Organizational Dynamics*, 1980, *9*(1), 42–62.

Hofstede, G. *Culture's Consequences: International Differences in Work-Related Values*. Newbury Park, Calif.: Sage, 1984.

Holmes, T. H., and Rahe, R. H. "The Social Readjustment Rating Scale." *Journal of Psychosomatic Research*, 1967, *11*, 213–218.

Horney, K. *Neurosis and Human Growth*. New York: Norton, 1950.

Kluckhohn, F., and Strodtbeck, F. L. *Variations in Value Orientations*. New York: HarperCollins, 1961.

Kohls, L. R. *Survival Kit for Overseas Living: For Americans Planning to Live and Work Abroad*. (2nd ed.) Yarmouth, Maine: Intercultural Press, 1984.

Kolb, D. *Experiential Learning: Experience as the Source of Learning*. Englewood Cliffs, N.J.: Prentice Hall, 1984.

Komarovsky, M. "Class Differences in Family Decision Making." In H. Kassarjian and T. Robertson (eds.), *Perspectives in Consumer Behavior*. Glenview, Ill: Scott, Foresman, 1968.

Lanier, A. R. *Your Manager Abroad: How Welcome? How Prepared?* New York: American Management Association, 1975.

Lawrence, R., and Lorsch, J. W. *Organization and Environment: Managing Differentiation and Integration*. Homewood, Ill.: Irwin, 1969.

Lee, Y., and Larwood, L. "The Socialization of Expatriate Managers in Multinational Firms." *Academy of Management Journal*, 1983, *26*(4), 657–665.

Lévi-Strauss, C. *Structural Anthropology*. New York: Basic Books, 1963.

Lewin, K. *Resolving Social Conflicts: Selected Papers on Group Dynamics*. New York: HarperCollins, 1948.

Lewis, T., and Jungman, R. *On Being Foreign: Culture Shock in Short Fiction*. Yarmouth, Maine: Intercultural Press, 1986.

Louis, M. R. "Surprise and Sense Making: What Newcomers Experience in Entering Unfamiliar Organizational Settings." *Administrative Science Quarterly*, 1980, *25*, 226–251.

McClelland, D. C., and Dailey, C. *Evaluating New Methods of Measuring the Qualities Needed in Superior Foreign Service Information Officers*. Cambridge, Mass.: McBer and Co., 1973.

Mendenhall, M., Dunbar, E., and Oddou, G. "Expatriate Selection, Training and Career-Pathing: A Review and Critique." *Human Resource Management*, 1987, *26*(3), 331–345.

Mendenhall, M., and Oddou, G. "The Dimensions of Expatriate Acculturation: A Review." *Academy of Management Review*, 1985, *10*(1), 39–47.

"Nehru, a 'Queer Mix of East and West,' Led the Struggle for a Modern India." *New York Times*, May 28, 1964, p. 16.

Newman, J., Bhatt, B., and Gutteridge, T. "Determinants of Expatriate Effectiveness: A Theoretical and Empirical Vacuum." *Academy of Management Proceedings*, 1976, pp. 340–345.

Oberg, K. "Culture Shock: Adjustment to New Cultural Environments." *Practical Anthropology*, 1960, *7*, 177–182.

Osland, J. *The Hero's Adventure: The Overseas Experience of Expatriate Businesspeople*. Unpublished doctoral dissertation, Case Western Reserve University, 1990.

Osland, J. "International Diversity and Expatriate Acculturation." In R. Sims and R. Dennehy (eds.), *Diversity and Differences in Organizations*. Westport, Conn.: Quorum Books, 1993.

Pinchot, G. *Intrapreneuring*. New York: HarperCollins, 1985.

Pool, I. "Effects of Cross-National Contact on National and International Images." In H. C. Kelman (ed.), *International Behavior*. Troy, Mo.: Holt, Rinehart & Winston, 1965.

Proust, M. *La Prisonniere, Bk. 6: A la Recherche du Tempes Perdu*. France: Editions Gallimard, 1989.

Quinn, R. *Beyond Rational Management*. Cambridge, Mass.: Ballinger, 1988.

Quinn, R., and Cameron, K. *Paradox and Transformation*. Cambridge, Mass.: Ballinger, 1988.

Ratiu, I. "Thinking Internationally: A Comparison of How International Students Learn." *International Studies of Management and Organization*, 1983, *13*, 139–150.

Russell, B. *Principia Matematica*. Cambridge: Cambridge University Press, 1913.

Sanger, D. "Mitsubishi's Unlikely Leader: After Stay in U.S., Is He Japanese Enough?" *International Herald Tribune*, Apr. 14, 1992, p. 14.

Schein, E. *Organizational Culture and Leadership*. San Francisco: Jossey-Bass, 1988.

Schutz, A. "The Stranger: An Essay in Social Psychology." *American Journal of Sociology*, 1944, *49*, 499–507.

Smith, K. K., and Berg, D. N. *Paradoxes of Group Life: Understanding Conflict, Paralysis, and Movement in Group Dynamics*. San Francisco: Jossey-Bass, 1987.

Solomon, C. M. "Success Abroad Depends on More than Job Skills." *Personnel Journal*, 1994, *73*(4), 51–54.

Storti, C. *The Art of Crossing Cultures*. Yarmouth, Maine: Intercultural Press, 1990.

Szanton, D. "Cultural Confrontation in the Philippines." In R. B. Textor (ed.), *Cultural Frontiers of the Peace Corps*. Cambridge, Mass.: MIT Press, 1966.

Torbiorn, I. *Living Abroad*. New York: Wiley, 1982.

Triandis, H. C. "Interpersonal Relations in International Organizations." *Organizational Behavior and Human Performance*, 1967, *2*, 26–55.

Triandis, H. C., and others. "Individualism and Collectivism: Cross-Cultural Perspectives on Self-Ingroup Relationships." *Journal of Personality and Social Psychology*, 1988, *54*(2), 323–338.

Tung, R. "Selecting and Training of Personnel for Overseas Assignments." *Columbia Journal of World Business*, 1981, *16*(1), 68–78.

Tung, R. "Expatriate Assignments: Enhancing Success and Minimizing Failure." *Academy of Management Executive*, 1987, *1*(2), 117–125.

Underhill, E. *Mysticism: A Study in the Nature and Development of Man's Spiritual Consiousness*. New York: Dutton, 1911.

Voris, W. "Considerations in Staffing for Overseas Management Needs." *Personnel Journal*, 1975, *54*(6), 332–333, 354.

Whitehead, A. N. *Science and the Modern World*. New York: Macmillan, 1925.

Index